Library of
Davidson College

Songs of Death

"The wretched, bloody, and usurping Boare," an illustration from Staunton's edition, 1858–60. Courtesy of the Folger Shakespeare Library, Washington, D.C. PR 2752, 1858–60, c.1 v2, Sh. Coll., p. 537.

R. Chris Hassel, Jr.

SONGS of DEATH

Performance, Interpretation, and the Text of Richard III

University of Nebraska Press
Lincoln and London

Acknowledgments for the use of
previously published material
appear on pages ix–x.
Copyright 1987 by the
University of Nebraska Press
All rights reserved
Manufactured in the
United States of America
The paper in this book meets the
minimum requirements of American
National Standard for Information
Sciences–Permanence of Paper for
Printed Library Materials,
ANSI Z39.48-1984.

Library of Congress Cataloging-in-Publication Data
Hassel, R (Rudolph) Chris, 1939–
   Songs of death.
   Bibliography: p.
   Includes index.
   1. Shakespeare, William, 1564–1616.
King Richard III. 2. Richard III, King
of England, 1452–1485, in fiction,
drama, poetry, etc. I. Title.
PR2821.H37   1987   822.3'3   86-14659
ISBN 0-8032-2341-2 (alk. paper)

To my students

Contents

List of Illustrations, viii
Acknowledgments, ix
Introduction, 1
1 Interpretation and Performance in Richard III, 6
2 Richard versus Richmond: Aesthetic Warfare in Act 5, 35
3 The Wooing of Elizabeth, 57
4 "Rotten Armour": Richard's Play for the Citizens, 74
5 Perceptions of Providence in Richard III, 89
6 "Odde Old Ends": Textual Cruxes and Interpretive Problems, 122
Epilogue, 145
Notes, 161
Textual Bibliography, 181
General Bibliography, 185
Index of Authors, 191
Index of Actors, Characters, and Directors, 194

Illustrations

"The wretched, bloody, and usurping Boare", *frontispiece*
Laurence Olivier as Richard, 8
Ron Cook as Richard, 11
Laurence Olivier with Claire Bloom as Lady Anne, 14
Laurence Olivier's crosslike sword, 32
"Dispaire and dye", 105
Antony Sher as Richard, 147
Antony Sher with Frances Tomelty as Queen Elizabeth, 152
Richmond's avenging sword, 156

Acknowledgments

I gratefully acknowledge the support and assistance of my family, my colleagues and friends, and the secretaries of the English Department, especially Alberta Martin. Scott Colley deserves special thanks for his generous and thoughtful readings of this manuscript, Ginger Pyron and Susan Gilroy for their careful assistance, and Luigi Monga for teaching me to use the word-processor. My colleagues here and in the world of Shakespeare have challenged and encouraged my work in person and in print. Among them I would like particularly to thank Bill Alexander, Antony Sher, John Andrews, Leeds Barroll, Werner Habicht, Barry Gaines, Robert Turner, Richard Knowles, Ann Cook, John Halperin, and Laurence Lerner. Charles Shepherdson helped me understand some contemporary currents in literary criticism and their relationship to this work. The publication of this book was assisted by a grant from Vanderbilt University. The Research Council at Vanderbilt has supported several visits to the Folger Shakespeare Library, whose staff, like the staffs at the Heard Library at Vanderbilt and the Shakespeare Birthplace Trust in Stratford-upon-Avon, has been patient and helpful. Penny Peirce and her staff at Vanderbilt's Learning Resources Center have also been unusually helpful. I would especially like to thank my students at Vanderbilt, who are a joy to teach and who helped me study the performance history of *Richard* III and the range of possible responses to the Olivier film of 1955 and the BBC videotape of 1982. I hope they remember that semester of Shakespeare as fondly as I do. I also gratefully acknowledge the following permissions I have received to reprint in this book portions of my previously published work: " 'Odde Old Ends': Some Textual and Interpretive Cruxes in *Richard*

III," *Bulletin of the New York Shakespeare Society* 1 (1983): 13-17; "Military Oratory in Richard III," *Shakespeare Quarterly* 35 (1984): 53-61; "Richard Versus Richmond: Aesthetic Warfare in Richard III," *Deutsche Shakespeare-Gesellschaft West Jahrbuch*, 1985, pp. 106-16; "Context and Charisma: The Sher-Alexander Richard III and Its Reviewers," *Shakespeare Quarterly* 36 (1985): 630-43; "Providence and the Text of Richard III," *The Vpstart Crow* 6 (1986): 84-92.

Introduction

Out on ye, Owles, nothing but
Songs of Death—*Richard* III

† The role of Richard III has challenged the best of Shakespearean actors and producers; some, like David Garrick and Edmund Kean, made it the centerpiece of their careers.[1] But even in this company, Laurence Olivier stands out with extraordinary power. This would probably have been true if Olivier had simply continued the success of his famous stage villain in the 1944 and 1948 Old Vic productions. But of course he revived and preserved that success in the brilliant film of the next decade. Antony Hammond suggests its extraordinary influence: "The total previous audience for the play would have been numbered in the thousands. After the film, the number must be reckoned in the millions. Our collective awareness of the play as performed will never be the same again." Roy Walker calls it "a permanent and satisfying record of one of the most remarkable Shakespearean performances of our time." Jack Jorgens concurs: "His *Richard* III properly remains one of the most admired and popular of Shakespeare films." Olivier was called "spellbinding," "breathtaking" as Richard, the film a "tour de force," all these in one of the few mixed reviews, and one of the most intelligent. Harry Schein refers to Olivier's "extraordinary competence as actor and director," and James E. Phillips to the "most celebrated of Olivier's performances." Their remarks are characteristic of the film's almost unanimous (and lasting) critical acclaim. Claire Bloom, Sir John Gielgud, Laurence Naismith, Alec Clunes, and Ralph Richardson also received deserved praise for their parts in the 1955 film, as did William Walker for the musical score.[2]

On the other hand, such success has extracted a cost on the theatrical and interpretive traditions of the play, a cost that is almost as widely acknowledged as the quality of the film. Walker, for example, offers this comment: "One only doubts whether such [filmed] performances as Olivier's *Richard* III might not be almost overwhelmingly influential, standardizing stance, stage business and intonation by sheer force of example." Robert Speaight wonders similarly if "anyone now producing it faces the difficulty that Sir Laurence Olivier's spectacular performance has seemed to put the part out of contemporary reach." As late as 1978 and 1981, some twenty-five years after the film, Hammond and Ralph Berry can still address problems relating to the film's great success: "In its very permanance ... it establishes a theatrical text for the play." In this light it is particularly "regrettable" to Hammond "that Olivier elected to perform a bastardized text."[3]

Speaking of English actor-dramatist Colley Cibber's "rearrangement" of *Richard* III in the early eighteenth century, Nicholas Brooke observes a similar distortion of the textual, the interpretive, and the theatrical traditions, one influencing productions all the way through Olivier's:

> It concentrated exclusively on Richard himself; omitted scenes in which he did not appear, minimized Margaret's role (which was often cut entirely), and drastically pruned the formalized patterning of language which is so conspicuous a feature of the play. This selective procedure is still often followed, most notably in Sir Laurence Olivier's film. And although the critics usually did read Shakespeare's text, their attention was for two centuries as selective as the actors.[4]

The impact of Cibber's adaptation was also exaggerated, of course, by its own great theatrical success. Stanley Wells has recently called it "for a couple of centuries probably the most popular play on the English stage."[5] As we consider the Olivier film in some detail in the next chapter, I will suggest that Cibber's version may have had a similar influence on the discussion of interpretive issues in *Richard* III since 1956. Like Hammond, Berry puts the influence in quasi-Jungian terms: "The problem is always Olivier's Richard, a permanent layer on the collective consciousness."[6]

In creating this extraordinarily compelling Richard, Olivier acknowledged the enduring interpretive problems of *Richard* III essentially by eliminating most of them from the production. Margaret challenges Richard's early preeminence; her role is completely cut. In act 4 Elizabeth may resist Richard's blandishments and threats and wither his growth with ironies; the whole scene is hacked out. In act 3 the Scrivener exposes as cynics and cowards the Mayor and the Citizens whom Richard supposedly gulls. Olivier elects to stage a completely successful deception; the Scrivener is conveniently eliminated. So, essentially, is Richmond. In Shakespeare's text he shares act 5 almost evenly with Richard. In Olivier's film Richmond receives hardly a dozen lines and even fewer camera shots. The ghosts, voices of judgment from beyond the grave, are similarly truncated in the last act. With them go also the voices of the dying lords throughout the last three acts, voices affirming the just hand of providence in their reversals and invoking a similar providence against Richard. The ritual patterns of repeated language and action are also largely eliminated from Olivier's film.

Most of the best critics of the film acknowledge these losses of complexity and significance, even as they praise the film's great accomplishments.[7] What their complaints reveal is the apparently inevitable conflict at the very center of Shakespeare's play (or between the play and its notorious adaptations) between our moral and our aesthetic responses. Making Richard Shakespeare's Pavarotti of evil (the Cibber-Olivier libretto) adds theatricality to the play but subtracts significance. Giving fuller play to Richard's antagonists—Margaret, Elizabeth, the Scrivener, the ghosts, Richmond, providence itself—as Shakespeare's own text seems to do, firms up the play's moral structure but disappoints the aficionados of Richard's ravishing villainy. Since Olivier's film, a number of stage productions of *Richard* III join the 1982 BBC videotape in playing some of these oppositions and conflicts against the ravishing appeal of Richard. In fact, this balance has never been realized more brilliantly than in the 1984–85 Royal Shakespeare Company's *Richard* III, directed by Bill Alexander and starring Antony Sher. I will discuss in the epilogue this production's achievements and their relationship to the theatrical and the interpretive traditions. Such productions bring back into focus some legitimate problems in the play; they also restore a moral and aesthetic richness to *Richard* III that it was denied for more than 300 years.

That richness is the subject of this book. It begins as it ends, with a careful look at the theatrical tradition, focusing particularly on the Olivier film and the recent BBC videotape, but playing as well with other stage productions, like that of Sher and Alexander. Those productions focus our attention on centers of energy and turbulence that can be investigated as productively in the study as on the stage. Chapters 2 through 6 deal with the most interesting of them. Is Richmond armed in act 5 against Richard's continuing aesthetic power? Shakespeare's modification of his chronicle sources and the evidence of Renaissance military manuals both suggest that Richmond is a better orator and a less pietistic character than most of his recent critics have been willing to concede. Does Richard seduce Elizabeth to his will in 4.4; on the other hand, is she something other than his "shallow changing woman" during their final confrontation? The complexity and coherence of her characterization, her relentless ironies during the scene, her perception of Richard as the Tempter, and the evidence of Shakespeare's sources can all be marshaled against Richard's perception of victory. Do Richard and Buckingham actually deceive the Mayor and Citizens in act 3, or do the cynicism, greed, and cowardice of these Londoners create an unusually receptive audience to an amateurish performance? Its words and its actions, its literary analogues, and its historical sources all suggest that the scene can legitimately reverberate with the jarring tones of a rotten charade and a rotten audience.

Perhaps the most challenging questions in the text and on the stage concern the operation of providence in *Richard* III. Some have suggested that it is problematic because it is indirect and imperceptible, too much like the judgment here that returns to plague the inventor, too little like the hand of God. Others argue that providence is sullied by such imperfect "representatives" as the vengeful Margaret or the "vacuous" Richmond, and is therefore "repulsive." Is providence impotent, uncaring, arbitrary, or even malicious in the play? Modern critics have embraced all these positions. The recent BBC videotape refracts them in its closing tableau of a cackling Margaret embracing a deposed Richard, both placed in the pose of a ghastly pietà upon a hideous pyramid of corpses. I will argue that the Olivier film has encouraged such theatrical and critical visions. In fact, it has been widely criticized both for diminishing the agents of providence and the words that credit their agency and then for implying in Richard's brutal death an arbitrary and therefore a repulsive providence. The more carefully Richard is protected from aesthetic and moral opposition in acts 3–5, the more likely this final execution of justice is to seem arbitrary, not to mention aesthetically disappointing at the end of a performance. A reconstruction of some Renaissance understandings of the theology of second causation, unanswered prayers, and the inscrutable will of God helps us confront such questions with renewed sophistication.

All these questions about providence and the effectiveness of Richard's adversaries have a direct bearing on our response to Richard's artistry in evil, on the stage and in the study. So do the many textual cruxes in this fascinating play. In fact, the question of providence, the relative attractiveness of Richard and Richmond in act 5, and the attempted seduction of Elizabeth can all be significantly affected by the hundreds of meaningful variants that have sparked off the flints of the clashing Folio and Quarto texts. Neither players nor readers can afford to ignore the interpretive implications of this kaleidoscopic text. This is particularly true since the theatrical text and the literary text of *Richard* III have both been so relentlessly modified throughout the play's history.

Approaching *Richard* III through such varied perspectives as performance history, historical and literary sources, military manuals, theology, textual cruxes, and a close attention to the language and the dramatic sequence of the play will provide a fresh look at some of the toughest interpretive questions in Shakespeare's histories.[8] Richard emerges less magnetic and more sinister. Elizabeth and Richmond come out of the fray less vacuous and more attractive. The play too seems richer and more coherent with this new balance, neither a mouthpiece of Tudor (or Christian) propaganda nor an amoral celebration of charismatic evil with a shameless, discontinuous reversion to propriety at the end. Richard has his day, but it may not be as long a day as some recent critics and the powerful Olivier film have claimed. The apocalyptic overtones, the advancing aesthetic and moral power of Elizabeth and Richmond, our own growing disgust with Richard's cruelty and his isolation from all that is worth swearing by, and Richard's own flagging energy and inventiveness are all possible harbingers of that approaching dusk. But Richard's most threatening "songs of death" are the angry heavens themselves, the previously inscrutable will of providence, which even Richard finally perceives in the low'ring, frowning skies at Bosworth Field. "Nothing but Songs of Death?" As we move beyond Richard's initial brilliance, I will argue that on the stage as in the study this is the contrary music we, and Richard, should increasingly hear. The Sher-Alexander production vividly illustrates that these songs of death can become a rousing motif in a major key to Richard's exciting but destructive tonalities.

1

Interpretation and Performance in Richard III

✝ Performances of Richard III on stage and screen have contributed uniquely to its interpretive feast. I refer not so much to items like the extravaganza of 1856 in Astley's Amphitheatre, whose playbill promises a stage "covered with DYING AND DEAD HORSES," but to the more wholesome dishes served up by the Garricks and the Irvings, the Keans and the Oliviers, over the last three centuries. None of these performances can be said to prove one interpretive position, of course. Still, by letting us compare old productions, and by inspiring new ones, they all enrich our banquet.[1] In this chapter I will focus most of my attention on the two performances of Richard III that are widely available to students of the play, the 1955 Olivier film and the 1982 BBC videotape, starring Ron Cook and directed by Jane Howell. Unlike the reported and reviewed stage performances which I shall also discuss, these two films are on record and are therefore subject to the repeated scrutiny of other scholars and players. I will look carefully at the ways the two films handle or evade each of the major interpretive issues in the play. But the overriding issue, the one I will start with and never completely leave, concerns the complex attractiveness of Richard himself. On the stage as in the study, the seasoning of that dish has usually determined the flavor of the whole feast. We will start, and end, with Olivier's film.

Besides being a "thrilling" film, "dramatically exciting, superbly acted, a joy to eye and ear," what is it about Olivier's Richard III that has exerted such influence since 1955? One of the common themes of the reviews is the extraordinary power of his characterization of Richard. Olivier cuts whole scenes to "leave Richard always in the centre of the action." Garrick and Kean enjoyed a similar monopoly of the stage in the Cibber versions they acted. So, for that matter, did Henry Irving, who restored Shakespeare's lines selectively enough to keep Richard always in the spotlight. Olivier's Richard impresses us with his intellect, in harmony with Charles Lamb's idea, which was also realized in Kean's performance, "that evil is somehow made splendid by the aspiring genius of the wrongdoer." Jorgens expresses for Olivier's hero "a sympathy of the imagination for a man more cunning than his adversaries, a brilliant wit and poseur." Richard's cynicism and self-awareness "are so complete that they annihilate the pathos of the situation." J. C. Trewin agrees: "Other players have achieved the Red King, boar, cockatrice, bottled spider, and developed the part with a burning theatrical imagination." None "has made us so conscious of the usurper's intellect."[2]

In a similar vein, others praise Olivier's Richard as a "virtuoso role-player": Olivier is "more a splendid entertainer than psychologist or realist, but rarely has so external a performance fit the work so well." How is this Richard theatrically effective? Jorgens urges Olivier's striking appearance, long sharp nose, jet-black hair, sinister good looks, mobility. He is also askew, oblique, out of place and therefore noticeable in a horizontal and vertical world. His entrances are always spectacular, calculated, and his costumes "either boldly declare his evil nature (Satanic blood-red or funereal black) or parody high fashion." One method of achieving this theatricality was "the daring device of looking straight at the camera. . . . The effect is arresting, suggesting the diabolic impudence of Richard's villainy." Further, Olivier's "infinitely beautiful diction" adds elegance to the role. This Richard projects "great charm and confidence." He has "presence, command, and rapidity."[3]

Still, Olivier's attractive and superficial villainy has not pleased everyone. Arthur Bryant, for example, prefers Shakespeare's multifaceted, darker vision to the bright surface of Olivier's film: "*Richard* III is a play in which Shakespeare sets out to tell how England was outraged—not by a foreign conqueror, but by a maniac who subjected her laws, her transmitted decencies, her morality of Christian justice to his power-mad will. . . . Shakespeare's play as written comes rather closer to doing this than the film version." Phillips also faults the Olivier film for failing to depict either the ugliness of Richard's villainy or the loss of "alacrity and spirit" at the end. Shakespeare depicted a "thoroughly human breakdown of the central character mainly in Richard's soliloquy following the . . . ghosts." Phillips continues, "it is a revealing [and] also a deeply moving expression by a man whose brilliant self-confidence has at last and inevitably been

Laurence Olivier as Richard, from the 1955 film. Courtesy of the Museum of Modern Art/Film Stills Archive.

broken." In the film this deeply human moment is cut, lost entirely. Richard's one moment of self-scrutiny and moral awareness, of complexity, is sacrificed to the false heroism of the final battle.[4] If Olivier was like Kean "full of life and spirit and dazzling rapidity," he was not like Garrick "an exact imitation of nature."[5]

9   *Interpretation and Performance*

Recent Richards have tried more for this imitation of nature, for a psychological and moral plausibility that Olivier's Richard lacks, for all its theatrical power. At the Stratford Festival, Canada, in 1967, Alan Bates played a neurotic Richard, more malicious than exultant, nervous, restless, with little of "the joyful and robust energy of the clown," little "love of the theatrical and the hypocritical." Similarly, David Pryce-Jones found "nothing magnificently evil or Machiavellian" about Ian Holms's Richard (Stratford-upon-Avon, 1963). In fact, this Richard was troublesome to several reviewers, suggesting as he did a "psychotic violence lurking beneath an innocent façade." Brian Bedford's (Stratford Festival, Canada, 1977) was "morose and embittered." Norman Rodway's (Stratford-upon-Avon, 1970) was described "as mad as Hamlet, ambling, jigging, and ridiculous." Terry Hands (*Comédie Française*, 1973) directed Robert Hirsch as Richard "the maniac cripple rather than the cunning Machiavel." Most grotesque might have been the touring Georgian production of 1969-70, where one was "transported into a region of irredeemable degeneracy." There the "seedy grotesque evil of Richard was everywhere, down to the very coffin-bearers." His mutilated hand and his hump have been exaggerated, as have the ugliness of his henchmen and his "gratuitous violence"; most vivid are "the bleeding corpse of Henry 6, [and] the two Murderers bound to a wheel."[6] When Alan Bates's Richard begins to "wane" after he reaches the throne, the critics howl. Of Robert Helpmann's (The Old Vic, 1957) they similarly complain, "But having arrived, he seems to weaken." He has lost his "sardonic relish." Helpmann reduces Richard after the coronation to a "white-faced Petrouchka puppet, jerked by strings, hardly human."[7]

One could argue that these diminished Richards are no less appropriate than the glorified villain of the Cibber-Olivier tradition. Still, as Julie Hankey suggests about all of these more somber, more thoughtful, more signifying Richards, there is a nostalgic dismay for the loss of "roaring melodrama" and "virtuoso performance." As far back as 1802 George Frederick Cooke tried a darker Richard who struck Lamb as "intolerably coarse," his hypocrisy "glaring and visible," his humor the "clumsy merriment of a low-minded assassin."[8] Richard Mansfield's Richard seems to have avoided such dissatisfaction. Presented at the Globe Theatre, London, in 1889, his Richard "visibly declines from earlier and more carefree days" after the Battle of Tewksbury, when "he was only nineteen years of age (his strength, his vast ambition, his imperial mind and reckless courage all fresh in him)." In sharp contrast is "the haggard, conscience-stricken, and care-worn tyrant Shakespeare paints him fourteen years later." By emphasizing the passage of so much time, Mansfield apparently made Richard's decline both credible and dramatically effective.[9] But Cibber's superficial touches, like the added line, "Richard's himself again" in act 5, seem to be what the public prefers; it is certainly the Richard Olivier and Cibber gave us, and we have canonized them for love. Theirs is a tasty theatrical morsel, without doubt. But is it Shakespeare's?

Comparing the 1982 BBC videotape of Richard III with Olivier's film will be an interesting way to begin to address that question in some detail. Whatever its faults, and they are considerable, the BBC tape does not imitate Olivier at all. In fact, it is often an effective departure from the Olivier maelstrom, and an interesting restoration of Shakespeare. By looking at the interpretation of Richard, the seductions of Anne and Elizabeth, the gulling of the Mayor and the Citizens, the relative attractiveness of Richard and Richmond in act 5, and finally, the force of providence in both films, we should learn more about these interpretive issues and more about these two films which inevitably embody them. We will also see that the BBC version, though it can hardly compete with the charisma of Olivier's Richard, is much more successful than its competitor in embodying the psychological, historical, and moral significance of Shakespeare's whole action.[10]

Act 1

On first and lasting impression, Cook's Richard is less attractive and less heroic than Olivier's. He lacks Olivier's bravado, carefully closing two doors before he cautiously speaks to us. He walks with an exaggerated limp, and his whole side seems crippled along with the arm, almost paralyzed at times. His hair is usually unkempt, long and unclean, while the other nobles often wear attractive headgear. Also, he is undignified, even childlike. He sprawls "Richard III" on the blackboard before he utters a syllable. Is he about to lecture us on English history? Cook's speech is stage-Cockney on occasion, as though the blood royal were no different from the newly minted bloods from Elizabeth's line.

Most noticeable, however, is the lack of vitality and command. Olivier's Richard is all magnetism, from the first words to us to the last battle. Cook looks right at the camera too, but he does not rivet our attention, and he does not mesmerize other characters. He rather insinuates himself into their favors and into their groups with his hypocrisy. Even that hypocrisy is not so accomplished as Olivier's. With Clarence in the first scene, and then with Anne in the next, his false tears are too obviously false to be believed. Is Cook playing Richard as a bad actor? If so, is the production playing all those around him too dumb to notice? We are never quite sure. Cook's Richard lacks more than acting ability and

Ron Cook as Richard, from the 1982 BBC videotape. © BBC/Time-Life Films.

intellectual energy. He is also grotesquely small. Most of the lords tower above him. Even Queen Elizabeth and Lady Anne match his height. For Kean and for Garrick, theatrical magnetism overwhelmed their small stature. Cook lacks magnetism and stature, and the attractiveness of his Richard is therefore circumscribed from the start.

With the wooing of Anne, however, he rises in our esteem. Olivier had only to mesmerize an exhausted Claire Bloom. She was very pretty but not very bright—all heart, no mind. In fact, their exchange is almost all pantomime, with the stichomythic exchanges reduced to no more than four or five couplets during the whole scene. Cook must take on a terribly angry woman who is almost his size and fully capable of standing up to him intellectually as well. He faces a band of soldiers bearing the coffin, rather than a band of priests. To his credit, he faces down the halberdier with steel eyes and will. Olivier undoes his halberdier with quick hands and feet, giving him a little gratuitous kick after he has put him down.

Cook also has to face down a corpse that bleeds profusely. It shocks him a bit, but he recovers. This touch of vulnerability to people and events will be repeated throughout the production. It makes Cook's Richard more human than Olivier's, and therefore less demonic, less melodramatic. Cook and his Anne begin their exchanges like two children having a word-fight: "You did. I did not." The match is fairly even. Anne's first wavering comes when Richard calls her "Angel." Zoe Wanamaker as Anne is made to look as plain as Claire Bloom is beautiful; she is therefore apparently more vulnerable to Richard's flattery. With Richard's "Your beauty," she is again drawn into his web, looking back at his face, which she has tried to avoid. She spits, effectively, but her own vehemence and the resultant shock on Richard's face both frighten her. She involuntarily covers her mouth with her hands, disarmed by her own violence. Cook's Petrarchan speech confuses her further. She seems now as much puzzled as angry, pleased at this gentle if extravagant praise. Richard speaks very softly throughout the scene, and when he weeps (again unconvincingly, at least to us), his words become almost a whisper. Anne begins to believe his humility as well as his love. She does threaten him with the sword, and she seems pretty good with it, too. But by the end of the scene, Cook has convinced her of his love and his repentance. She is glad of the repentance, too full of grief to respond to the love. There is honesty to this scene, integrity on both their parts. Magic plays no part in the seduction of Anne, unless it be the magic of Richard's clever psychological thrusts against Anne's peculiar vulnerabilities of heart, mind, and body.[11]

Claire Bloom is more vulnerable from the start. Though Olivier has her mourning the corpse of her husband Edward rather than her father-in-law Henry, she looks too pale and sensitive, seems too weak emotionally, mentally, and physically to withstand Olivier for long. He seems supernaturally strong, his black shadow framing their scenes as it does the whole play. Most of Anne's invective and most of her curses are cut. So then is most of her rhetorical strength, which is her only strength against Richard here. The Gregorian chant seems to fit her tearful face and pathetic, sniffling, trembling voice, rather than representing the strength of the church. Its irony is emphasized by the heroic if sinister music that precedes it in the scene, Richard's music.[12]

Olivier also splits the wooing into two scenes, with the idea of adding more plausibility to the result.[13] Time passes; in the second sequence Edward is in the tomb and Anne is praying over cold stone, not warm blood. Has she armed herself in the interval against the troubles Richard must surely bring her? Apparently not. Even during the first exchange, she seems drawn physically to him. She spits dramatically, and feels momentarily exhilarated. But Richard stares her down, and when she signs the cross at the end of the first sequence, it is more to protect herself from his mysterious attractiveness than to bless the corpse. Anne catches herself looking back at him in fatal fascination. Then as she leaves with the religious figures, she almost looks again into the shadows for this Richard. The Gregorian *"In paradisium"* ends the scene aurally, but Richard's greater power is as clear as his shadowy surroundings at the end. He is somewhere in those shadows, and he knows he has won. "I'll have her" comes right here in the Olivier film.

The second sequence opens with Anne praying over the tomb of her husband, Richard's shadow in the foreground. Richard is all black in the scene, she all white. Their physical intertwining is particularly effective as a symbol of his increasing success. Richard plays the consoling friend rather than Cook's repentant sinner. He also intimidates and hypnotizes this Anne; he does not deceive her. He grabs her white wrist with that black hand. His face is often close to hers. Even after she spits for the second time, she also looks into those menacing eyes and feels fatally attracted. He hovers over her at the tomb; then by the arches of the walkway he again surrounds her, black hand over white arm, black arm around white body. She is swaying, almost swooning, incredulous, but too tired and too hypnotized to resist or to understand.[14] She could almost be drugged. Olivier allows his voice to break only slightly when he proclaims that he is blind with weeping. It is enough. Anne is effectively awkward with the sword, as girls used to be with bats and balls. She could not use the sword even if she could will its use. Then Olivier almost sticks the sword into his own neck as he offers to kill himself for her. That bowed, tense sword frightens Anne, and she moves to remove it, and him, from danger. Now she is won. She caresses his cheek in passing. She kisses him twice, once passionately. "Dissembler" becomes her submissive, complimentary epi-

14   Interpretation and Performance

Laurence Olivier with Claire Bloom as Lady Anne, from the 1955 film. Courtesy of the Museum of Modern Art/Film Stills Archive.

thet for this dominant man. And then the shadow falls on Anne standing before the bed, the altar of their love, as she knelt before the tomb of Edward when the scene began.

The energy, the excitement of the whole enactment is extraordinary. Olivier is sinister, composed, mysterious, worldly. Of course, in Shakespeare's play his total command, of himself and of the world around him, is about to be circumscribed by Margaret's awesome presence, but Olivier completely eliminates Margaret from the film. In one stroke, he thus also eliminates Richard's toughest early competition, morally, psychologically, and dramatically. At the same time, he severely reduces the providential dimensions of the play.[15] Margaret can steal the scene if she is allowed to play it. If she is eliminated, Richard can romp through the first two acts unchecked by the hand of God or man.

A glance at the discomfort Julia Foster's Margaret causes Cook's Richard in the BBC videotape reveals some of the problems Olivier avoided by eliminating Margaret from his film. Foster is wonderful, dressed all in black, a homespun woolen clout wrapped under her chin and around her head, wild gray hair, bags under her eyes. She is more unkempt even than Richard. Foster hides behind the throne, undercutting Richard's lies and his presence. She commands our attention. She also commands the camera, as she would in any production of the scene. In the BBC version, she is often closer to the camera than Richard, who babbles in the background while we stare, still fascinated, at Margaret. Foster also speaks eloquently; she is no Cockney here but a true queen. Only her features are coarse, with grief. Made up to look unmade, and with her plain clothes of mourning and poverty, she seems almost a peasant. But in stage presence she is clearly Margaret of Anjou.

She also commands Richard effectively. I wonder what Olivier could have done to avoid her riveting presence. As the curses begin, Cook tries to move away. He may be bored; he may be a bit frightened. But when Margaret commands him to stop, he stops. It is in the text. It has to happen. Just as Richard has stopped the procession to the prison and the procession to the grave, Margaret stops him in his tracks. The tables are turned, quickly, visually, verbally. As the curses continue, Richard is also inevitably in the rhetorical background, merely a lord among these other lords. Oh, he cleverly mobilizes them against her. That he has so recently insulted the pack of them makes this new amity impressive. But most of our attention is still pinned on Margaret; so, not incidentally, is Richard's. He watches, fascinated, the effects of Margaret's curses on Elizabeth. Her cane punctuates those curses. So do the stubby fingers protruding from the worn-out gloves.

Richard tries to leave when the curses finally reach home. Margaret stops him again with "stay Dog." Then he tries to avoid her eye, as Claire Bloom tried to avoid Olivier's. His face is impassive, but she is right behind him fixing him there in place, and fixing our attention still. She begins to circle Richard's warped body as she talks about his deformity from birth. He is cool; he is also being humiliated. By the end of her scene, her agonies themselves indict this Richard and this company. Never mind that she has her share of guilt; never mind that Richard finally makes her cry when he seems to frustrate her curse. The scene stresses her righteous indignation and her deep woes; it evokes pity and fear for the tragic queen. Her grief is as compelling as Anne's in the previous scene. But this woman also dominates Richard dramatically for much of the scene, and she only leaves when she wants to. Richard's control is severely threatened, as are his theatrical presence and his moral and physical being. Olivier avoided a lot of complexity by deleting Margaret. He also radically distorted the play's narrative logic and its aesthetics by doing it this violence.[16]

Act 3, Scenes 5–7

In the Olivier film and in the theatrical tradition in general, the sequence with the Mayor and the Citizens, 3.5–3.7, is usually another tour de force of Richard's acting ability. The actor playing Richard naturally wants to put on a successful performance before the Mayor and the Citizens, a mirror of his own successful illusion. In Kean's *Richard III* and in Olivier's, the audience on the stage is therefore made gullible and pliable, stupid but successfully deceived. Hankey talks of the tradition through the eighteenth and nineteenth centuries of a comic Mayor, which makes this deception easier to play convincingly.[17] Some twentieth-century productions have followed this tradition.

However, the last few decades have heard interesting voices of dissent. At Ashland, Oregon, in 1967, Richard Risso succeeds with his audience through the "sheer virtuosity of his villainy," but is finally "carried away by his own actor's skills" during 3.7. At the Colorado festival in 1970, Richard and Buckingham are depicted as "herding feckless fools into crowds and leading them to fifteenth-century political meetings. The cynicism here was brilliantly conceived." At Stratford-upon-Avon in 1970, "Richard's acting in 3.7 [was] cynically presented by Buckingham as a play-within-a-play. [It] was not designed to convince, but offered as a party-joke." Of this same production, Marder writes, "when Hastings' head is brought in, Richard kisses it and throws it to the Lord Mayor, who faints dead away.... [Later], when the Lord Mayor will not acknowledge Richard, his arm is twisted." Finally, at San Diego in 1972, "Richard's mock-prayer scene with the bishops doesn't fool the Citizens. A few judiciously cut throats and spurting blood force the people to reluctant knees."[18] Though the reviewers predictably dislike some of these interpretations, and though they may stem from a political cynicism that is more contemporary than Renaissance, the sources and Shakespeare's text can be shown to support these competing versions over the older theatrical tradition.

The most interesting touch of the BBC version of 3.5 is its early portrayal of the Mayor. Arthur Cox comes in as the red-faced buffoon of the earlier theatrical tradition, sixtyish, flustered by the great men he has so seldom seen. With Richard's "What? thinke you we are Turkes or Infidels," this Mayor is also clearly intimidated by Richard's vehemence, rather than convinced of his sincerity. But several uncertain looks at Michael Byrne's Buckingham as the scene goes on begin to suggest something other than the buffoon. Cox's Mayor wants to respond as Richard and Buckingham want him to respond, but he is not quite sure of the scenario they have devised. He seems, like many characters in this *Richard III*, afraid to look Richard in the eyes. He also seems to be shooting those glances off to his director Buckingham to see whether his acting in this little play is itself believable. So far, so good. The scene explores some delicious ambiguity, and this ambiguity does no credit to Richard the arch-deceiver. This complexity continues as the Mayor apparently loves the intimacy these lords are granting him. He leans close to Buckingham's face, visibly pleased that a lord would condescend to lay a hand on his shoulder, or shake his hand as he leaves. As we shall see in chapter 4, this is the Mayor of Shakespeare's historical sources, and it may be the surest interpretation of this dramatic moment in the tradition.

However, the buffoon-Mayor is then uncomfortably spliced onto this more complex version. Richard the naughty boy tries to make a complete ass of the Mayor as this first sequence ends, by giving back the now tear-stained and dirtied handkerchief the Mayor lent him. Is it a relic the Mayor would cherish? Cox takes it, somewhat puzzled, and leaves with his people. Richard cannot contain his joy and his disgust until the Mayor is out the door. The laugh is indistinct, however; although the Mayor hears something, he may dismiss it as more of Richard's grief for the fallen friend, Hastings. Or does he hide his distaste at the dirtied handkerchief, and his surprise at the actor's (and the lord's) indiscretion? We cannot be sure in this production, but in a sophisticated Mayor these would be fine touches. The bloody head of Hastings prefaces their conversation, and clearly gives some point to the possibility that the Mayor is intimidated rather than gulled. *Sic semper* "no-men." But by the end of the scene, we are not sure of the Mayor. He may be "convinced" by the first half of the deception merely because he wants power and the company of powerful men. He may be deathly afraid of Richard; he may be the fool Richard seems to assume him to be. Or Richard may be fooling himself by thinking this Mayor a fool.

With such possibilities of cynicism and self-deception, Richard's as well as the Mayor's, the next scene, the one with the Scrivener, is particularly effective in undercutting Richard and his cronies. The Scrivener is presented in the BBC production as a frightened but honest bureaucrat. Whispering, looking around before he will confide in us, he is at once fearful and embarrassed at his fear. Almost as wrinkled as Margaret, he is very old, gray-bearded. He looks straight at us, after all the shifting eyes of the previous scene. In contrast to the flurry of activity in the two scenes of deception and intimidation that surround him, he is quiet and still. He is also outspokenly against that cynicism. All of these qualities undercut Richard, undercut these surrounding scenes of crowning achievement. We are drawn to the Scrivener as one of us; we are therefore drawn still further from the monstrous Richard. Conveniently, Olivier also leaves out the Scrivener. Like Margaret, he goes against the grain of Olivier's upbeat, heroic, external villainy. Buckingham and Richard are having such a good time and the crown is so close. Why spoil it all with reflectiveness, or worse, mixed reviews?

After the intriguing complexity of its 3.5 and 3.6, the BBC film disappoints us by portraying 3.7 as a tour de force for Richard and Buckingham. Buckingham puzzles us briefly by speaking with more and more of a Cockney accent. Is this a touch of baseness or merely the clever politician playing down to his new constituency? Nicely, Buckingham is visibly embarrassed when he refers to Richard's form that he praised so highly to the Citizens. That little charade obviously does not stand the light of day. So Richard is briefly crestfallen when he learns that the Citizens did not cry "God save Richard, Englands Royall King" (2235; 3.7.22). With him, we are therefore astonished when Buckingham soon reports, "The Maior is here at hand" (2258; 3.7.45). Whence has victory come? This production does not vouchsafe a reply with its stage business. Since the play's text is no clearer, we are left darkling. For a moment, here and in the Olivier, one wonders if Buckingham is sadistically drawing out the moment. But then all is bustle, and on with the charade.

The scene itself is presented in the BBC film as the best acting of Richard and Buckingham in their careers. The Mayor is our chief stumbling block. He seems completely duped, heartily in favor of Richard's coronation. Gone are the fear and the uncertainty that he showed in 3.5. Gone as well are the glimmers of intelligence that lay behind those darting eyes. He is so gullible, so pliable, that he almost leaves when Catesby says "Next day" (2276; 3.7.60). Buckingham has to restrain him. Then, the Mayor and the Citizens are eager to see Richard and offer him the crown. They are Buckingham's allies, but they seem sincere and enthusiastic in their alliance, not bought and sold. The Mayor is absolutely transfixed at Richard's show of piety. He shakes his head, smiles knowingly at Richard's apparent naiveté about their meaning some harm to him. He is chagrined at the "ignoble Plants" (2348; 3.7.127) that have debased the royal stock. And he is always looking up, adoring Richard with his Citizens, rapt, serious, responsive to Richard's every word. This Mayor kneels to entreat Richard to take the crown, even before Buckingham. The Citizens follow.

As a further inconsistency, when Buckingham earlier describes the failed meeting with the Mayor and the Citizens, he seems really disturbed that the Mayor has neither taken him at his word nor pretended to do so. "Thus sayth the Duke, thus hath the Duke inferr'd, / But nothing spoke, in warrant from himselfe" (2245–46; 3.7.32–33) is spoken with anger and disappointment. If this is true, what has happened in the interim to change the Mayor's mind? If it is not true, is Buckingham putting Richard on? The contradiction may lie in Shakespeare's compression of more than a week of action and several more speaking characters in the sources into this one dramatic moment with the Mayor. But it still must be resolved into a coherent dramatic moment in production. If the Citizens are here and glad, why must the Mayor explain their lack of response earlier? If they are bought and sold, why is it not obvious in their looks and gestures? All that remains of the Mayor's doubts and fears are those nervous thumbs.

If the Mayor is gulling Richard and Buckingham along with his Citizens, he is too good at it in the BBC version. That is, neither we the audience of the film nor Richard and Buckingham the fellow actors can see through his acting. The irony of Richard's failure to see would be compounded when he similarly deludes himself into believing he has seduced Elizabeth in 4.4. But if we cannot see the hypocrisy either, then the irony is again lost. I think the production gives us a whiff of complexity in 3.5, but then somehow drops it from the menu. The meal is not as successful without it.

More interesting is Buckingham's reversion to melodramatic acting as the scene ends. "And in this resolution here we leave you. / Come Citizens, we will entreat no more" (2439–40; 3.7.218–19) is grossly but intentionally overacted, apparently to get the attention of the stupid Citizens. When Richard answers "I will," the Mayor clasps his hands in ecstasy and shrieks (well, sighs) "Oh," full of joy. "Long live Richard." Their play is completed to rave reviews. "Amen." A curtain closes on Richard and the holy men, as it had opened to reveal them on their balcony as the scene began. To my taste, the visible theatrical metaphor is more obvious than effective here. The curtain and the melodramatic acting are pretty touches, but without some ambiguity in the response of the audience on stage, they have less point.

Olivier cuts this sequence severely, though parts of 3.7 are brilliantly realized. First, crucially, the Scrivener's condemning words are as completely eliminated as Margaret's haunting severity in 1.3. In Shakespeare,

Rivers, Grey, and Vaughan go to their deaths at Pomfret with similar moral and prophetic words. In the Olivier film, they disappear without a trace, and therefore without affirming Margaret's prophecies or foretelling Richard's doom. Neither prophecy nor doom is much in favor in Olivier's heroic recipe. Neither is the reflectiveness of their remorse. Hastings is allowed a little scene, but the best of his lines are also cut, like the ringing and prophetic "O momentarie grace of mortall men" (2069-74; 3.4.96-101). In their place is a snide remark from another play about the cat, the rat, and the dog. We may see an impressive Last Judgment over his head in fresco as the lords back away in fear. We may also see a death's head. But these are both indistinct images, and they seem to suggest ironies against only Hastings.[19] Richard remains untouched by them. Catesby has just been so entertaining in his own ironies against Hastings, so pleasantly amoral. It is all a jolly joke. Why spoil it all with high sentence, particularly when it is not the least bit obtuse?

There is also almost nothing of 3.5 in the Olivier film. We jump from Hastings's few last words to a carriage carrying the Mayor and Buckingham to Baynard's Castle. Somehow Lovell, Ratcliffe, and Catesby have leaped from Pomfret into the carriage, and sit there sinister and smirking as Hastings works on the Mayor. In fact, the cutting also makes a shambles of the following conversation between Richard and Buckingham. Since Buckingham has just broached the subject to the Mayor, and the Mayor is left as he is about to address the Citizens from a soapbox, what does Buckingham have to report to Richard? The Citizens have not yet been tried. The ominous silence cannot have occurred. Yet Buckingham dutifully reports to Richard anyway.

The Mayor in the Olivier film is an easy mark, corpulent and gullible, though not intimidated. He seems to believe the rationalization about Mistress Shore and Hastings's dark future. Buckingham's cronies are amused at either his gullibility or his cynicism. Little more is made of this crucial scene. Similarly, Buckingham is curiously unconcerned as he relates his failure with the Mayor and the Citizens to Olivier, who is himself thunderstruck. Olivier stares at the dead fireplace throughout most of their chilling conversation. But Buckingham is hungry, and a buffet is near at hand. He draws a glass of wine; he cuts a piece of cake; seasons his food; wipes his hand. A little snack, a little chat, and then back to business. It is as though the difficulties of the sequence were all swept under the table with the crumbs. Again, since Buckingham knows from the start of the conversation that the Mayor is either convinced or a willing if cynical ally, why all the dialogue? A real problem in the text is again glossed over in performance. The eating and drinking may suggest just a dash of sadism. It will be the last power Buckingham wields over Richard. In fact, when this scene ends, Olivier's Richard extracts subservience with a vengeance.

Out in the courtyard, the Mayor is comically conceived, and effectively so. Once again, this keeps us from taking the scene too seriously. He echoes Buckingham's words, "Generall good" and "two deepe Divines" (2284, 2291; 3.7.68, 75), as though he were the Recorder for the eager if scruffy Citizens. Then to the Mayor's "say us nay," they almost comically echo, "say us nay." All are caught up in this little litany of legitimacy. After the charade is over and the Citizens are gone, Richard swings down on a bell-rope, exultant but horrifying, even to Buckingham. He demands that his accomplices kneel and kiss his misshapen glove. Finally, he is overwhelmingly ugly, white-faced and ghastly; playing has been superseded by a reality none of them quite anticipated. Though the moment is brief, it is memorable. Olivier's Richard is seldom as real, or as hideous, as here. His curtain opens as the charade ends.

Act 4, Scene 4

Unlike the Olivier film, the BBC *Richard* III gives full play to the mourning queens, and to Richard's disintegration as king in act 4. Particularly interesting is the BBC treatment of Richard's attempted seduction of Queen Elizabeth. Olivier may have cut this whole scene to save a whopping 400 lines.[20] But again, as with Margaret, Hastings, Rivers, Grey and Vaughan, and Clarence with the Murderers, Olivier is also cutting significance, particularly significant ritual opposition to Richard and significant upstaging of him. It is easier to seem invulnerable without this chorus of past, present, and future truths always sounding about his ears. It is easier still without the embodiment in their ordered rhetoric of the ritual order of the providentially controlled universe they all manifest and inhabit. It is finally easier to be the Cibber-Olivier "myself again" in act 5 if the fabric of that invincible self has not been shredded by potent words and potent women in the earlier acts.[21]

The exchange with Elizabeth is prefaced by Annette Crosbie's strong and sure Duchess of York in the BBC version. She puts Richard to much the same disadvantage that Margaret did earlier. Despite the din of drums and trumpets, she faces Cook's Richard down. She reviews to his ugly face his ugly childhood and early manhood. Richard tries to leave, as with Margaret, but again he is frozen with "a word." Words are the most potent weapons of these adversaries, after all, and they have ironic power over this nominalist Richard. Olivier has systematically disarmed the women by taking away most of their words. Cook's Richard cannot face his mother down during her assault. Her words are stronger than his will. He plays the bored teenager, but the scene wears him down. At the end he is weary, and his eyes evade hers.

Then it is Elizabeth's turn. Made up to look old, tired, plain too, as unpainted as Margaret in 1.3, she is at first more vulnerable than his mother to Richard's intimidation. The din forces her to cover her ears, while Richard does not even flinch when she menaces his eyes with her nails. Despite these disadvantages in the BBC production, Rowena Cooper's Elizabeth holds the upper hand throughout most of the scene. Her rich grief, anger, and truth all pour out in the devastating irony of her words. Richard keeps assuming a success that never comes; thus he is repeatedly deflated. He is as confident about the battle ("when this Arme of mine hath chastized") as he is about the seduction ("Go then, [my mother]") [3110, 15; 4.4.325, 330]). He smiles, tries to charm, kneels for the blessing he is sure to receive. Cook is very persuasive here, and Elizabeth's resistance is therefore all the more impressive. Richard's resilience is awesome, too. Only occasionally does he look tired, discouraged. But as the scene goes on there is a growing edge of frustration. His voice rises as he feels the impotence of his words and the power of hers. His anger shows more and more as Elizabeth remains calm in the midst of her finer anger. Hers is a grand dignity throughout; his presumption cloys. Once Elizabeth walks around Richard, forcing him to turn and see more insults, more rebuffs, more truth in her ironies. We recall Margaret behind his crooked back, repulsed and scornful, in 1.3.

The soldiers are omnipresent, but impassive. As in the scene with Anne, when they are always in the frame, one wishes for some clue, some response from them. But when Cook's Richard reaches a peak of frustration, when he stops trying to persuade and starts trying to intimidate with the purely physical threats of wholesale destruction, the soldiers, still there, take clearer symbolic shape. After Elizabeth has stripped Richard of all he can swear by, the soldiers may be the only power Richard has left. This coward will use them relentlessly, all these men against one woman.

At the end of the scene she is "tempted of the Divel thus," by force, not by guile. She yields, but she is not persuaded. Already grief-worn, Cooper's Elizabeth is exhausted by their exchange. But Cook's Richard is ludicrous to assume that she is "shallow changing." She hears this monster, this devil, promise to destroy Elizabeth, Dorset, the whole world, before he will accept a denial. What else can she do? Certainly not lose more children to save face. Richard demands a parting kiss; she grants it. Her face, impassive now as the soldiers, is also very tired. During their nose-to-nose confrontation, she blinks; afterwards, her voice becomes pitiable. Her "shall I's" are apparently concessions. Dazed, exhausted, she seems finally dominated by the parting kiss. After all of the superb resistance, after the mighty will of the earlier Elizabeth, I would prefer some sarcasm at the end, some hint that she is not broken nor really even bending, just deceiving Richard. Cooper does not vouchsafe us such a detail. The moral and the logical victory is clearly Elizabeth's. But this sudden turn at the end gives Richard victory too, a literal conquest of physical domination. Interestingly, Richard intimidates Lord Stanley in similar fashion in the scene that follows. We see a sinister smile as they stand nose-to-nose in a battle of wills. Then Stanley's lips quiver. Richard is horrifying, to Stanley and to Elizabeth. He is neither persuasive nor deceptive. Both Stanley and Elizabeth will renege on these forced compacts in the next act. At best, Richard's victories here are Pyrrhic.

At the moment of Elizabeth's apparent capitulation in the Cibber *Richard* III, an inserted speech makes it absolutely clear that she is merely deceiving Richard:

> What shall I say? still to affront his love,
> I fear will but incense him to Revenge.
> And to consent I should abhor my self,
> Yet I may seemingly comply, and thus
> By sending *Richmond* Word of his Intent,
> Shall gain some time to let my Child escape him.
> It shall be so.

Though the lines are not Shakespeare's, they reveal how the scene was acted and interpreted throughout much of the eighteenth and nineteenth centuries. I think her motivation and her strong will are also implicit in the logic of character and scene and play. In Cibber, it is inescapable that Richard is fooled, and self-deceived. The confusion with the messengers and the forgotten orders just cap off this massive defeat. In Irving's "restored" *Richard* III, the speech is deleted, but so are most of Elizabeth's following questions, with their ambiguity. In fact, Irving's Elizabeth still adds "[Half aside] What were best to say" before her "Shall I be tempted...."[22] This is essentially the entire theatrical tradition Olivier inherited. His only recourse was apparently to delete the whole debacle. How else could his Richard remain invincible and clever?

Several modern productions have also stressed the great complexity of this scene, usually to Richard's disadvantage. In one, Elizabeth finally yields, but to torture, not persuasion: "Elizabeth is not a 'shallow, changing woman.' As Richard coaxes her to yield up her daughter, his torturers are applying other kinds of pressure." Maggie Smith's Elizabeth (Stratford Festival, Canada, 1977) played "the inquisitor for all the part's steely logic in the great confrontation scene of IV.iv. That ... was the high plateau of theatre in the season's set, a memorable duel between the Company's stars." Lynne Porteous's Elizabeth in the 1981 production in Brisbane also illustrates how brilliantly the scene works on the stage if Elizabeth's resistance holds: "The passionate battle between Richard and Elizabeth became one of the most electrifying scenes in the play. . . . There was no need for the brief interpolated aside . . . by Queen Elizabeth . . . assuring us that . . . she was only playing for time." The production in Warsaw, 1969, has "Richard caressing Elizabeth, kissing her cleavage, and practically seducing her—all to her visible loathing."[23] I wish the BBC film had stuck to its guns, or fired them more on target, as its interpretation of the scene ended. Such an ending would have found good company in the theatrical tradition for Elizabeth's consistent devastation of Richard.

Act 5

Act 5 is superb in the BBC videotape, and usually true to the words and the dramatic sequence of Shakespeare's play. A pattern of contrasting actions punctuates the entire act, usually to Richmond's advantage and almost always to moral and aesthetic effect. In fact, one realizes after seeing this version how completely Olivier distorted the order and significance of these most crucial scenes. This is not to say that the BBC version contains no distortions of its own. The last tableau, however modern in its cynicism and irony, is perversely contradictory of the thematic integrity of the play's final act, as the BBC performs it. But until that last vignette, this act is another of those grand moments the BBC series has consistently produced in the history plays. Because it is so much more effective than the Olivier film, and so much closer to Shakespeare's text, I will describe it in considerable detail.

First we see the somber but still intelligent Buckingham, understated at last. By not playing for anyone but himself, he conveys most effectively the truth of his reflections on All Souls, the accuracy of Margaret's prophecies, and the justice of providence. Some of the play's most crucial issues come to the foreground in this quiet, dignified, thoughtful moment. Michael Byrne's Buckingham is impressive throughout; he is clearly superior in concept to Ralph Richardson's bemused gull in the Olivier.[24]

Antony Browne's Ratcliffe remains the impassive and imposing figure he has been throughout, menacing but inscrutable. More and more he suggests the undertaker.

If there were one area in which this production could easily better the Olivier, it would be in the presentation of Richmond and his men; the BBC takes full advantage. Richmond's first scene is much brighter, rousing but never melodramatic. The soldiers are orderly and confident in their drill. Brian Deacon's Richmond is armed and handsome, very personable, and in control. He has a manly Welsh accent and an open, honest, but never vacuous smile. In immediate contrast, Richard is nervous, but attending to the business of the moment. (One may need to add that the contrast is built into Shakespeare's play.) Richard is also particularly unattractive, small and ugly in shape as well as spirit, now that we have seen Richmond. Richard's face is as closed as Richmond's is open.

A golden sunset flashes off Richmond's armor and face in the next scene. His lords cluster round him; they will continue to do so throughout the play. Obviously this leader is as well regarded as Richard is feared. Richmond's men all kneel with love around their lord. Right afterward Richard's lords stand all apart in a darker setting. One betrays the same sense of atrocity in his face that Tyrrel showed after the princes had been murdered. The lost cheer of mind and alacrity of spirit come across in Richard's slower-paced words and movements. A reflective if not morose Richard is left brooding at a table with one candle lighting his face and the room. We cannot forget Clarence's last night in prison; the settings are effectively similar, even to the bowl of wine and Ratcliffe's undertakerly airs.

"Rites of love" also dominate our next scene with Richmond and his men, even in these troubled times. Like Richard, Richmond is now out of his armor. As his friends leave the tent, bidding good night, all touch him with affection. There are smiles here, eagerness to kneel in love and eagerness to engage the enemy. This is a handsome band, serious but hopeful of success. We sense *comitatus*, troops of friends, not mouth honor, breath. Like Richard, Richmond too sits at a candlelit table before he sleeps. In striking contrast, the table suggests an altar instead of a symbol of doom or judgment. Richmond's softly spoken prayer in that strong and honest Welsh accent is attractively pious, manly, and devout. He snuffs the candle with his moistened fingers, places his head on his arms, and sleeps.

The ghost sequence continues this effective alternation of Richard and Richmond, and it continues to work as film while signifying psychologically, morally, and spiritually the meanings of the roles these two men are playing out. It particularly dramatizes the psychological weight of Richard's crimes, and the alliance of providence and the wronged souls with Richmond. Like the courtship of Elizabeth, this scene can devastate Richard's remaining shreds of attractiveness. Characteristically, Olivier leaves almost all of it out.[25]

We look through Richard's open but sleeping eye to begin the sequence. In his dream that lies behind that eye, we see him as he dreams himself. With surprising effect this Richard is made aware of all that the ghosts say to him and also to Richmond. Except for the wine spilling grotesquely out of Clarence's mouth while he speaks his lines to Richard, and then pouring over the camera lens as he addresses Richmond, everything is visually and thematically impressive. Even here, Clarence offering a cup of wine to Richmond on the throne suggests the community of good fellowship and divine assistance against Richard's aloneness, his impending despair, death, and damnation. We see and hear Rivers, Grey, and Vaughan signing Richard's death warrant. The scratching quills are particularly rasping reminders of the judgment to come; perpetual torment might be always hearing those scratching pens, and seeing their syllables of recorded judgment. When we see Hastings it is across a table with many candles burned almost away. Then Richard must watch Hastings's blessing of Richmond on the throne. The princes in concert crown Richmond; Richard watches again.

Suddenly, Anne is in bed, Richard on the floor, frantically stuffing a bloodstained pillow. All of the feathers are strewn about, like untrammeled consequences. Richard tries to smother her with the pillow. But no sooner has he covered her ghost's face than she is blessing Richmond, now sleeping again at the table. Only now does Richmond seem aware of Richard in his dream. Richard frantically ascends the dias and puts on the crown. Buckingham curses him on the throne. It is overwhelming, this parade of all eleven ghostly witnesses against Richard and for Richmond, and the better it is done on the stage or screen, the more devastating it must be to Richard. The refrains "Dispaire and dye" and "live and prosper" come alive in this representation more effectively than they do in the text. The only way to minimize their power is to cut most of the ghosts and their words to Richmond and Richard. That, essentially, is what Olivier chooses to do, following the successful theatrical precedent of the past three centuries.

Olivier also cuts almost all of Richard's soliloquy. The action goes better, of course, more quickly, less ambiguously. But Richard's disintegration is almost certainly the point here. It is fascinating how loath critics, actors, directors, and audiences have been to let him go. In the BBC version, the soliloquy is not astonishingly effective, but at least it is there. Richard is talking to a candle, fascinated like a moth, sweating, deeply shaken. Who could be otherwise after such horrors? Unlike his earlier successes with the women, he cannot stare this candle down. Nor can he stare down his other self. The I who will despair, the self who acknowledges morality and divine retribution stares down the Machiavel. Cook's Richard has trouble recovering from these moments, as well he should. His time is almost up, if the audience or the actor is thinking about what all this signifies. Ratcliffe is still more the undertaker, silent, grave, inscrutable, hovering over the doomed Richard.

Richmond awakes with a fresh, bright face; his lords enjoy his hope and his refreshment. As he addresses his men, they are serious, orderly, attractive. His lords remain near him. Brian Deacon's Richmond is not a triumphant orator, but he is effective, personable and convincing. He is not the stiff, pious, or platitudinous Richmond so many critics have seen since the Olivier film.[26] He is inspiring, and he is loved. All smile when he mentions their wives welcoming home the conquerers. All say "Richmond and victory" with raised swords as the oration ends. Richard's lords are all frowns, or totally inscrutable. The frozen but vaguely pained mask is a common face in Richard's camp. Friend and foe are indistinguishable, as Richmond said. These are friends for fear. Though Richard is first as visibly bothered by the omens as he was by the ghosts, he is controlled when he must busy himself with command. In fact, this accustomed command gives theatrical vigor and some tragic dimensions to the end of this play, as it does in Macbeth. It reminds us of Richard's lost potential, the true gifts that were falsely used, the waste. Richard's desperation is also exciting; it does not have to be heroic as well. The BBC production is not particularly successful in making this difficult distinction between bravery and bravado, "true hope" and despair. The Olivier version fails completely.

Richard's men are quite different from Richmond's. They look like a gang of thugs. Their lines are uneven, their ranks broken at the end of the oration by the messenger. But there is much more response. Richard seems to stir them up more than Richmond stirred his men, even though it is often with the slurs on Richmond and his troops. We can understand this response as coarseness, or as overconfidence. But the BBC production also does not make that distinction as clearly as it might.[27] After the thoughtful alternations of an attractive Richmond and an unattractive Richard throughout the act, one is surprised and a bit disappointed to see the distinction blurred at this crucial moment. Richard could be less stirring, his troops less responsive, his lords more loath to follow. There are some undercutting touches, but not enough.

The death of Richard is fascinating but not completely successful. Four or five spears penetrate his body and are broken off and left there before he falls. Even then he will not die. This "pierced boar" scares Richmond's men away and rushes at Richmond with his dagger. Richmond's broadsword does the trick, but still Richard never falls prone. We look again and again at this sitting, crouching thing, wondering with Richmond and his men if he is indeed dead, if, in fact, he can die. "The bloody dog is dead," Richmond proclaims; but no one is sure. Richard's mace earlier in the battle is effectively brutal. Richmond's sword with its crosslike hilt is finally decisive. But like the Olivier film, the BBC production focuses too much of our attention on Richard's death and Richard's corpse, too little on the deserving and victorious Richmond.

The rest of the BBC videotape is unambiguously heroic and joyful, that is, until the final tableau. Stanley's "long usurp'd royalty" is the crown itself, and we gladly see it placed on this Richmond's head. Richmond's first "Amen" is not coercive but smiling; he knows that his men will affirm this good wish. Effectively, his final speech has three distinct parts: to the men, to the audience, and to God. On that final manly note of order and *comitatus*, Richmond ends good and triumphant.[28]

Curiously, the BBC production does not end with Richmond's last speech. In a touch reminiscent of Roman Polanski's 1972 film *Macbeth*, the king's words of order, providence, and justice are not the last words. In the Polanski film, Donalbain goes back to visit the witches. In the BBC's *Richard III*, we are served up a pyramid of dead bodies, dashed with Margaret's cackling laughs. And then, as the camera ascends, who should be at the apex but this Margaret, holding her Richard like a Christ just brought down from the cross. The emblem is unmistakable, and the effect is quite contradictory to all that has been going on during the last act of this production. Providence is either identified with the cackling Margaret or all of the wanton violence that she has invoked. Our last taste is not of the restoration of order and good governance, but of chaos and arbitrary violence. If there is a providence at all, it is bloodthirsty. The last picture might be modern; it is certainly cinematically effective. But neither the words nor the actions are Shakespeare's.[29]

The final act is the least impressive part of the Olivier film. In large measure this is probably because Olivier's heroic, witty, dashing, dauntless Richard cannot survive the relentless logic of Shakespeare's conclusion. Olivier's solution of this problem is to cut almost everything in the last act, replacing it with heroic spectacle. Most perverse to anyone who knows the play is the shabby treatment of Richmond and his men. Thirteen lines are their total allotment for the fifth act, and therefore for the whole play. Thirteen lines.[30] And nine of them come during Richmond's prayer. The whole system of instructive contrasts built so carefully into the act is thus demolished to save Richard's image. Richmond is nothing but a "vacuum in shining armor" because Olivier has taken away most of his lines and those of his friends, and all of their loving companionship and rich humanity. Constance Brown's excellent review of the film in 1956 coined the striking phrase to describe Olivier's Richmond that Robert Hunter would use twenty years later in his excellent book on the tragedies:

> He is too perfect a heroic figure to be believably human. He is, as Richard calls him, "shallow Richmond," an utterly humorless being who bears no scars of psychological conflict, who apparently never engaged in a battle with his conscience. In Olivier's film he is endowed with a conventional square jaw, a melodious Welsh accent, and a head of blond hair with not a curl out of place. He cannot even be credited with defeating Richard. It takes Richard to do that. Richmond has all the compelling properties of a vacuum.[31]

It is clear that Olivier's Richmond, not Shakespeare's, became the whipping boy of the critics of the sixties and the seventies. Having seen this powerful and widely acclaimed film, a whole generation of viewers was seduced by a Richard and repulsed by a Richmond who were not Shakespeare's. Cibber's "Richard's himself again" is a big enough lie. We would all grant this today. But Olivier's Richmond is an equal perversion of Shakespeare's character and his play. If its chief agent is deprived of an appropriately compelling portrayal, providence too must come across as vacuous, or worse, repulsive in its bad taste for the delicacies of the stage.

Olivier's act 5 opens with neither words nor lords eagerly clustering around this attractive deliverer. Instead, we see Richmond (we guess) alone and wordless, gazing out over a bright plain. He is blond, broad-shouldered, elegantly manicured, his hair as freshly curled as Chaucer's Squire. But without those good words and those good lords, with only the heroic music and the brightness, he does seem vacuous. And so one gladly leaves him for the morose, intense, and fascinating Richard of Olivier.

Richmond is given his thirteen lines in the next scene, four before the prayer and nine during it. He will not speak again; in fact, we will hardly see him again. The four lines bid goodbye to his men. The moment is too brief for any sense of relationship to be established. Olivier's Richmond is again almost as alone as Richard. He does have God to speak to, however, and in a virile Welsh accent he prays as the scene concludes. Just before, he has again looked heroically off into the distance, handsome but not interesting. We do not hear him planning, reassuring his friends, expressing hopes or fears, doing anything human except praying. And then he practically disappears.

How much of a butchery is this?[32] In the BBC videotape, and in the play Shakespeare wrote, the act is about half Richmond's, half Richard's. Further, the close system of contrasts and parallels works consistently to Richard's disadvantage. He is falling apart; Richmond is building the Tudor dynasty, in this play at least with good thoughts, good men, and good enterprise. The ghosts promise him "success and happy victory." But in the Olivier film, there are hardly any ghosts either, and those who do appear speak nothing to Richmond. Clarence whispers to a prone Richard, a mysterious speaking head. The cousins are disembodied voices; Hastings says only "Think on Lord Hastings, despair and die." Claire Bloom, as Anne, is allotted more of her ghostly lines, with her romantic leitmotif sounding in the background and white ghost tears trilling down her cheeks. Buckingham merely roars as he charges the sleeping, dreaming Richard. We sense Buckingham's rage rather than Richard's guilt. In fact, all of these ghosts seem rather to victimize Richard. Perhaps this is because the prevailing idea of providence has been so thoroughly excised from the film. If one thinks of providence at all here, it seems rather a bad sport.

We also wonder whether the ghost sequence is anything but a dream in the Olivier film. It appears not. Richmond receives no similar visitations. The pairing of those visits makes them most surely supernatural. Their rhetorical order and power is cut just as much as that of the wailing queens and the dying lords earlier. So again the formality that lies behind the rhetoric, embodying as it does the order of the universe, the governance of providence, is sacrificed to cinematic expediency.[33] Richard would have loved it. The BBC production serves up a straightforward (though very effective) representation of the eleven ghosts visiting Richard and Richmond. They know about providence; they are among its agents, and they exist in a supernatural realm. They witness to truths that transcend what is popularly called in modern reviews of *Richard* III "historical Nemesis" or the like. But in the Olivier film they are almost as invisible as Margaret. Their curses, their blessings, their moral and supernatural force are eliminated. So is eliminated another component of Richmond's attractiveness and his power, the realm of angels and departed souls, the realm of God.

Richard is also deprived of his final soliloquy in the Olivier film. Instead, we receive three quick reactions to the dream: basically, where is my horse, bind up my wounds, and, indistinctly, "Have mercy, Jesu." Several early reviewers of the film heard nothing of the soliloquy.³⁴ Then, after just a bit more uncertainty, a minute or less by my reckoning, "Richard's himself again." "Somebody" elicits his smile. "Not shine today"? No problem. The confidence is building again. The odd interlude of uncertainty is over.³⁵ With renewed vigor, as though he had slept as well as Richmond, whom we still have not seen since the prayer, Richard uses his sword like a magic wand to outline the troop formations for the battle to come. Then the lines become lines of troops themselves, and Richard, all armed, is in their midst. The lowering skies have miraculously disappeared.³⁶

All of these are Richard's "miracles," Olivier's manipulations of the feelings and events of the last act. Richmond is supposed to have supernatural agency here, not Richard. This is also where Olivier reassures us with Cibber's immortal line, "Richard's himself again." How perverse. Does this mean that he has proven superior to the powers of providence and the visitation of the ghosts, that he is splendidly amoral again as well as heroically irreligious? Does it simply mean that he is confident, warlike, in control? It could mean all of these. That is why it so distorts Shakespeare's play at this most crucial moment. Then Richard gallantly addresses his troops from his horse, white Surrey. All are around him on horse and foot. The moment is made all the more heroic because we are yet to see the first of Richmond's men, or to hear a word from Richmond, since the prayer. We do see Richmond on horseback for about two seconds, then Stanley for one. We see Richmond, far away, directing a small troop of horse. This time he receives three seconds, tops. Even during these shots what we see most of is Richard's face as he watches the ebb and flow of the battle. Richmond is allotted no battle oration here, just as he was deprived of the rousing words to his troops at the beginning of act 5. In fact, neither he nor his men will speak a word more.

Few of Shakespeare's lines interfere with the scenic and musical effects of Olivier's last act. Fifty at most would be my guess. We see a crown rolling in the dust, kicked by horses, found in bushes. We see fields and commanders looking at them, as unaware as we are of the flow of battle. Norfolk, killed by an archer (is it friend or foe?) rolls off a bridge into the stream below. One of Richard's horses is stabbed; another is killed with an arrow. All this is striking stuff; it certainly happens too fast for anyone to think too much about what it all means. In fact, when Richard is swarmed

Laurence Olivier's crosslike sword, from the 1955 film. Courtesy of the Museum of Modern Art/Film Stills Archive.

over by the avenging hordes of Richmond's troops, we feel disgusted by their brutality and sorry that this handsome, hardly limping fellow has to die.[37] Is that sword that Richard holds in his pathetically withered hand as he dies only accidentally silhouetted as a cross?[38] Consistent to the end, our last shots are of Richard thrown over a horse (at last), with his garter showing ostentatiously. Stanley engages Richard in the final battle. Richmond is not even granted the privilege of killing the bloody dog. Nor is he allowed a word at the end of the film.[39] We see Stanley with the crown and a triumphant look, and we have to assume that Richmond will be crowned. He might be that small figure in the middle of the field. We cannot be sure, but it must be Richmond. Witness the vacuum in shining armor. With neither words nor action, what else can he be?

Hankey talks about the two extremes of interpreting the character of Richard in the theatrical tradition. One of them investigates too closely a psychology that is finally not all that complex, and that demanded little analysis among Shakespeare's contemporaries:

> By the time Shakespeare wrote his play, then, Richard was vividly alive in the popular imagination. He was bad and damned, almost by definition. He needed no explanation. The analogy with that other self-defined villain, the Vice from the morality plays, fitted perfectly.... United here with the historical tyrant, ... he is perfectly realized, without being psychologically elaborated.... [In fact,] the idea of historical Nemesis which pervades the play draws its strength from the impenetrability of its chief agent, Richard. It is very often at the cost of this theme that Richard's character is "psychologized" in production.

The other makes too much of the heroic Richard:

> Whatever its shortcomings as a closet play, Cibber's version was a gift to the actor.... When Richard falls into an ecstasy at the prospect of the crown ... when he indulges himself over the captive prince ... when he defies the tugs of complaining Nature, energy alone will get him respectably by. These moments are all designed for the flourishes of contemporary acting, and when finally the revamped fifth act turns Richard into a heroic warrior, it is obvious that Cibber was interested in writing a good part, not a searching account of personal immorality.[40]

Olivier does more than get respectably by. His film has enjoyed unprecedented success and influence. He does, however, take Cibber's gift and make of it a film that also severely reduces one's sense of historical, moral, or theological context. The Mayor and the Citizens are too easily and too absolutely deceived. So are Hastings and Buckingham, especially the latter. The ladies are virtually eliminated, Margaret completely, Anne and Queen Elizabeth as effective adversaries. There are almost no prophecies, and even fewer verifications of their accuracy or of their providential dimensions. The four ghosts who appear in act 5 seem more dreams than spirits. Even Richmond is almost eliminated from the play. Without the women to confront and expose his immorality and his ugliness, without the ghosts or Richmond to challenge him in the final scenes, Richard is everything. But Richard without the women, without the context of the morality plays and Tudor history, and without Shakespeare's condemning words and tightly made dramatic structure is not Shakespeare's Richard at all. With every change, Olivier's Richard becomes more invulnerable, but his *Richard* III becomes less significant. It would be fascinating to see an actor of Olivier's accomplishments attempt a Richard who must face other extraordinarily gifted actors in pruned but not hacked-up roles, and live with the consequences. I suspect we should see a play of unexpected power, and unexpected depth, where the chief actor still could shine, but with a brilliance derived from the moral and psychological possibilities of the role, properly conceived as part of a larger dramatic structure and moral universe. In fact, this is not a bad description of the Sher-Alexander *Richard* III that I discuss in the epilogue.

The subsequent chapters respond to the challenges of the Olivier film, and of the productions that have followed it, by taking their most interesting disagreements, their richest possibilities, their strengths, and their shortcomings, back to the study. After all, these problems of performance are also matters of interpretation. The director, like the scholar, can put them to the tests of Shakespeare's historical and literary sources, Renaissance military manuals and theological commonplaces, and a close look at the words and actions of these challenging dramatic sequences, as well as their most arresting textual variants. But finally the director, the actor, can go only one way. The scholar has the luxury of exploring the problems in all their complexity, resolving some perhaps, but also leaving others delightfully suspended. The scholar can talk about possibilities that might work better for the reader than for the player; the scholar can also suggest several possibilities for the player without having to settle on one of them. To their credit, Olivier and Cibber have established both a text and an interpretation of *Richard* III that have overwhelmed the critical and the theatrical communities for more than two centuries. It is time for the critical community to join the theatrical community in reevaluating that influence.

2

Richard versus Richmond: Aesthetic Warfare in Act 5

☦ Laboring under the unusual influence of the Cibber-Olivier tradition, only a few twentieth-century critics find Richmond's orations in act 5 of *Richard* III to be affirmative, ringing assertions of what is right and just. To E. M. W. Tillyard they represent the "properly pious utterance of the chief instrument of God's providence." To Emrys Jones they circumscribe Richard's dramatic power, and provide a morally fitting and aesthetically satisfying conclusion to the play. More numerous are the readers who concede the rightness of Richmond's cause, but are unimpressed by his personality and his oratorical style. Hunter, referring to the platitudes of his last two orations, calls Richmond "a vacuum in shining armor." John Palmer refers to his "pious twaddle," M. M. Reese to his "flat, unimpassioned utterance." A. P. Rossiter seems more attracted to the powerful stage presence of Richard, the "artist in evil," than to the man he acknowledges to be his legitimate and divinely appointed successor.[1]

Those critics who question the providential scheme of the play are even more inclined to find the counterpoint of Richmond's concluding speeches aesthetically unattractive next to Richard's continued public energy and inner turmoil. David L. Frey calls Richmond's speech to his troops "a set piece," "sans personality, sans teeth, sans everything." It annoys him as "flat, stiff, limp, pious, formal, rhetorical, and platitudinous." Brooke finds the whole providential scheme "repulsive." Wilbur Sanders argues that Richmond's last words leave "the closing minutes of the play sadly contracted to the stature of Tudor propaganda."[2] Olivier would almost certainly have agreed.

But several recent Richmonds, most notably Richard Gale's (the Old

Vic, 1957) and Brian Deacon's (BBC videotape, 1982), have apparently made the character attractive enough to challenge Richard's supremacy in act 5. The BBC's Deacon was particularly effective in his moral and aesthetic opposition to Cook's Richard. David Wheeler (Boston, 1973) directed a Richmond as noble and as fresh as Deacon's, "strong," "solidly assuring change and reconstruction." Gale gave the last oration "a touch of real fervor," "leaving no doubt at all about the sunburst that heralds the Tudor dawn."[3]

Is the "Sword unsway'd," the "Empire unpossest" as the play concludes? Such diverse responses to and portrayals of the orations of Richard and Richmond suggest that the aesthetic warfare between the two has proven less conclusive than their trial of arms. In fact, Richard clearly retains the upper hand, on the stage and in the study. Looking again at their last speeches in the light of Shakespeare's narrative and dramatic sources and Renaissance military manuals on the art of battle oratory can help us arbitrate their claims anew. Such new evidence is not likely to close out the debate, of course. My purpose is more modest. I hope to reinvigorate the discussion and the appreciation of act 5 of *Richard* III by exploring through this evidence the possibility that Shakespeare might have been manipulating our final response toward Richmond and away from Richard, however difficult it is for us today to say "amen."

The Sources
The Tudor historian Edward Hall is a major source for the two battle orations, and indeed for much of the public utterance of Richmond and Richard during act 5. As we know, Hall is particularly good at contriving speeches for his public figures, thus injecting into his history a drama his successor Raphaell Holinshed seldom achieves alone. It is therefore instructive to watch Shakespeare adapting Hall's orations to his own purposes. We can listen at the same time to what Hall apparently found attractive in a Richmond that he was almost certainly praising. Repeatedly, though not exclusively, Shakespeare seems to be making changes that diminish the attractiveness of Hall's Richard and enhance that of Hall's Richmond, particularly to suit the aesthetics of the stage. I will emphasize Shakespeare's omissions from Hall for two reasons. Geoffrey Bullough's widely read and indispensable work on Shakespeare's sources is heavily biased toward what is included or paraphrased, and therefore rather disguises the importance and the scope of Shakespeare's omissions. Even more important, what Shakespeare omits from Hall seems particularly relevant to our consideration of the aesthetic counterpointing of Richard and Richmond in act 5.[4] The crucial details of Shakespeare's modification of Hall follow.

First, Shakespeare omits the tour de force of Richard's audacious hypocrisy at the opening of his speech to his chieftains. In Hall the speech begins,

> Most faithfull & assured felowes, most trusty & welbeloved frendes and elected captains, by whose wysedome & policie, I have obteyned the crowne . . . , by whose puissaunce and valiauntnes I have enjoied & possessed thestate roial & dignite of ye same, maugre ye yl wil & sedicious attemptes of all my cancarde enemies & insidius adversaries. . . . I have omitted nothing appertaining to ye office of a juste pri[n]ce, nor you have pretermitted nothing belongyng to ye dewtie of wise & sage counsailers. So y^t I may saie & truely affirme, that your approved fidelite & tried constancye, maketh me to beleve firmely & thinke, y^t I am an undoubted kyng & an indubitate prince.[5]

Shakespeare dramatizes none of this attempt to claim just cause. Words like "faithful, assured, trusty, well-beloved, wisdom, valiantness, justice, fidelity, constancy," have long since lost their currency for Richard and his followers. Queen Elizabeth makes that loss clear with her relentless ironies during the second seduction scene in act 4. As against her there, Shakespeare's Richard also apparently lacks the energy, the wit, and the will to create in his oration another illusory world of legitimacy. This suggests that his revels now are ending.

The same might be said of Shakespeare's second omission from Hall, Richard's contrived admission of considerable guilt:

> although in ye adepcion & obteinyng of ye Garlande, I being seduced & provoked by sinister counsail and diabolical temptacion did commyt a facynerous & detestable acte. Yet I have with strayte penaunce and salt teryes (as I trust) expiated and clerely purged thesame offence, which abhominable cryme I require you of frendship as clerely to forget, as I dayly do remember to deplore and lament thesame. (fol. liiii)

In Hall, the cleverness, the will to deceive, the enormous energy and delight in religious hypocrisy which Shakespeare has so effectively used in his Richard of acts 1-3, is still there, still full of dramatic potential. He essentially says, "The Devil made me do it, but I have repented, clearly purged the sin away. You would be less than Christian men if you did not forgive me as God has forgiven me." Shakespeare completely eliminates this audacious attempt. Neither of these moments would have been beyond Richard's power in the first few acts. Now he is apparently both too depraved and too weary to carry them off.

Richard's next plea in Hall, to the natural bonds between prince and subject, subject and prince, is also completely absent in Shakespeare's version of the oration:

> yf ever amitie and faythe prevailed betwene prynce and subjectes or betwene subjecte and subjecte: or yf ever bond of allegians obliged the vassall to love and serve his naturall sovereigne lorde, or yf any obligation of dewtie bounde any prynce to aide and defende his subjectes: All these loves, bondes and deuties of necessite are this daie to be exper[i]mented, shewed and put in experience. (fol. liiii, verso)

What are allegiance, bonds, duty, or love to this king and these followers? What can they swear by now? The constraints of the stage have deprived Shakespeare's Richard of the multitudes that Hall's might still try to deceive. Everyone on stage has known this Richard too well for too long for such an appeal to have much chance of success, or any need to be uttered. For these followers still to be his men they must either be friends for fear or almost as depraved as Richard himself. Indeed, Richard announces the forfeiture of such an argument as preface to his oration: "Conscience is a word that Cowards use, / Devis'd at first to keepe the strong in awe, / Our strong armes be our Conscience, Swords our Law" (3779–81; 5.3.309–11).[6] So be it. Might makes right. But then right cannot also make might. Having claimed a universe of raw power, Richard cannot also claim just cause. In Shakespeare he has at least the honesty to know it.

Further omitted in Shakespeare's oration is a passage from Hall which Shakespeare would surely have appropriated for his more clever and vigorous Richard of acts 1 or 2. The passage directly celebrates the wit and policy of the Machiavel:

> For yf wyse men saie trew, there his some pollycie in gettyng, but muche more in kepyng. The one beyng but fortunes chaunce, and the other high wyt and pollicie, for whiche cause, I with you: and you with me, must nedes this daye take labour and payne to kepe and defende with force, that preheminence & possession which by your prudent devises I have gotten and obteyned. (fol. liiii, verso)

Wit and policy were once Richard's stock in trade. Now they are becoming his potent adversaries, denied him at this most crucial moment by

Shakespeare's excising hand. Richard is finally being put to school, by events and consequences he can no longer control.

Finally, Shakespeare mutes the still-ringing rhetoric of most of Richard's speech in Hall. Four good examples have already been quoted. Another occurs as Hall's Richard is rousing his troops again:

> we must live to gether like brethern, fight together like lions, & feare not to dye together lyke men. And observyng and kepyng this rule and precept, beleve me, the fearefull hare never fledde faster before the gredy greyhound, nor ye sylye larke before ye sparowhauke, nor the symple shepe before the ravenous wolfe, then your proud bragging adversaries astoned & amaised with ye onely sight of your manly visages, wil flee, ronne, & skyr out of the felde. . . . [W]e have manifest causes, and apparant tokens of triumph and victorie. (fol. liiii, verso)

Such persuasive rhetoric is denied Richard at his ultimate moment in Shakespeare's play. Like Falstaff, he is "fall'n away vilely" since the earlier action. He lacks even the wit to turn the tokens to his own advantage. "Do I not bate? Do I not dwindle?" Shakespeare's deletions from Hall imply that the answer is "Yes." "The sheriff with a most monstrous watch is at the door." Shakespeare's Richard has less to say on his own behalf than Hall's.[7]

What Shakespeare chooses to keep from Hall is equally revealing. Shakespeare's Richard retains the insults, the "downward comparisons," "base epithets," and "unsavory similes" that are more appropriate to a tavern lord than to the king of England. Most of Richard's address to his troops contains insults, the desperate ad hominem assaults of a pathetic, nearly impotent foe. Of Richmond he rants:

> the devell continuall enemie to humane nature, disturber of concorde and sower of sedicion, hath entered into the harte of an unknowen welshman. . . . [H]e is a Welsh mylkesoppe, a man of small courage and of lesse experience in marcyall actes and feates of warr, brought up by my brothers meanes and myne like a captive in a close cage . . . and never saw armie, nor was exercised in marcial affaires. (fol. liiii, verso)

Of Richmond's troops, Hall's Richard sputters:

> a compaigny of traytors, thefes, outlawes and ronneagates of our awne nacion, . . . a nomber of beggerly Britons & faynt harted French-

men be with hym arrived to distroy us our wyfes and children.... What wil you make of them, braggers without audacitie dronkards without discrecion rybaudes without reason cowardes without resisting & in conclusion ye most effeminate & lascivious people, y^t ever shewed them selfes in Frunt of battaile. (fols. liiii, verso-lv)

Even in the midst of these Rabelaisian epithets with which Shakespeare so lavishly stocks Richard's final battle oration, there are revealing omissions. Excluded are the preposterous claims that Richmond is the Devil's man, and that a "divine plage" will devastate Richmond's troops; gone is the equally pathetic hope that Richmond's men will desert to his side "remembryng there oth promise & fidelitie" (fols. liiii, verso-lv). In fact, even when Richard invokes Saint George, as in Hall, Shakespeare makes him associate him with "the spleene of fiery Dragons." In Shakespeare's hands it is clear enough from the dramatic context who the Devil's man is. Richard himself prefaces his oration with "hand in hand to Hell" (3783, 3822; 5.3.313, 315).

Shakespeare also places Richard's speech after Richmond's. As Bullough says, "the order of the orations is reversed, possibly to disgust the reader with Richard's base appeal."[8] Why might Shakespeare have reduced Hall's Richard at the end of the story? I would argue that it could be precisely to avoid the misunderstandings that might be evoked by a continuation of his aesthetic appeal during the first two acts, particularly act 1. Hall has an easier expedient. Because his is a narrative rather than a dramatic mode, he can simply warn the reader of Richard's deceptive aesthetic power after he has "reported" his culminating speech:

> This exhortacion encouraged all such as favoured hym, but suche as were present more for dreade then love, kyssed them openly, whome thei inwardely hated other sware outwardely to take part with suche whose death thei secretely compassed and inwardly imagened, other promysed to invade the kynges enemies, whiche fled and fought with fyrce courage against the kyng: other stode stil & loked on, entendynge to take parte with the victors and overcommers: So was his people to hym unsure and unfaithfull at his ende, as he was to his nephewes untrew and unnaturall in his beginnyng. (fol. lv)

Following the effective peroration Hall gives Richard, and the power of his whole speech, such a warning is necessary; it also allows Hall to exploit to the hilt Richard's final rhetorical powers, without worrying about their ultimately confusing the audience. Shakespeare may have attempted a similar theatrical undercutting in the bitter words of the Scrivener in 3.6, the ironies of the women in 4.1 and 4.4, even as early as Richard's scenes with the Mayor and the Citizens. However, the history of our responses to his charismatic evil, especially as it was canonized in Cibber's adaptation, suggests that the audience also needed Hall's words of warning, as melodramatic as they might have seemed 400 years ago. In fact, it is probably no coincidence that the recent return to Shakespeare's text in stage productions has been accompanied by a heightened complexity in these scenes, and an increasingly tarnished Richard.

The contrast between Richmond's orations in Shakespeare and Hall is equally suggestive. Unlike Richard's speech to his troops, Richmond's is in spirit and in content essentially the same in both versions. The omissions often brighten Richmond's portrayal, simplify it, make it more natural and less ambiguously upright than the source. In Shakespeare's hands the platitudes and the piety that are so characteristic of Hall's Richmond are softened; so is the stiff, Ciceronian formality of Hall's rendition of Richmond's prose. In the light of these changes, Richmond's critics might want to reconsider their isolation of the very chinks in Richmond's aesthetic armor that Shakespeare seems to have gone to considerable lengths to hammer out. It is equally ironic that they would chafe against a handsome portrayal that is less ambiguous than the source, and at the same time more relaxed.

First, Shakespeare completely avoids three of Hall's most pious and platitudinous passages in Richmond's oration. The first begins the speech, and concerns his "trewe, Godly, and vertuous" cause:

> If ever GOD gave victorie to men fyghtynge in a just quarell; or yf he ever ayded suche as made warre for the welthe and tuycyon of ther awne naturall and nutritive countrey; or yf he ever succoured them whyche adventured there lyves for the relefe of innocentes, suppressynge of malefactores and apparaunt offenders; No doubt my felowes and frendes, but he of hys bountefull goodnes wyll this daye sende us triumphaunt victorye and a luckey journey over our prowde enemyes, and arrogant adversaries: for yf you remember and consider the very cause of our just quarell, you shall apparantlye perceyve the same to be trewe, Godly, and vertuous. In the whiche I doubte not but GOD will rather ayde us (ye and fyght for us) then se us vanquished and profligate by suche as neyther feare hym nor his lawes, nor yet regarde justice or honestie. (fol. lv, verso)

For God's minister, there is nothing wrong with the sentiment. But the Ciceronian style, however effective it might be in a prose history, would be devastatingly stuffy for a dramatic character. Shakespeare cuts the whole speech.

The second, equally full of high sentence, asserts the "infallible" rule,

> that as il men daily covyte to destroy the good, so God appoynteth the good to confounde the yll, and of all worldly goodes the greatest ys, to suppresse tirauntes, and releve innocentes, wherof the one is ever as muche hated as ye other ys beloved. If this be trewe (as clerkes preche) who will spare younder tyraunt Richard duke of Gloucester untrewely callyng hym self kyng, consideryng that he hath violated, and broken bothe the lawe of God & man. (fol. lvi)

Shakespeare's battlefield is no such bully pulpit as this; his Richmond is also spared this preachment.

Omitted as well is the labored, Ciceronian analogy Hall's Richmond draws between Richard and Tarquin and Nero, classical tyrants:

> I have hard of clerckes saie, y^t Tarquyne ye proude for the vice of the body lost the kyngdome of Rome . . . yet was not his fault so detestable as the facte of cruel Nero. . . . Beholde younder Richarde whiche is bothe Tarquine and Nero: Ye a tyraunt more then Nero, for he hath not only murdered his nephewe, . . . bastarded his noble brethern and defamed the wombe of his verteous and womanly mother, but also compased all the meanes and waies y^t he coulde invent how to stuprate and carnally know his awne nece under the pretence of a cloked matrimony, whiche lady I have sworne and promysed to take to my make and wyfe as you all know and beleve. (fol. lvi)

Though the allusions are pertinent, the passage in Hall would seem particularly offensive on the stage in its formality and its platitudinous piety. Note particularly the second preacherly "Yea" ("Ye a tyraunt"; "ye and fyght for us"). By omitting this passage completely, Shakespeare apparently tries to lessen again the stuffy, overblown style and the righteousness modern critics have found so objectionable in Richmond.

Three other omissions from Hall are equally suggestive. Hall's Richmond refers boldly to his lineal claim to the English throne. He argues that Richard's forces wrongefully deteyne and usurpe ouer lawefull patrymonye and lyneall inherytaunce. For he that calleth hym selfe kynge, kepeth from me the Crowne and regymente of this noble realme and countrey contrarye to all justice and equitie. (fol. lv, verso)

Shakespeare, by omitting this claim, focuses our attention more on Richard's obvious wrongs than Richmond's questionable rights. Further, Hall's Richmond suffers from the conqueror's ambitious vainglory:

If we had come to conquer Wales and had acheved y^t, our praise had bene great, and our gayne more? but yf we wyn this battaill ye hole riche realme of England with the lordes and rulers of the same shall be oures.... The smaller that our nombre is, the more glorie is to us yf we vanquishe, if we be overcome, yet no laude is to be attributed, to the victors, consyderyng that .x. men fought agaynst one: and yf we dye so glorious a death in so good a quarell, nether fretyng tynne, nor cancarding oblivion shal be able to obfuscate or race out of the boke of fame ether our names or our Godly attempte. (fol. lvi)

Before and after the battle Shakespeare's Richmond modestly attributes all of his success and victory to God. The difference is crucial, striking out as it does Richmond's bloated sense of election.

Shakespeare also chooses to underplay the appeal that Hall's Richmond makes to his soldiers' greed:

while we were in Brytaine we had small livynges and lytle plentye of welthe or welfare, now is the tyme come to gett abundaunce of riches and copie of profit which is the rewarde of your service and merite of your payne. (fol. lvi, verso)

There is nothing particularly wrong with any of these sentiments or statements. Shakespeare's modifications seem to emphasize Richmond's Christian heroism, his faith, and his humility; at the same time they lessen or eliminate Hall's potential ambiguities. Gone are Richmond's vainglorious motives in Hall, his appeal to greed, and his questionable claim to lineage; lessened is his rhetorical formality and stuffiness. If this makes Shakespeare's Richmond "a vacuum in shining armor," and I think it does not, it also makes Richard's villainy and his pettiness even more obvious in the final scenes. Personally, I find Shakespeare's version of Richmond's oration a moving affirmation of just cause and honorable conflict. It is time for a good man to stand up effectively against the tyrant Richard, and Richmond is that good man. Richmond's speech inspires his men, clarifies the values at issue, and finally produces its intended result, for England, and not incidentally, for Shakespeare's own Queen Elizabeth, a Tudor victory at Bosworth Field. In this most obvious sense, Richmond's speech works and Richard's does not. To this reader it even works aesthetically, if those two responses are actually inimical, particularly after comparing it with its source in Hall.

Another modification of Hall has the effect of softening Richmond's consciousness of his own heroism, and yet certifying it in other voices. Shakespeare spreads parts of Richmond's one long battle oration in Hall throughout act 5, and even places part of it at the end of act 4. He also gives portions of it to other characters. Richmond's brief battle speech in 5.2, though it is grander than Hall's and much more vivid, is influenced by that source:

> Lykewise, hys mates and frendes occupie your landes cutt downe your woodes and destroy your manners, lettyng your wifes and children range a brode for ther livyng. (fol. lv, verso)

Richmond says in Shakespeare:

> The wretched, bloody, and usurping Boare,
> (That spoyl'd your Summer Fields, & fruitfull Vines)
> Swilles your warm blood like wash, & makes his trough
> In your embowel'd bosomes: This foul Swine
> Is now even in the Centry of this Isle. (3412–16; 5.2.7–11)

Similarly, the impassioned responses to Richmond's oratory by Oxford, Herbert, and Blunt contain pieces of Hall's one oration:

> Or cause them beinge greved and compuncted with the pricke of ther corrupt consciences cowardely to flye and not abyde the battaill: besyde this I assure you that there be yonder in that great battaile, men brought thyther for feare and not for love, souldieurs by force compelled and not with good will assembled: persons which desyer rather the destruccion then salvacion of ther master and captayn: And fynally a multitude: wherof the most parte will be our frendes and the lest parte our enemies. (fol. lv, verso–lvi)

In Shakespeare, immediately following Richmond's speech just quoted, we hear,

> *Oxf.* Every mans Conscience is a thousand men,
> To fight against this guilty Homicide.
> *Her.* I doubt not but his Friends will turne to us.
> *Blunt.* He hath no friends, but what are friends for fear,
> Which in his deerest need will flye from him. (3422–26; 5.2.17–21)

As we see, Richmond's men follow Hall's rousing words very closely. Their hope, inspired by Richmond's words, mirrors Hall's assertion at the end of Richmond's oration: "These cherefull wordes he sett forthe with suche gesture of his body and smylyng countenaunce, as though all redye he had vanquyshed hys enemies and gotten the spoyle" (fol. lvi, verso). Shakespeare's systematic modification of Hall's battle orations leaves little reason to question a similar efficacy in the play. Richmond's oration plainly works, on his troops as individuals and as a group. I have tried to suggest that there is good reason to believe that Shakespeare meant it to work on the audience as well, at least from the testimony of his adaptation of Hall.

The patterns of this adaptation seem clear. Shakespeare's Richmond effectively senses and counters the fear of his men; he is in turn encouraged by their love and their good cause. His language is more relaxed, his motives are less grandiose, and his inducements lack the appeal to greed. Richmond's rhetoric is orderly but not stiff; he urges confidence against fear, but he is never complacent, even in his hope that he is God's minister. Richard seems to become pettier and duller in Shakespeare's hands, base if bustling in his colloquialism, repetitive and unimaginative in his oratorical strategies. Opportunities to display Richard's continuing wit and audacity are passed up more than once as Shakespeare modifies Hall. Opportunities to make Richmond glorify himself or appear otherwise more ambiguous are similarly declined. All of these revisions suggest the same possibility. Richmond's victory over Richard can be affirmed aesthetically as well as morally. Richmond is still larger than life, as befits God's "ministers of Chasticement." He is neither unreal nor repulsive as a result. Richard, on the other hand, is well on the way to becoming that "paltry Fellow" he calls his noble adversary, sans wit, sans hope, sans good cause, horse, kingdom, eternal blessedness. He is about to fall victim to the very foes he has tried to reduce to "scum," "Pezants," "Rascals," and "Run-awayes." Poor rat, he is about to hang himself (3556, 3793, 3786–87; 5.3.113, 323, 316–17). With Richmond's help, and God's, he will die betimes.

The Military Manuals

Though Richmond's victory over Richard Hunchback at Bosworth Field was memorialized in chronicle and verse throughout the sixteenth century, the question of the aesthetic victory in Shakespeare's *Richard III* remains alive. Does the "artist in evil" continue to beguile us, even as he falls? Or does God's chosen, Richmond, drown Richard's book even as he takes his crown? Because the interpretive questions involve at least two *non disputanda*, questions of taste and questions of doctrine, the issue is unlikely ever to be resolved. That merely adds to its fascination. The influential treatises of Niccolo Machiavelli, Matthew Sutcliffe, Barnabe Rich, and others on the art of war often address the topic of military oratory. They therefore become another useful Renaissance prism through which we can view and try to judge the relative attractiveness of Richmond and Richard during their controversial final scenes.

In *The arte of warre* Machiavelli calls a good oratorical style essential to military leadership:

> It was requisite that the excellente Capitaines were oratours: for that without knowyng how to speake to al the army, with difficultie maie be wrought any good thing. . . . This speakyng taketh awaie feare, incourageth the mindes, increaseth the obstinatenes to faight, discovereth the deceiptes, promiseth rewardes, sheweth the perilles, and the waie to avoide theim, reprehendeth, praieth, threateneth, filleth full of hope, praise, shame, and doeth all those thynges, by the whiche the humaine passions are extincte, or kendled.[9]

Machiavelli's contemporaries add such crucial particulars as the effective exploitation of God and good cause, and the favorable interpretation of signs. They say that a military leader should stress the weaknesses of the foe and the potency of the leader's own valiant past. Finally, he should invoke love of captain and country.

Barbara Tuchman in *A Distant Mirror* thoroughly discusses the importance of God and just cause in Medieval and early Renaissance warfare: "While desirable in any epoch, a 'just war' in the 14th century was virtually a legal necessity as the basis for requisitioning feudal aids in men and money. It was equally essential for securing God on one's side, for war was considered fundamentally an appeal to the arbitrament of God."[10] Sutcliffe's influential military manual begins with a lengthy argument for just cause: "first, I require religion," he says, for "God he is Lord of Hostes, and giver of victories; and sure it is not probable, he will give it to those, that aske it not at his handes." Elsewhere Sutcliffe writes that the "Generall [must] be religious, and a mainteiner of religion, . . . if hee expect the favour of God, and good successe in his affaires." In other Renaissance military manuals the appeal to God and good cause can smack as much of opportunism as it does of piety. Onosander suggests that "the sugred talke of the Captaine maye move thym . . . unto great actes for the love of vertue." Machiavelli writes, "Enterprises maie the safelier be brought to passe by meanes of religion." Machiavelli even advises citing dreams as evidence of God's favor, whether or not they have occurred:

> Many have tolde how God hath appered unto them in their slepe, who hath admonished them to faight. In our fathers time, Charles the seventh kyng of Fraunce, in the warre whiche he made againste the Englishemen, saied, he counsailed with a maide, sent from God, . . . the which was occasion of his victorie.[11]

Whether pious or practical, the invocation of God and just cause was an essential weapon in the arsenal of the military orator.

Though with none of this cynicism, Richmond can honestly and effectively report to his captains:

> Me thought their Soules, whose bodies *Richard* murther'd,
> Came to my Tent, and cried on Victory:
> I promise you my Heart is very jocond,
> In the remembrance of so faire a dreame. (3695-98; 5.3.230-33)

We have seen these souls and heard their unanimous testimony that "God, and our good cause, fight upon our side" (3706; 5.3.240). Think how often the motif occurs. "Vertuous and holy be thou Conqueror," says the Ghost of Henry VI. "Good Angels guard thy battell, Live and Flourish," says Clarence. The two young princes bless Richmond: "Good Angels guard thee from the Boares annoy." Richard's Anne promises: "Thou quiet soule, / Sleep thou a quiet sleepe: / Dreame of Successe, and Happy Victory." Buckingham completes this chorus affirming God and good cause: "God, and good Angels fight on Richmonds side" (3575-3636; 5.3.128-75, passim). Richmond and his allies often claim God and good cause in their military oratory. They march "In Gods name, cheerely on." Their good "Conscience is a thousand men" (3419-27; 5.2.14-22, passim). Richmond is assured of God and good cause in his devout prayer and in his battle oration (3551-57, 3706-36; 5.3.108-14, 240-70). When Richmond reminds his men of these two potent allies, he is telling the truth as well as exploiting an effective first strategy of military oratory, not mouthing pious platitudes. In the last battle they are strengthened in these beliefs. Richard, in sharp contrast, can neither shake off the horrifying effects of his dream of despair and death nor dissemble otherwise before his allies:

> O Ratcliffe, I have dreamd a fearefull dreame,
> What thinkst thou, will our friendes prove all true?
> (3674+1&2, Q1; 5.3.212–14)[12]
> ....
> By the Apostle *Paul*, shadowes to night
> Have stroke more terror to the soule of R*ichard*,
> Then can the substance of ten thousand Souldiers
> Armed in proofe, and led by shallow R*ichmond*. (3677–80; 5.3.216–19)

Again we have witnessed the unanimous testimony of the ghosts; as Richard knows, it is more substance than shadow. He has stabbed a king, butchered two princes, punched another king "full of holes," washed a brother to death, killed Rivers, Grey, Vaughan, Hastings, "wretched A*nne*" and Buckingham. His cause is overwhelmingly bad; all of these "wrongs" are in Richard's bosom, weighing him down like lead. "Bloody and guilty" becomes the countering epithet to Richmond's "Vertuous and holy," that and "dispaire and dye." Near the middle of this chorus, all chant to Richmond, "Awake, / And thinke our wrongs in R*ichards* Bosome, / Will conquer him. Awake, and win the day" (3564–95; 5.3.119–45, passim).

Not only is Richard without supernatural sanction or good cause for the upcoming battle; he is also without the wit or the will to pretend to have them. This is true when he wakes; it is also true during his battle oration. Not incidentally, Hall's Richard is more than equal to this challenge. Shakespeare's is not. Apparently he knows that he is "One that hath ever beene Gods Enemy." Richmond's corollary is inescapable: "Then if you fight against Gods Enemy, / God will in justice ward you as his Soldiers" (3718–20; 5.3.252–54). Only Richmond can invoke such an ally in Shakespeare's version of the battle orations or during the final act. By any standards, then, whether Sutcliffe's idealism or Machiavelli's cynicism, Richard is Richmond's clear inferior in terms of God and good cause. He does not even invoke them as an oratorical technique.

On the other hand, Richard is probably better than Richmond at the time-honored strategy of insulting his enemy, even though Richmond has better material to work with. Machiavelli advises his military orator to "make thy men to esteme little the enemie, as Agesilao a Spartaine used, who shewed to his souldiou[r]s, certain Persians naked, to the intent that seyng their delicate members, thei should not have cause to feare them." Sutcliffe suggests declaring "the enemies wantes, and weakenes, and disadvantages." Jaques Hurault cites the example of Lysander at the siege of Corinth, who said to his troops, "Are you not ashamed to be afraid to assaile those enemies, which are so slothfull and negligent, that hares sleep quietly within the precinct of their walles."[13]

Richard's speech is composed almost exclusively of such deprecation of his enemies. He insults Richmond's troops:

> Remember whom you are to cope withall,
> A sort of Vagabonds, Rascals, and Run-awayes,
> A scum of Brittaines, and base Lackey Pezants,
> Whom their o're-cloyed Country vomits forth
> To desperate Adventures, and assur'd Destruction.
> (3785–89; 5.3.315–19)

He calls them "straglers," "over-weening Ragges of France," "famish'd Beggars," "poore Rats," "bastard Britaines" (3785–3803; 5.3.315–33, passim). He insults Richmond in the same key:

> And who doth leade them, but a paltry Fellow?
> Long kept in Britaine at our Mothers cost,
> A Milke-sop, one that never in his life
> Felt so much cold, as over shooes in Snow. (3793–96; 5.3.323–26)

Without just cause or God's name, Richard's recourse to this tactic smacks of desperation and of pettiness. But he does play this Machiavellian card for all it is worth.

Richmond is not totally deficient in this unpleasant if time-honored strategy. Against Richard he says,

> For, what is he they follow? Truly Gentlemen,
> A bloudy Tyrant, and a Homicide:
> One rais'd in blood, and one in blood establish'd;
> One that made meanes to come by what he hath,
> And slaughter'd those that were the meanes to help him:

A base foule Stone, made precious by the soyle
Of Englands Chaire, where he is falsely set:
One that hath ever beene Gods Enemy. (3711–17; 5.3.245–51)

Earlier, Richmond had also attacked Richard as a "foule Swine," "The wretched, bloody, and usurping Boare" (3412–15; 5.2.7–10).

Both speakers, then, use this tactic freely. Is there any difference in their usage? One-fourth of Richmond's military oratory is ad hominem, as against nearly three-fourths of Richard's. Further, Richmond's assaults against Richard are mostly true. That is to say, they are not so much ad hominem argument as articulations of just cause, as witness the deserved final epithet as "Gods Enemy." That Richard speaks ad hominem almost exclusively attests further to his loss of wit and vitality at this crucial moment. He himself admits "I have not that Alacrity of Spirit, / Nor cheere of Minde that I was wont to have" (3513–14; 5.3.73–74). In Richmond's mouth, attacking the man asserts Richard's unjust cause. Paradoxically, it may also add some attractive dents of humanity to the surface of Richmond's shining armor. If Shakespeare follows Hall more closely in this respect than in others, perhaps he too wanted that healthy dose of anger, which sometimes "hath a privilege" even in God's minister.

Incidentally, Richard may also take his own oratory too literally here. Hurault advises against overconfidence before battle, a fault Richard betrays in his oration. Of the defeat of Darius by Alexander, Hurault says: "The thing that undid him, was his overweening opinion that he should overcome Alexander with ease, which is the thing that overthroweth all such as upon disdain to their enemies, do set no good order in their affairs, and in the leading of their armies."[14] Richmond's oration acknowledges the military power as well as the moral impotence of his foe.

As further advice, Sutcliffe urges the military orator "to confirme them with hope and report of their former valiant actions." William Garrard stresses "the example of magnanimitie in their forefathers."[15] Richard has the better of Richmond in this area. He can effectively remind his troops of the battles of Poitiers and Crécy and Agincourt, all major English victories over the French: "And not these bastard Britaines; whom our Fathers / Have in their owne Land beaten, bobb'd, and thump'd, / And on Record, left them the heires of shame" (3803–5; 5.3.333–35). Richard's troops should be encouraged that they are again engaging these French. In the light of recent history, Richmond's must be more than a little unsure.

In fact, Richmond might be countering that fear by leaning so heavily on God's help and on the theme of hope: "In Gods name cheerely on, couragious Friends, / To reape the Harvest of perpetuall peace, / By this one bloody tryall of sharpe Warre." Again he urges, "Then in Gods name march, / True Hope is swift, and flyes with Swallowes wings, / Kings it makes Gods, and meaner creatures Kings." Even at the end of his oration, he encourages them similarly, "Sound Drummes and Trumpets boldly, and cheerefully, / God and Saint George, Richmond, and Victory." Without the precedent of recent victory, Richmond must emphasize his good hope in God's cause and their own. He must encourage them as Englishmen, invoking Saint George. His reassurances have a psychological validity, an insight into human nature and human need, an awareness of his own vulnerability and that of his troops, that further humanizes Richmond. Like Hal inspiring the troops before Agincourt, Richmond is effective because he is one of them. They are truly "Fellowes in Armes," and "most loving Frends" (3406–29; 5.2.1–24, passim; 3735–36; 5.3.269–70). Richmond may thus turn this apparent disadvantage to his favor; in the process he becomes a more attractive character as well.

With "Encourage them with promises, and hope of rewarde," Sutcliffe sounds another common theme of military oratory. Garrard urges reciting "benefits to soule and bodie," crisply combining the appeal to greed with that to just cause. Machiavelli says that any good orator "promiseth rewardes."[16] Interestingly, Richmond is much more lavish than Richard in numbering the rewards of battle. However, Shakespeare has refined his appeal considerably from that recounted in Hall:

> Therefore labour for your gayne and swet for your right:
> while we were in Brytaine we had small livynges and litle
> plentye of welth or welfare, now is the tyme come to get
> abundance of riches and copie of profit, which is the reward
> of your service and merite of your payne. (fol. lvi, verso)

Shakespeare's Richmond replaces material gain with these nobler spoils:

> Then if you fight against Gods Enemy,
> God will in justice ward you as his Soldiers.
> If you do sweare to put a Tyrant downe,
> You sleepe in peace, the Tyrant being slaine:
> If you do fight against your Countries Foes,
> Your Countries Fat shall pay your paines the hyre.
> If you do fight in safegard of your wives,

Your wives shall welcome home the Conquerors.
If you do free your Children from the Sword,
Your Childrens Children quits it in your Age. (3719–28; 5.3.253–62)

God's reward, peaceful sleep, a welcome home, love, honor in old age—these are the rewards of noble combat in Richmond's good cause. "Countries Fat" is his one concession to the more materialistic interests of his men. Even Brutus would not be embarrassed by this Cassius.

Richard, being in power, leans instead on threats to the status quo, fear of shame and fear of loss:

You sleeping safe, they bring you to unrest:
You having Lands, and blest with beauteous wives,
They would restraine the one, distaine the other.
(3790–92; 5.3.320–22)

Lost lands, stained wives, unrest; these are the threats of the established but reeling king: "Shall these enjoy our Lands? lye with our Wives? / Ravish our daughters?" (3806–7; 5.3.336–37). The repetition can again suggest desperation. It may also betray a lack of cause and a loss of ingenuity, not to mention a dearth of abstract value in Richard's universe. On the other hand, all of these arguments are also established parts of the arsenal of military oratory. Sutcliffe says, "Feare them with shame." Machiavelli and Garrard urge threatening "present peril."[17] Richard uses what little stock he has. However, his inventory of invention is running almost as low as the number of causes he can claim.

Of "love of Captain and country" we must infer the effectiveness of Richard and Richmond from their words and from the responses of their men.[18] Both leaders invoke the patron saint of England, Saint George. Richmond connects him with God, Richard with "the spleene of fiery Dragons" (3822; 5.3.350). Hope and despair are fairly obviously the respective companions of Richmond and Richard in this little counterpoint. Both men harp on defending their land, their wives, and their children. Richard can have little moral leverage with the last two points. Richmond addresses "most loving Frends" and "loving Countrymen," and seems surrounded by them in Oxford, Blunt, Herbert, and Stanley. Richard has Surrey, Norfolk, Ratcliffe and Catesby, loyal chiefs if not loving friends. But when Blunt says "He hath no friends, but what are friends for fear" (3425; 5.2.20), we cannot believe him far wrong. Can we imagine anyone rushing in to embrace this Richard? Richard addresses no friends in his oration, only the "Gentlemen of England" (3809; 5.3.338). Their only true cause is country, not king. Even the diminished Richard is apparently aware of this liability in his words of address.

Elaborate signs precede the battle, and the public reactions of both leaders to them are instructive. Thomas Proctor says, "some people doe stumble muche at sygnes or tokens which befall before battaill, . . . wherefore the wyse captayne will chearefullye expounde all suche chaunces for his advauntage . . . [as] a happy sygne of the victorye falling unto him."[19] Richmond has an easy time of this, because his signs are good and his heart is jocund. He has had "the sweetest sleepe, / And fairest boading Dreames, / That ever entred in a drowsie head." The ghosts have promised "Successe, and Happy Victory." Therefore Richmond does not have to feign when he cheerfully proclaims, "Me thought their Soules, whose bodies Richard murther'd, / Came to my Tent, and cried on Victory" (3623, 3691–96; 5.3.165, 227–31, passim). Richard does have to feign good cheer, and he cannot. His vaunted ingenuity fails him yet again, as it has failed him consistently ever since he became king. To Ratcliffe he admits, "I have dreamd a fearefull dream." He adds, "shadowes to night / Have stroke more terror to the soule of Richard, / Then can the substance of ten thousand Souldiers / Armed in proofe, and led by shallow Richmond." To the troops there is a similar admission, only barely masked by ineffective bravado: "Let not our babling Dreames affright our soules: / For Conscience is a word that Cowards use" (3674+1, 3677–80, 3778–79; 5.3.212, 216–19, 308–9). Unless all of his troops are as cynical, as skeptical as Richard himself, this piece of oratory does not augur well for his cause, or speak well of his presence of mind.

Richmond also ignores the darkling sky. Richard is enveloped by it, as by guilt: "Who saw the Sunne today?" he asks; "Then he disdaines to shine. . . . A blacke day will it be to somebody." All of this is spoken out loud, before Ratcliffe and Catesby. Then "The Sun will not be seene to day, / The sky doth frowne, and lowre upon our Army. / I would these dewy teares were from the ground." Even when Richard rouses himself to shake off the omen, he still attests unconsciously to its power: "the selfe-same Heaven / That frownes on me, lookes sadly upon him" (3744–55; 5.3.277–87, passim). Heaven frowns on Richard; on Richmond it looks sadly. They are not the same. Richard knows it, and he cannot pretend otherwise. The good face that he puts on immediately afterward remains colored gray by these frowning skies. The desperation and emptiness of the oration which follows is darkened too by Richard's encounters with these signs and tokens. His despair must affright the souls of all but the most depraved of his men.

Finally, Richmond's more orderly style of public oratory might be more effective than Richard's because it matches his substance, and because this is the ultimate moment to assert order and control and community values and beliefs. Richard is superb one-on-one, with the audience, and with individuals in the play. His soliloquies and his earliest dialogues are masterpieces of personal, colloquial rhetoric, full of energy, wit, and inspiration. But Richard as military orator is sometimes a victim of what he is not. "What shall I say more then I have inferr'd?" (3784; 5.3.314) is an interesting admission of this victimization. Richard has denied God. He has forsaken all traditional values, all abstractions even. "Conscience is a word," says this nominalist, "Air—a trim reckoning." Like Falstaff's "catechism,"[20] Richard's comment here glosses his ultimate impotency. He is himself alone. So is his language limited to his condition of being. After the brief interlude of the Vice, he is base, inferential, uninspiring. Richmond, in contrast, because he is allied with God and good cause, is eloquent precisely because he is not alone. He believes in God, in virtue, in family, friends, and country; he believes in order, in justice. Shakespeare's Richmond knows truth; he does not infer it. Thus he can assert truth and be believed in that assertion. Richmond exploits this advantage to the hilt, but because he also believes it, there is no dissimulation. Truth arms his oratory. Style and substance are one. Richard is no longer clever enough or sufficiently in command of himself to use Richmond's rhetorical strategies, even cynically. Words, so often abused by Richard, take their own revenge.

Rich says of the captain's oratory that "it encourageth the minds either of hope, either else of despair."[21] There could hardly be a clearer illustration of these polar opposites than during the battle orations in *Richard III*. Richmond's unequivocally ends on the note of hope, as it should since his cause is just and his conscience clear: "Sound Drummes and Trumpets boldly, and cheerefully, / God and Saint *George*, *Richmond*, and Victory." Richard's strains are much as the ghosts predicted, chaotic, sulphurous, full of valiant fury, signifying nothing. He prefaces his oration, "March on, joyne bravely, let us too't pell mell, / If not to heaven, then hand in hand to Hell." He ends it with "Our Ancient word of Courage, faire S. *George* / Inspire us with the spleene of fiery Dragons: / Upon them, Victorie sits on our helpes" (3735–36, 3782–83, 3821–23; 5.3.269–70, 312–13, 349–51). It does, like a vulture or a leering Beelzebub. Saint George is not the Dragon, nor is he just a word. If Richard had the time or the composure, even he might appreciate this last revenge of language and truth upon himself.[22]

In the final act of *Richard III*, and in the chronicle tradition too, military oratory consistently, though not simplistically, proves to be one of Richmond's strengths and one of Richard's weaknesses. After Richmond's oration, Hall reports, "These cherefull wordes he sett forthe with suche gesture of his body and smylyng countenance, as though all redye he had vanquyshed hys enemies" (fol. lvi, verso). The effect of Richard's oration was quite different:

> This exhortacion encouraged all such as favoured hym, but suche as were present more for dreade then love, kyssed them openly, whom they inwardely hated other sware outwardely to take part with suche whose death thei secretely compassed and inwardely imagened, other promised to invade the kynges enemies, whiche fled and fought with fyrce courage against the kyng.... So was his people to hym unsure and unfaithfull at his ende. (fol. lv)

Shakespeare seems to have followed Hall very closely in these respects. Richard's battle oration did not work, in Hall or in Shakespeare. Richmond's did. Hall also offers in this passage a plausible explanation for this success and failure. The murderous Machiavelli could have schooled Richard better on military oratory. But then, there was no "good thing" that he could have wrought by the final scene of his life, except his death, except his death, except his death.

This evidence from Shakespeare's sources and Renaissance military manuals suggests that Richmond may be Richard's equal or his superior in military oratory in act 5 even before he defeats him in the Battle of Bosworth Field. Richard knows the rules, and employs some of them energetically. But his oration is less audacious, less imaginative, less hopeful, less rousing than it was in Hall. In style and substance, it is both more narrow and more desperate. In contrast, Shakespeare's changes in Richmond's oratory project a rousing but thoughtful speaker who is also a good man. Further, unlike Richard he has good men to respond to his good words. Not every reader will want to change his allegiance as a result of this look at Shakespeare's handling of some of his sources; not every reader will agree that the evidence points as exclusively in Richmond's favor as I have argued here. If my discussion plausibly restores some energy to the aesthetic combat of Richard and Richmond act 5 of *Richard* III, it will have achieved its major goal. While theatrical Richmonds like Gale and Deacon do not "prove" this reading of the aesthetic conflict of Richard and Richmond any more than the sources, they certainly establish its equal plausibility on the stage. If God and good cause fight on Richmond's side, so do considerable personal and rhetorical skills. The power of his ordered rhetoric may even predict his subsequent success at arms. Richmond's words have been weighed too lightly in the past. Perhaps filtering them through these military manuals and chronicle sources will help to right the balance.

3

The Wooing of Elizabeth

> On this dialogue 'tis not
> necessary to bestow much criticism,
> part of it is ridiculous, and
> the whole improbable.—Samuel Johnson

Dr. Johnson's opinion notwithstanding, its length, its placement, its carefully polished rhetoric and its concentration of ironies suggest that Shakespeare considered Richard's wooing of Elizabeth to be a fairly important scene.[1] It is all the more ironic that when critics have stooped to interpret it, they have disagreed so radically about what finally happens. E. K. Chambers states one view: "In his last bout [Richard] is palpably outwitted.... Elizabeth is the deeper dissembler. She is already far in the plot with Richmond, and although her daughter shall be a queen, she shall assuredly not be Richard's queen." Tillyard completely disagrees: "Are we to think, with E. K. Chambers, that Elizabeth had outwitted Richard and had consented only to deceive? That is so contrary to the simple, almost negative character of Elizabeth and so heavily ironical at Richard's expense that I cannot believe it."[2] Predictably, scores of critics, good readers and bad, have lined up on both sides.[3] Despite Dr. Johnson's caveat, we obviously need to play more dexterously upon this scene, sound it from its lowest note to the top of its compass, the better to hear its contradictory music.

First, we need to test the stops of two of Tillyard's unproven assumptions about the scene. Does Elizabeth's deception make the scene "too heavily ironical at Richard's expense"? Can we agree that her character is "simple, almost negative"? Second, we might fret the sources again, Hall and Holinshed in particular, but also *The true tragedie*, to hear their music in consort with Shakespeare's. Elizabeth's line, "Shall I be tempted of the Divel thus" (3209; 4.4.418), coming as it does near the end of the scene, also deserves a better hearing.[4] The rave reviews of Maggie Smith's and Lynne

Porteous's enactments of the scene in 1977 and 1981 might further expand our sense of the possibilities of the scene, and its continuities with what precedes and follows.[5] So should Olivier's decision to cut the scene entirely from his film. Listening to each of these tones might reveal that there is much music, excellent voice, in this little organ, even if we cannot pluck out the heart of its mystery.

Elizabeth's Characterization

First, Elizabeth's characterization is probably more complex than Tillyard is willing to concede. In her earlier scenes Elizabeth emerges as a tough, smart political creature. She holds her own fairly well in confrontations with Margaret and Richard. She is also clever enough to anticipate future events tending to the downfall of her house, and aggressive enough to try to manage them. The unusual malignancy and ruthlessness of Richard and Buckingham frustrate some of her efforts, but not all of them; she also survives Margaret's curses better than most, though obviously with major casualties. After all, Dorset escapes and her daughter will marry Richmond at play's end, keeping her family close to the center of political power for the next century. Finally, surrounded by many characters, Richard included, who either rationalize their relationship to divine providence or uncritically accept the old clichés about it, Elizabeth has the courage and the intellect to try to discover for herself what this God, this providence, must be like. Tempted by her own bitter experience to believe in Gloucester's sadistic gods in *Lear*, and by Margaret's apparently successful curses to believe in Shylock's ferocious God of judgment (three eyes for an eye, my daughter for a ducat), she finally chooses neither. Rather she either remains suspended in agnosticism, or settles on a god of "ignorant uncaring, of sleep."[6] The final music of her belief, or unbelief, is so muted it is not easy to hear. But the strenuous honesty of this woman who maintains a strong moral sensibility and powerful political ambitions for herself and her family, even after "all harmes" (472; 1.3.8) have befallen her, hardly suggests a "simple, almost negative character." If there are negatives, they are the negatives of agnosticism, not of passivity or unimportance. In her is "most excellent music," both before and during her duet with Richard.

Richard, albeit sarcastically, himself testifies to Elizabeth's political cunning and strength early in the play. She and Mistress Shore "Are mighty Gossips in our Monarchy" (87; 1.1.83). She may have engineered the imprisonment of Hastings (70–72; 1.1.66–68). She has definitely been a successful advocate for the political promotion of her family (99; 1.1.95). Most complimentary of all, she is perceived by Richard as a threat, however much he jokes about it. He honors her with his distrust, and with his frequent public confrontations. If he and Clarence are not "the Queenes abjects" (112; 1.1.106), they are also not as influential as they were before her accession to Edward's bed and the throne.

We first see Elizabeth in 1.3, lamenting the coming death of her husband: "If he were dead, what would betide on me?" These apparently pathetic, almost melodramatic words have done Elizabeth a disservice, for they establish in our minds a whimpering, weak Elizabeth we will not see again. A closer look reveals the depth of honesty behind her lament, which is brief by the play's standards. In political terms her power is her relationship to Edward. Thus, plainly, "The losse of such a Lord, includes all harmes." The succession of her son to the throne guarantees little: "Ah! he is yong; and his minority / Is put unto the trust of *Richard Glouster*, / A man that loves not me, nor none of you" (469, 472, 475-77; 1.3.6, 8, 11-13). Always the realist, Elizabeth has seen and said the truth, no more, no less. She does so again, with clear political and philosophical wisdom, just thirty lines later: "Would all were well, but that will never be, / I feare our happinesse is at the height" (505-6; 1.3.40-41). She is too honest and too wise to rest on that tempting, false cliché. And so she corrects her note, and correctly perceives her precarious position at court and in this world of chance and change. Few around her are either as perceptive or as honest.

What else do we see of Elizabeth in this scene? She bristles under the insults of "the nobility," people like Derby's haughty wife. She has "too long borne" Richard's "blunt upbraidings, and . . . bitter scoffes" (568-69; 1.3.102-3). She also stands up to Richard. No less than three times early in the scene she contradicts his baiting innuendoes (528-34, 539-41, 548-54; 1.3.62-68, 73-75, 82-88). The men in Henry VI's funeral procession showed far less courage. But the scene's major confrontation is between Richard and Margaret. Margaret, in fact, undercuts Richard's blatant lying here with an irony that nicely parallels Elizabeth's main weapon against him in her culminating scene.

When Elizabeth next appears, she is basically indistinguishable from the rest of the court. Richard appears and manipulates all of them equally well. But when Edward dies, and Elizabeth laments his death, we begin to hear neither pious platitudes nor thoughtless wailing but the beginning of what I submit is her serious questioning of transcendental things, particularly divine providence. Full of grief, she enters "*with her haire about her ears,*" threatening suicide: "Ile joyne with blacke dispaire against my Soule, / And to my selfe, become an enemie." But if she will not "make an act of

Tragicke violence," not follow her Edward "To his new Kingdome of nere-changing night" (1306-20; 2.2.34-46, passim), she has in her own words given in to a theological despair that is suicide's close cousin. She has projected the dark night of her soul onto the Christian universe she has hitherto assumed, and found it dark indeed. "Nere-changing night," not eternal life, is the kingdom she proclaims after death. The Duchess's comments, in contrast, are shallow, reserved for the affairs of this world only.

Elizabeth's son Dorset knows how close his mother is to the deeper grief of despair, and he tries to confront her lack of faith directly: "Comfort deere Mother, God is much displeas'd, / That you take with unthankfulnesse his doing." It is much more "ungratefull, / . . . to be thus opposite with heaven, / For it requires the Royall debt it lent you" (1362–68; 2.2.89-95, passim). Elizabeth will no more respond to his attempted correction of her opposition to providence than she does to his attempted political and personal consolations which follow. "The dimming of [her] shining Starre" (1377; 2.2.102) is more than Edward's death. From that loss she will recover; from her loss of faith she will not. Her lack of response to Dorset, to Rivers, and to Richard henceforth in the scene is a crucial subtext, expressing a despair too deep for words. Elizabeth, in fact, will always distrust words; she will also never again completely trust providence.

We see Elizabeth only twice more until 4.4. In each scene small talk is interrupted by devastating news that provokes her brief but profound response. Learning of the imprisonment of Rivers, Vaughan, and Grey in 2.4 leads her to proclaim the amoral natural and political universe of an Edmund:

> The Tyger now hath seiz'd the gentle Hinde,
> Insulting Tiranny beginnes to Jutt
> Upon the innocent and awelesse Throne:
> Welcome Destruction, Blood, and Massacre,
> I see (as in a Map) the end of all. (1542–46; 2.4.50-54)

Apocalypse now, where innocents are ravaged by tyrants and beasts, tooth and claw. She has not moved far from the "nere-changing night" of her recent despair. In response to this vision, however, Elizabeth is not frozen. She immediately resolves upon sanctuary. She will try to remove herself and her other son from this world.

But the world affords her no sanctuary. Barred just a few scenes later from the Tower by the Lord Protector, a particularly apt political title given her present theological despair, Elizabeth knows the news to be "dead-killing," to her sons and possibly also to her remnants of faith. England is truly a "slaughter-house," and she is about to become "thrall of *Margarets* Curse, / Nor Mother, Wife, nor Englands counted Queene" (2514-26; 4.1.35-46, passim). This time she has more words, words of compassion for Anne, and a mother's desperate words of prayer. Desperate? She prays not to God, but to the Tower for her sons:

> Pitty, you ancient Stones, those tender Babes,
> Whom Envie hath immur'd within your Walls,
> Rough Cradle for such little prettie ones,
> Rude ragged Nurse, old sullen Play-fellow,
> For tender Princes: use my Babies well;
> So foolish Sorrowes bids your Stones farewell. (2580-85; 4.1.98-103)

Prayers to stones could only be provoked by "foolish Sorrowes." In Elizabeth's universe they are not likely to be heard, or heeded. They do suggest how long the impulse to pray, to something, anything, endures, even in a woman as disillusioned and as honest as Elizabeth.

And then "The tyrannous and bloodie Act is done." How else could this Elizabeth respond to "The most arch deed of pittious massacre / That ever yet this Land was guilty of" (2705-7; 4.3.1-3) but by doubting again God's providence:

> Wilt thou, O God, flye from such gentle Lambs,
> And throw them in the intrailes of the Wolfe?
> When didst thou sleepe, when such a deed was done?
> (2793-95; 4.4.22-24)

God, providence, not content with sleeping during this atrocity, seems to Elizabeth to have participated in it. Why? When? "Ah who hath any cause to mourne but wee?" (2805; 4.4.34). Such questions would be inescapable for anyone at such a moment, but for Elizabeth they have become characteristic. She has voiced such doubt since Edward's death. If "God is much displas'd" with such unthankfulness, as Dorset earlier admonished her, so be it.

With Margaret continually gloating over the downfall of Elizabeth's house and the fulfillment of most of her own curses, Elizabeth must also confront her possible "thralldom" to Margaret's curses. She does concede an apparent potency to these curses, and evidences a certain curiosity about their power:

> O thou did'st prophesie, the time would come,
> That I should wish for thee to helpe me curse
> That bottel'd Spider, that foule bunch-back'd Toad.
> (2850–52; 4.4.79–81)

Unlike the other victims of Margaret's curses, however, Elizabeth concedes nothing about their efficacy in the destruction of her family. Her request, "Teach me how to curse mine enemies" (2888; 4.4.117) is as close as she comes to such a confirmation. Perhaps her pride refuses such a concession, such a further humiliation as Margaret's victory. Perhaps her silence transcends pride, and relates again to her continuing agnosticism about supernatural agency in human affairs. In such a world as this, where prayers for innocents are apparently denied, where beasts and tyrants destroy lambs and children, could curses really work?

Elizabeth directly confronts this question just before Richard enters the scene, and her answer is a resounding "No." What are these words provoked by calamities, these curses, prayers, and lamentations?

> Windy Atturnies to their Clients Woes,
> Ayery succeeders of intestine joyes,
> Poore breathing Orators of miseries,
> Let them have scope, though what they will impart,
> Helpe nothing els, yet do they ease the hart. (2899–2903; 4.4.127–31)

Prayers, curses, lamentations have no supernatural power. They are air, wind, breath, insubstantial expressions of misery. They may "ease the hart," but they "helpe nothing els." Faced with all this evidence of the accuracy of Margaret's curses, Elizabeth will not concede their potency. Perhaps that is why she has no "spirit to curse" Richard in the sequence that follows. She has plenty of spirit to devastate him in debate. The Duchess of York gives cursing a try. Elizabeth remains "Tongue-tyed," though she has "far more cause" to curse than Richard's mother (2904, 2976; 4.4.132, 197). She can hardly believe in the efficacy of curses when she has lost her faith in divine providence.

Elizabeth's Ironies

Like Edgar at the end of *Lear*, however, Elizabeth has not lost everything. She still believes in human decency, in standards of behavior to which she thinks all persons should attain, regardless of supernatural agency. She is still a moralist, and interestingly, she still bases her morality, in part at least, on the Judeo-Christian God who is often the basis of morality in Western thought. What results from this complex experience is an overwhelming sense of irony which she directs against the very character who has contributed most directly to its creation in her—Richard. Richard is powerless against her irony precisely because Elizabeth is so sure of the human values that endure even an apparently somnolent God and a vicious king. In fact, she must assert them all the more vigorously precisely because of her precarious human condition. Elizabeth clings tenaciously to her remaining children, to her remaining power, and to her remaining sureties. Richard has as grievously underestimated this woman as he will underestimate Richmond in the final act.

Paradoxically, Richard must fall victim to her ironies precisely because he has created them so well. He has driven her, like the evil characters in *Lear* drive Albany, Edgar, and Lear, to certain certainties beyond which she will not withdraw. "Nothing" is not enough for such characters. Richard has also created for himself a world in which all that might have value to him, to any human being, has been so wronged that it has been rendered inaccessible to him. Richard's vulnerability to Elizabeth's ironies in this scene is surely one of his most powerfully self-inflicted wounds in the play. If providence is directing this judgment against him through Elizabeth's second causation and his own, it is just indeed. Characteristically, Elizabeth says nothing about this possibility. But in the light of Elizabeth's present psychology and Richard's participation in it, her words cannot be "too heavily ironical at Richard's expense."

Elizabeth's ironies are so overwhelmingly effective that they should require only the briefest recitation. In fact, even Tillyard concedes them. He questions only their appropriateness to her character and to the logic of the dramatic sequence. Elizabeth immediately throws off Richard's courtship with the crushing assumption that he could only wish to destroy that which is "Faire, Royall, and Gracious" (2984; 4.4.205). She has good cause. Then it is she, not Richard, who purposefully misunderstands his words in a relentless exposure of his dishonesty. Richard has turned double meanings and false appearances to his advantage throughout the play. Now she makes him their victims. The cousins are cozened; advancement is "up to some Scaffold." His soul (he said it) is a shaky foundation for his promised love: "So from thy Soules love didst thou love her Brothers, / And from my hearts love, I do thanke thee for it" (3002, 3022, 3040-41; 4.4.223, 243, 260-61). Richard is aware that he is losing to Elizabeth's ironies, and he is as disconcerted as Wall or Moonshine by her rude but effective interruptions: "Be not so hasty to confound my meaning." What a witless, impotent response. Elizabeth's suggested wooing strategy is similarly devastating to him (3055-67; 4.4.271-83), cataloguing as it does all of his atrocities against her family as seals of his love. Is this not the very technique he used so successfully against Anne?

But Elizabeth is now the creator of ironies and the aggressor. The atrocities, like the cutting words that derive from them, have become too many and too damaging for Richard's continued manipulation. He can only admit his loss of inventiveness and his vulnerability to the power of her words and wit: "You mocke me Madam." He is right. Listing the murders of brothers Edward and York, uncles Clarence and Rivers, and good Aunt Anne is "not the way / To win [her] daughter." "Say that I did all this for love of her" (3002-3073; 4.4.223-88, passim) will not work twice, and Richard is all the more impotent for thinking that it will. Elizabeth's effective ironies become the sere, yellow leaves of Richard's impending fall.

Of course, Richard still has some time and energy left to spill and spend. He turns to Elizabeth's self-interest, and it is considerable. The result? More irony:

> What were I best to say, her Fathers Brother
> Would be her Lord? Or shall I say her Uncle?
> Or he that slew her Brothers, and her Uncles?
> Under what Title shall I woo for thee? (3122-25; 4.4.337-40)

There can be no answer, for Richard has forfeited all such titles of family relationship. So Richard retreats again, but only to expose other vulnerabilities. England's peace will be Elizabeth's war; Richard entreats that which God forbids; Elizabeth will only wail the title of queen; Richard's "everlastingly" will not last for ever, not if Richard can end "her sweet life" when he wills. Noble eloquence and honest plainness would both be obviously false from his lips. His George is profaned, his Garter dishonored, his Crown usurped.

Elizabeth's crescendo begins: "Sweare then by something, that thou hast not wrong'd" (3151; 4.4.366 ff.). Richard tries. Give him that. But the ironic litany is familiar to us all:

> *Rich.* Then by my Selfe.
> *Qu.* Thy Selfe, is selfe-misus'd.
> *Rich.* Now by the World.

> Qu. 'Tis full of thy foule wrongs.
> Rich. My Fathers death.
> Qu. Thy life hath it dishonor'd.
> Rich. Why then, by Heaven.
> Qu. Heavens wrong is most of all. (3160-67; 4.4.374-77)

Elizabeth is almost swept back to conventional belief as she undercuts each of Richard's answers. But if Richard has wronged Heaven most of all, Elizabeth says nothing of Heaven's avenging that wrong. "What canst thou sweare by now" announces the exhilarating victory she knows she has won. Richard's absolute forfeiture of all that is worth having, worth swearing by, of all that gives life meaning, has given him what he deserves, a life "full of sound and fury, signifying nothing." But Elizabeth can only promise judgment here. In fact, she knows only that children and parents will wail with her in the woes that Richard has stirred up for them in his "times ill-us'd repast." If Elizabeth were ever going to invoke divine providence, this would be the time. She does not.

All of the bluster of Richard's final attempt to persuade Elizabeth seems to reinforce his utter devastation during their debate. Paradoxically, if Elizabeth will not curse him, he curses himself, to Heaven and to fortune: if "with deere hearts love / Immaculate devotion, holy thoughts, / I tender not thy beautious Princely daughter." Since he does not so tender her, he tenders himself a fool. "Heaven, and Fortune" will "barre [him] happy houres" soon enough. And he will with their help "my selfe confound" as well. Then Richard tries blatant threats of physical violence against mother and daughter, "the Land, and many a Christian soule" (3188-3202; 4.4.396-411) if he is denied. For Elizabeth to yield at this point to the frustrated blustering of a thwarted bully would negate the purpose of the whole scene, thwart its climactic movement through Elizabeth's ironies, and make a shambles of their hitherto consistent if complex characterization. For Elizabeth to pretend to yield, to avoid Richard's suddenly threatened violence to herself, the land, and all Christian souls, makes eminently good sense and does no damage to her courage or her intellect. Richard has adduced no reasons to change Elizabeth's mind. And until his physical threats, she has had no reason to deceive him. The quick announcement of the engagement of her daughter to Richmond in the next scene demonstrates either that her mind is unchanged or that she is promising her daughter to both men (3349, 3355-56; 4.5.1, 7-8).

The final irony of the scene is that Elizabeth does not even have to be perceived as lying to Richard. If we look at the text carefully, Richard, not

Elizabeth, "relents" at the end of the scene by deceiving himself, and then exulting in the self-deception. Elizabeth has only six lines after Richard's bullying peroration, which addresses, incidentally, none of her earlier objections and so concedes their validity. Her lines follow:

> Shall I be tempted of the Divel thus?
> Shall I forget my selfe, to be my selfe.
> Yet thou didst kil my Children.
> Shall I go win my daughter to thy will?
> I go, write to me very shortly,
> And you shal understand from me her mind. *Exit Q.*
> (3209–20; 4.4.418–29, passim)

Where is her concession in the text? Three of these lines are rhetorical questions, the fourth a disgusted remembrance of the atrocities against her sons. She seems instead incredulous, obdurate even in the face of physical violence. If Richard is about to assault her physically, the lines could be said with uncertainty; but even that uncertainty might be a self-protective mask rather than weakness. The exit lines are also noncommittal, cleverly ambiguous perhaps but nothing more. Only a Richard desperate for another victory of any kind could be deceived by these final notes of their exchange. His confusion of mind in the following words with Ratcliffe and Catesby and the increasing threat of political chaos would seem consistent with this pattern. Without even having to lie, then, Elizabeth may have finally gulled this self-deluded Richard into believing her a "Relenting foole, and shallow-changing Woman" (3222; 4.4.431). If this is the case, Richard is really the fool here, and Elizabeth the overwhelming victor.

Though his remarks are ambiguous, Dr. Johnson must have nodded off at this moment. He seems to have assumed Richard the sudden victor and to have been offended by this "improbable" turn of events. Even worse, he may have considered Elizabeth's effective confrontation of Richard the most improbable dimension of the scene. After all, he elsewhere says of women: "Sir, a woman's preaching is like a dog's walking on his hind legs. It is not done well; but you are surprised to see it done at all."[7] This sentiment augurs poorly for his proper estimation of Elizabeth. Stylistically, the elaborate rhetorical exchanges may be too long and too formal for some tastes, even a bit "ridiculous." Still, Maggie Smith and Lynne Porteous recently used these words and this formality to affirm the theatrical integrity, indeed the brilliance, of a strong-willed Elizabeth. I have tried to show that in the study as on the stage, the scene can be relentless in its probability. This, at least, is the "utterance of harmony" I would command it to, had I the skill.

Elizabeth's Temptation

Elizabeth responds to Richard's final bullying speech with the intriguing question, "Shall I be tempted of the Divel thus?" (3209; 4.4.418). Such interrogatives characterize most of her last responses to Richard. I have argued that they drive an ironic wedge between the true Elizabeth and the Elizabeth Richard desperately wants to perceive. But her question is of particular interest because it suggests that Elizabeth considers Richard's wooing to be analogous to the Devil's temptations of Adam and Eve or of Christ. Renaissance understandings of those temptations reveal interesting analogies between them and this courtship sequence.

Throughout most of 4.4, Richard is either defending himself against Elizabeth's scathing words, or offering to her as attractively as he can the allurements of the world, the first of Satan's traditional triad of temptations. Richard correctly senses the world to be Elizabeth's particular weakness, even after all of her reversals. Her early questions of him would seem to confirm this intuition, while revealing as well the new wisdom her suffering has brought her: "What good is cover'd with the face of heaven, / To be discovered, that can do me good" is one such question. Another: "Tell me, what State, what Dignity, what Honor / Canst thou demise to any childe of mine?" Unlike her final rhetorical questions, which are actually devastating answers, or clever equivocations, these seem to invite answers, and Richard tries to provide them: "Th'advancement of your children, gentle Lady / . . . Unto the dignity and height of Fortune, / The high Imperiall Type of this earths glory." This is "the world" epitomized, and Richard the Tempter harps on it throughout the scene. Even the proffered sweetness of second motherhood may continue his worldly temptations, though it contains as well some appeal to the flesh, sensual delight: "To quicken your encrease, I will beget / Mine yssue of your blood, upon your Daughter." This motherhood will hurt less ("save for a night of groanes"), vex less, comfort more: "mine shall be a comfort to your Age." But when Richard adds, "And all the Ruines of distressefull Times, / Repayred with double Riches of Content" (3026–3109; 4.4.247–324, passim), we see that the world is still his primary thrust. Elizabeth will receive not "double Riches," but "ten-times double gaine of happinesse" if only she yield to him.

But Richard does not stop here. He goes on to try to make Elizabeth her daughter's tempter, much as Satan used Eve to tempt Adam:

> Go then (my Mother) to thy Daughter go,
> Make bold her bashfull yeares, with your experience,
> Prepare her eares to heare a Woers Tale.
> Put in her tender heart, th'aspiring Flame
> Of Golden Soveraignty: Acquaint the Princesse
> With the sweet silent houres of Marriage joyes:
> And when this Arme of mine hath chastised
> The petty Rebell, dull-brain'd Buckingham,
> Bound with Triumphant Garlands will I come,
> And leade thy daughter to a Conquerors bed:
> To whom I will retaile my Conquest wonne,
> And she shalbe sole Victoresse, *Caesars Caesar*. (3110–21; 4.4.325–36)

This time, Richard the Tempter has combined the world, the flesh, and the Devil. If young Elizabeth will share a conqueror's bed, the world and the flesh will be "retailed" to this "sole Victoresse, *Caesars Caesar*." Teach her to aspire to sovereignty; acquaint her with the joys of sex; ask her if she would be "lord of all the world." It has a familiar ring to it, this triple equation. The world, the flesh and the Devil, power and wealth, sexuality, and pride are all in Richard's package, as they are in the Devil's for Christ, Adam, and Eve.

Elizabeth devastates the proffered gift with her sarcasm. As we have already seen, her answer comes in the form of a series of questions ("What were I best to say . . . tender yeares?" [3122–27; 4.4.337–42] which cannot be answered. Richard tries anyway, but this simply adds to his frustration and his defeat. His wiles, his fraud, his guile have not worked. He has neither seduced Elizabeth nor convinced her to seduce her daughter to his will. Even with her recent disillusionment, she can still invoke God, law, honor, and love against Richard's temptations. Her daughter would apparently be even more likely to recoil at these unnatural, ungodly, illegal, immoral, and loveless suggestions. Elizabeth's "Reasons are too deepe and dead" for shallow, quick Richard, and she will "harpe on [them] . . . till heart-strings breake" (3147–49; 4.4.362–65). Richard has failed so completely that it takes him almost sixty lines to regain the offensive.

Even then, Richard has no new arguments, no counterarguments either. He asserts that he will "thrive," and that Elizabeth will plead his case to her daughter. He will have his way, or else:

> Without her, followes to my selfe, and thee;
> Her selfe, the Land, and many a Christian soule,
> Death, Desolation, Ruine, and Decay:
> It cannot be avoyded, but by this:
> It will not be avoyded, but by this. (3198–3202; 4.4.407–11)

Elizabeth responds: "Shall I be tempted of the Divel thus." With these words she clearly connects Richard's last thrust with the temptation of force, of violence, traditionally the last recourse of the Devil, his final and most desperate strategy. He uses it only when the other three have failed.

Elizabeth Pope discusses this final strategy in her book on *Paradise Lost*. As she suggests, "Many exegetes agreed that Satan did try to terrorize Christ," as part of the temptation in the wilderness. But the more traditional time for the temptation of violence was later, during the Passion: "Satan can tempt either by 'fraud' or 'violence': that is, either by persuasion or by fear. In the wilderness, he assailed Christ with persuasion only; afterwards, at the time of the Passion, he tried to shake him through threats of death and torture."[8] Lancelot Andrewes describes the tradition in a sermon on the temptations of Christ:

> Christ was too cunning for him in desputing: he meant therefore to take another course; for as James noteth, there be two sorts of temptations, one by enticement as a serpent, another by violence as a lion; If he cannot prevail as a serpent, he will play the lion.[9]

Elizabeth's allusion to the Devil's temptation just after Richard's crude threats of "Death, Desolation, Ruine, and Decay," to Elizabeth, her daughter, himself, and the whole world, effectively suggests this theological tradition, and invites its application to the play. Richard, frustrated by the obvious failure of his enticing fraud, must finally resort to violence. Failing as a serpent, he must become a lion. But Elizabeth, "too cunning for him in disputation," may also be too courageous for him in violence. Modifying a now-familiar rhetorical pattern, she may be understood to deflect his fury with a cleverly aimed series of questions, and deceive the dissimulator at the same time. Richard will no longer "thrive," any more than he intended to "repent." His last, threatening temptation of force has resulted merely in a potent curse against himself.

Elizabeth's Sources

The most important source of Elizabeth in 4.4 of *Richard III* is Hall's *The union of the two noble ... families of Lancastre and Yorke*. Two other sources are also worth our brief attention, Thomas Legge's *Richardus Tertius* (1579) and the anonymous *The true tragedie of Richard the Third* (1594). Considered together, the three provide another interesting perspective on Shakespeare's treatment of Richard's courtship of his potent adversary.

In Hall's account, Queen Elizabeth, courted by "diverse and often messengers," "men bothe of wit and gravitie," finally yields to Richard's proposals. She is not courted directly by Richard himself. Since Shakespeare so clearly uses Hall elsewhere in the play, and since Hall's account of the courtship is brief and revealing, it should be reproduced:

> [Richard] clerely determined to reconcile to his favoure his brothers wife quene Elizabeth either by faire woordes or liberall promises.... Wherfore he sent to the quene beynge in sanctuarie diverse and often messengers, whiche first shoulde excuse and purge him of all thinges before againste her attempted or procured, and after shoulde so largely promes promocions innumerable and benefites, not onely to her but also to her sonne lord Thomas Marques Dorsett, that they should brynge her yf yt were possible into some wanhope, or as men saie into a fooles paradise. The messengers beynge men bothe of wit and gravitie so persuaded the quene with great & pregnaunte reasons, then with fayre & large promises, that she began somewhat to relent & to geve to theim no deffe eare, in somuche that she faithfully promysed to submyt & yelde her selfe fully and frankely to the kynges will and pleasure. And so she putting in oblivion the murther of her innocente children, the infamy and dishonoure spoken by the kynge her husbande, the lyvynge in avoutrie [adultery, OED] leyed to her charge, the bastardyng of her daughters, forgettyng also ye feithfull promes & open othe made to the countesse of Richmond mother to ye erle Henry, blynded by avaricious affeccion and seduced by flatterynge wordes, first delivered into king Richards handes her v. daughters, as Lambes once agayn committed to the custody of the ravenous wolfe. After she sente letters to the Marques her sonne ... willynge him in any wise to leave the earle [of Richmond] and without delaie to repair into Englande, where, for hym were provided greate honoures and honorable promocions, asserteignynge hym ferther, that all offences on bothe parties were forgotten and forgeven, and bothe he and she highely incorporate in the kynges hearte. Surely the inconstancie of this woman were muche to be merveled at.... [K]ynge Rycharde had thus with glorious promyses and flatterynge woordes pleased and appeased the mutable mynde of quene Elizabeth. (fol. xlviii)[10]

Hall is perplexed at her inconstancy and her avarice, not to mention her naiveté, but he has no question that she has changed her mind. This is clearly the version of the scene that Richard perceives. The strategies sound particularly familiar: the excuses for Richard's villainy, the promised preferment of Dorset, and her own "promes promocions innumerable and benefites." The result is just what Richard hoped: "blynded by avaricious affeccion and seduced by flatterynge wordes," Elizabeth "delivered" her daughter. The tempter prevails over a shallow and changing woman, by appealing to her love of things and her love of praise, the world and the Devil. But Hall's Richard is not responding to the scene we have just witnessed. Shakespeare has transformed the bland negotiations of Hall's account into a vivid confrontation between Richard and Elizabeth. This Elizabeth may be neither mutable nor gullible enough for his wiles.

The differences Shakespeare introduces may therefore be more significant than the similarities. In the first place, Richard himself courts Elizabeth in the play, and his precarious position by now, both with her and with us, hardly presages well for his efforts. Further, Shakespeare's Elizabeth is shown "somewhat to relent," only if we mean deceitfully; she is never shown "faithfully . . . to submyt & yelde her selfe fully and frankely to the kynges will and pleasure." At most she offers some ambiguous final questions. Before that she adamantly refuses to yield an inch. "Deffe eare" would best describe her responses to all of Richard's blandishments. That and "articulate tongue." For Shakespeare's Elizabeth, unlike Hall's, is full of reasoned and emotional arguments which Richard cannot answer. Finally, the order of her final negotiations is reversed from Hall to Shakespeare. In Hall, Dr. Lewes, Richmond's physician, first proposes the Richmond-Elizabeth match to the queen in sanctuary. Her response is joyous: "lorde howe her spirites revyved, and how her heart lept in her body for joye and gladnes" (fol. xxxvii). She is thus all the more shallow and changing in Hall when she is later seduced by Richard's emissaries.

In Shakespeare, it is Richard who is quickly undercut by her subsequent agreement with Richmond, only a hundred lines after Richard proclaims victory. Her messenger Derby tells Sir Christopher, "tell *Richmond* this from me, . . . that the Queene hath heartily consented / He should espouse *Elizabeth* hir daughter" (3349, 3355–56; 4.5.1, 7–8). The close timing of this announcement would seem to emphasize Richard's self-deception, just like the intervening news of gathering rebellion by four messengers and Richard's confusion with Catesby and Ratcliffe. All of these "songs of death" are added to Hall by Shakespeare. All of them increase the probability of Elizabeth's successful deception of Richard at the end of the courtship scene.

The relationship between Legge's *Richardus Tertius* and Shakespeare's *Richard III* is ambiguous at best. Still, Legge's treatment of the essential action of 4.4 is interesting to compare to both Hall and Shakespeare. Legge conceives two wooing scenes, one in which Queen Elizabeth is persuaded by Lovell to yield to Richard's desires, and a second in which Princess Elizabeth resists Richard's personal proposals. Thus Legge, alone among the sources, may have provided Shakespeare with both a model for Richard's failure and a model for his success in this late courtship. In Legge, Lovell succeeds and then Richard fails, a further deflation. Young Elizabeth is given the glory of resisting the tempter. Not incidentally she is also insulated from her mother's past and present weaknesses in Legge by her direct victory. It is Princess Elizabeth who catalogues Richard's bloody crimes and his incestuous proposal with the most hyperbolic of classical allusions. Interestingly, when Legge's Richard sees the futility of persuasion, he turns like Shakespeare's to devilish threats of violence: "There is a double way for ruling for a prince, love and fear. It is advantageous for kings to try both." But this Elizabeth prefers not to consent, choosing death over dishonor. She even faces down a veiled threat of rape. Legge's Richard, unlike Shakespeare's, knows his impotence "in her madness" of honor, and decides to "postpone this business" until her fury diminishes. He is unequivocally defeated by her.[11]

From *The true tragedie* we receive only the most cryptic of notes about the scene from Lovell: "My Lord very strange she was at the first, / But when I had told her the cause, she gave concent." Then Queen Elizabeth and her daughter appear after the battle and the queen seals an earlier vow with Richmond. Her dutiful daughter consents to her will, and England rejoices.[12]

The sources suggest that Shakespeare may have added considerable strength of wit and will to Queen Elizabeth during the wooing scene, inevitably deflating Richard in the process. At the same time, Shakespeare has left her decision at the end of that scene much more ambiguous than it is in any of the sources. In them she always yields, then vacillates toward Richmond after his victory. Legge's young Elizabeth provides a better model than her mother for Queen Elizabeth's relentless denials in Shakespeare. Far from moving gradually from denial to curiosity to assent, Hall's pattern and Legge's, Shakespeare's Queen Elizabeth denies all of Richard's arguments with withering irony, names him the Devil he is in his final desperate attempt at physical intimidation, and never says yes to his demands. Her hard-won skepticism about divine providence seems to have made Shakespeare's Elizabeth much more careful—provident if you will—about her remaining son and daughter than the gullible and frightened mother of Shakespeare's sources. We have in her the first worthy adversary of the Devil Richard since Margaret. Elizabeth can be seen to outwit him in cunning and in controversy, assert over him moral superiority and courage to boot, and outlast him politically as well by returning with her daughter to Richmond's throne. In so doing she also survives some, though not all, of Margaret's curses. That survival, of kin and crown, reminds us of her stubborn refusal to credit their supernatural efficacy. This is a queen of which a descendant and a namesake, say Shakespeare's Elizabeth, could be justly proud.

4

"Rotten Armour": Richard's Play for the Citizens

Shakespeare's sequence with the Mayor and the Citizens presents the reader and the director with difficult inconsistencies and the challenge of an ambiguous overall impression. In the Cibber-Olivier tradition it is usually played as the culmination of Richard's deceptive villainy, a crowning achievement that leads him directly to the crown. More recently, the sequence has been presented as a sham success, a product of cold intimidation and/or the cynicism and stupidity that surround Richard and Buckingham. A number of productions since the Olivier film have exploited these darker, richer possibilities.[1] The BBC videotape seems to lean in their direction at first, only to revert to the buffoonish Mayor and the consummate actors of the earlier theatrical tradition.

The critics have been as divided as the players on this issue. Some, of course, find this one of Richard's finest hours. Robert Heilman calls it the "special triumph" for an actor with "an extraordinary passion for the taxing role, the impossible part." Rossiter enjoys the "magnificently sardonic fooling of the London bourgeoisie with a crisis-scare." David L. Frey similarly argues that "the day is his."[2] Even those who find the elaborate deception unconvincing tend to absolve Richard of blame. Charles Cowden-Clark finds it ludicrous that Buckingham thinks himself a good actor, calling him weak "morally and mentally." F. A. Marshall argues that "the difference between Richard and Buckingham was precisely that between the really great actor and the ranting tragedian of the fair-booth." W. A. Wright attributes to Buckingham only "a gift for what is now called melodrama." To Marshall, "Buckingham's acting could deceive noone but himself; but Richard's powers of dissimulation deceived even his most intimate associates."³

Others blame Shakespeare. Tillyard, though he notices that the "verse drops somewhat" during the scene, does not attribute this to Richard's flagging energy or effectiveness with the Mayor and the Citizens. W. J. Birch, equally dissatisfied, emphasizes the stupidity of Richard's Christian audience: "Shakespeare must have thought the ... religious people of his day thus easily won over by the appearance of piety, and the whole scene must have been intended to ridicule them. It is exaggerated, and the actors are made barefaced hypocrites."⁴

Only Stopford Brooke observes that this awkwardness may manifest Richard's declining powers, not Shakespeare's immature dramatic skills:

> Yet it is difficult to find fault with Shakespeare. It may be that he desired to mark, by their strained unnaturalness, that weakness in intellect which arises from the absence of love in his character. Intellectual power, without love, grown abnormal, unbalanced, and weak through pride of itself. Nay, more, Shakespeare felt that it would not only lose its power, but finally itself. It would be sure to make mistakes in dealing with mankind and the movements of the world; to overdo its cunning; to end, like the plotting Mephistopheles, in folly and failure.⁵

I would like to argue that the sources and analogues of these scenes lend strong support for Stopford Brooke's old and solitary distrust of the successful charade, and that the text does as well. So, again, does the recent theatrical tradition. In fact, a close look at the words and the sources of 3.5–3.7 might persuade us that the contrary tradition of Richard's overwhelming artistry in this sequence could only have dominated the critical and theatrical traditions for so long because of the influence of the Cibber-Olivier script.

First, Hastings's death speech is a somber prologue to their charade. "They smile at me, who shortly shall be dead" is an ominous cue line, in fact, for "*Enter Richard and Buckingham, in rotten Armour, marvellous ill-favoured.*" Like Hastings, these two tragedians live "like a drunken Sayler on a Mast / Readie with every Nod to tumble downe, / Into the fatall Bowels of the Deepe" (2069–80; 3.4.94–107, passim). Hastings's swan song further modulates Richard's manipulativeness into the minor key, undercutting his enthusiasm and his confidence, and coloring the whole deception with irony. The surface of their rotten armor might sound like military inexperience, desperate haste, and political naiveté, the characteristics they will try to sell to the Mayor. At the same time, they also look strangely like emblems of the same memento mori tradition Hastings has just evoked in his valedictory. Before long, both will be what Hastings and their costumes predict, rotting flesh.

As several of the critics have already suggested, their confidence as actors may also be undercut by their theatrical naiveté. Richard and Buckingham need to be schooled by Hamlet, so poorly do they seem to understand the actor's craft. They agree on a style that can only be called melodramatic:

> *Rich.*   Come Cousin,
> Canst thou quake, and change thy colour,
> Murther thy breath in middle of a word,
> And then againe begin, and stop againe,
> As if thou were distraught, and mad with terror?
> *Buck.* Tut, I can counterfeit the deepe Tragedian,
> Speake, and looke backe, and prie on every side,
> Tremble and start at wagging of a Straw:
> Intending deepe suspition, gastly Lookes
> Are at my service, like enforced Smiles;
> And both are readie in their Offices,
> At any time to grace my Strategemes. (2084–95; 3.5.1–11)

Quaking, blanching, halting, blushing, their looks are "ghastly" and their smiles "enforced." They are about to "out-Herod Herod," "tear a passion to tatters," to very rags. We might say with Hamlet, "Pox, leave thy damnable faces, and begin." Their understanding of playing is its parody, and this false understanding is apparently shared by both Richard and Buckingham.

Compare this confusion with the absolute confidence, the clear purpose, and the ruthless determination of Richard's soliloquy on acting in III *Henry* VI:

> Why, I can smile, and murther whiles I smile,
> And cry "Content!" to that which grieves my heart,
> And wet my cheeks with artificial tears,
> And frame my face to all occasions.
> I'll drown more sailors than the mermaid shall,
> I'll slay more gazers than the basilisk,

> I'll play the orator as well as Nestor,
> Deceive more slily than Ulysses could
> And like a Sinon, take another Troy.
> I can add colors to the chameleon,
> Change shapes with Proteus for advantages,
> And set the murtherous Machevil to school.
> Can I do this, and cannot get a crown?
> Tut, were it farther off, I'll pluck it down. (3.2.182-95)

This speech never confuses political with theatrical acting, much less bad melodrama with good politics. It gives epic and mythic dimensions to Richard's deceptiveness, as well as a frightening naturalness. Finally, it is neither undercut by the tableau of the dying Hastings, nor subjected to the scathing review of the Scrivener. We have little reason, therefore, to distrust its sophistication or its success.

In *Richard* III, even if the "artist in evil" had simply chosen such a poor supporting actor as Buckingham, his masterpiece would have been marred. Worse, Richard is Buckingham's confederate in theory as well as practice. Unless the Mayor and the Citizens are the most ignorant groundlings, habitués of the bearbaiting or cockfighting pits; or unless they are incredibly cynical, all of them, the charade can hardly work. Nowhere is the BBC's *Richard* III more effective than in its treatment of this first part of the scene. Buckingham and Richard overact just as badly as their theories would suggest, and the Mayor is plainly puzzled as well as frightened by their strangeness. But he is eager to please these mighty lords, and quick to perceive the role they want him to play. Richard's vehemence in "What? thinke you we are Turkes, or Infidels?" (2127; 3.5.41) may frighten him at first, but by the end of the sequence the Mayor is flattered to think himself a member of their company. He is not so much fooled as ambitious. His eyes rapidly cutting to Buckingham's, to test out his own acting, mark this entirely plausible portrayal.

Simply looking at the text of their exchange with the Mayor yields no definitive evidence as to how to play him or them during the first scene. Buckingham lays out the conspiracy theory. The Mayor can play his response either gullibly or incredulously: "Had he done so?" On his interpretation of this first line hinges much of the rest. Even if the Mayor is at first incredulous, Richard's acting may change his mind. In a few lines the Mayor seems of their party: "Now faire befall you, he deserv'd his death, / And your good Graces both have well proceeded, / To warn false Traytors from the like Attempts" (2133-35; 3.5.47-49). Mistress Shore, their pathetic shred of evidence against Hastings, is thrown out repeatedly. The Mayor apparently accepts their report of Hastings's "timorous" confession, their regret at his overhasty death, the whole package:

> *Maior.* But, my good Lord, your Graces words shal serve,
> As well as I had seene, and heard him speake:
> And doe not doubt, right Noble Princes both,
> But Ile acquaint our dutious Citizens
> With all your just proceedings in this case. (2148–52; 3.5.62–66)

The Mayor may be deceived. He may also be as accomplished an actor as Richard and Buckingham. If they do not perceive his acting, they are the poorer players for it. In fact, how can such awful evidence as the dukes provide, presented in a style that most critics concede to be terribly melodramatic, possibly persuade? The Mayor has to be a buffoon, as he often is in the theatrical tradition, or as cynical and self-serving a politician as Richard and Buckingham to be "deceived."

Because there are no stage directions and the evidence of Shakespeare's text and the theatrical tradition is not definitive here, the major sources can again serve our turn. At the very least, they suggest what Shakespeare's audience might have expected to see. In both of them, Hall and the literary analogue *Richardus Tertius*, the evidence is overwhelmingly in favor of a cynical, self-serving Mayor. He has neither been deceived nor intimidated; he is simply playing along. Hall describes his presence at the council plotting the deposition of Edward V:

> To this counsaile they toke diverse such as they thought mete to be trusted and likely to be enduced to that parte and hable to stand theim in steade, eyther by powre or by polycye. Emong whom, they made a counsaile Edmond Shaa then Mayre of London, whiche upon trust of hys awne avauncement, where he was of a proude harte highly desirous, toke on hym to frame the cytie to their appetite. (fol. xvii, verso)

The theatrical tradition might have been quite different had this historical commonplace been more widely known in the eighteenth and nineteenth centuries. Shakespeare's audience would have expected political duplicity on the part of the Mayor. The charade did not fool the Mayor because it did not need to; all that was required was the appearance of a motive for Hastings's death, or the removal of the princes. The Mayor was already in their pocket.

So also were the Citizens. In Hall, a number of substantial Citizens of London also witness the charade of Richard and Buckingham in 3.5. They all see them "Harnessed in old evill favoured brigandiers," implying that "sodeyne necessitie had constraigned them." They all hear Richard and Buckingham implicate Hastings in an assassination attempt. This time the details are closely followed by Shakespeare:

> Then the Lord protector shewed them, that the lord Hastynges & other of his conspiracy had contrived to have sodeynly destroyed hym and the duke of Buckyngham there the same daie in counsail ... which sodeyn feare drave them to put on suche harnesse as came nexte to their handes for their defence, and so God holpe them, that the mischiefe turned upon them that woulde have done it, & thus he required theim to report. (fol. xvv, verso)

However, in Hall, the result is again only a surface success for Richard's deception: "Every man answered fayre, as though no man mistrusted the matter, which of trueth no man beleved." If anything, Richard is deceived by the Citizens' hypocrisy. Thomas Legge's *Richardus Tertius*, which Bullough calls an analogue derived essentially from Hall, is even clearer:

> *Citizens.* We loyal [Citizens] will sedulously execute [your] command. [*Then after Gloucester departs.*] O obdurate villain, hiding [your] slaughter with a lie and [hiding] such evil confined by [your] mild aspect; who does not know about the monstrous deceits of this savage Duke? and [who] doubts that the noble man [Hastings] has been taken by fraud?[6]

In Hall, as in Legge, Richard may have intimidated these people, but he has not deceived them. The Mayor is a willing accomplice; the people are less pleased, but they go along.

If the Scrivener's scene had not so often been deleted from the productions of *Richard* III, Shakespeare's text could have made this point almost as clearly as the historical and dramatic sources. For the Scrivener is also not fooled, and like the moral voices in Legge's play and in Hall, he is deeply disturbed at both the villainy of the protagonists and the fear and cynicism of the Citizens. Like the connivance of the Mayor, this cowardly and depraved citizenry can further undermine our sense of the artistry of

Richard's evil. For the rotten charade would apparently have worked even if it had been ten times more melodramatic. Listen more carefully to the Scrivener's scathing words. They undercut Richard morally, of course; they also undercut him aesthetically:

> Here is the Indictment of the good Lord *Hastings*,
> Which in a set hand fairely is engross'd,
> That it may be to day read o're in *Paules*.
> And marke how well the sequell hangs together:
> Eleven houres I have spent to write it over,
> For yester-night by *Catesby* was it sent me,
> The Precedent was full as long a doing,
> And yet within these five houres *Hastings* liv'd,
> Untainted, unexamin'd, free, at libertie.
> Here's a good World the while.
> Who is so grosse, that cannot see this palpable device?
> Yet who so bold, but sayes he sees it not?
> Bad is the World, and all will come to nought,
> When such ill dealing must be seene in thought.
> (2199–2212; 3.6.1–14)

The charges against Hastings are a "palpable device." "Who is so grosse, that cannot see?" Eleven hours to write the indictment; at least as long for the precedent: "And yet within these five hours *Hastings* liv'd, / Untainted, unexamin'd, free, at libertie." No one has been fooled; yet no one has spoken either, not the lords, not the Mayor, not the Citizens, not even the Scrivener, except, of course, to us. He asks us, as fellow humans, to share his distress and to understand his fear. Cynicism and intimidation are everywhere. Even the boldest "sayes he sees it not." In such a world, Richard will grow and prosper. He needs no art at all.

This time we need not try the sources to clarify Shakespeare's intent. In the text the Scrivener's interpretation is clear and unconfused, even if it is also fearful. Actually, Hall and the others present more confusion than Shakespeare at this point. The sham is clear enough: "Every chyld might perceyve that [the proclamation] was prepared and studyed before" (Hall, fol. xvi), and therefore bogus. The responses of the Citizens are mixed, however, in spite of this obviousness:

> So that upon the proclaimyng thereof, one that was scolemayster at
> Paules standyng by and comparyng the shortenesse of the tyme with

the length of the matter sayed to theim that stoode aboute hym, here is a gaye goodly cast, foule cast awaye for hast. And a marchaunte that stoode by hym sayed that it was wrytten by inspiracyon and prophesye. (Hall, fol. xvi)

Legge makes less of the skepticism, and more of the gullibility:

> *Second Citizen.* These things have been written by the profound spirit of a prophet, for how else could so many [beautiful] words be thought up or so [well] expressed in so short a time? The documents seem extremely beautifully [done] to me, and the little proclamation . . . delineated beautifully, and . . . excellent for speaking. Yet it seems especially wondrous that so many beautiful things were prepared in so short a time. (Legge, p. 342)

"True wit is nature to advantage dress'd."[7] The surface is beautiful; why worry about the substance? In the sources and analogues, then, some of the people are fooled all of the time. In Shakespeare the eyewitness Scrivener reviews a performance that is flawed morally and aesthetically. It is too palpable to have fooled even the grossest mind, but the citizenry is too bad and too fearful to reject it. The Scrivener credits Richard with no deception, nor are we given the merchant's deceived response. Cynicism and cowardice, not artistry, are the causes of this effect.

Though they have been voices crying in the wilderness, some critics too have suggested that we must revise our estimation of Richard's deceptive skills after this Scrivener's speech. Cowden-Clark laments its traditional excision from productions of the play:

> This slight passage appears to me accurately suggestive of the smothered feeling of indignation that boils in men's minds under a tyrannical dynasty; and, indeed, so well is this under-current of opinion depicted in the subordinate characters in Shakespeare's historical plays, that they ought in nowise be omitted in the representation, since they form part of the . . . whole.

F. A. Ordish concurs: "The scrivener perceives the villainy at work, and in the succeeding lines demonstrates it as grossly apparent. Yet the city has connived, and the indictment is about to be read in public, presumably by the city's recorder."[8]

This undercurrent of connivance and indignation can also influence our response to the concluding scene at Baynard's Castle. Only if the Scrivener's searing words are not heard can we fail to know that the Citizens have already seen through the first charade, but remained silent. Only if the Mayor is portrayed as the gull of Richard and Buckingham, rather than their confederate, can we miss his connivance. The cut and oversimplified theatrical versions of the last 300 years have probably contributed heavily to our underestimation of the complexity of these scenes.9 If that is true, so has the naiveté of Richard and Buckingham. For the Mayor must be a better actor than either of them, and a consummate manipulator of his people as well, for their plan to work. Yet they seem persistently to underestimate his roles as actor and director in their city pageant. They may even be gulled by his role playing into thinking themselves more successful actors than they really are. So much for Richard's continuing discernment and self-irony.

Nowhere would their poor acting become more obvious than in the Citizens' responses to Buckingham's attempts to act out Richard's scenario about the bastardy of Edward's children. Despite their cleverness and intimidation, their audacious enterprise often fails. These failures are compressed in the script into the beginning of 3.7, but the failures are unequivocally there. Early in 3.7, Richard asks, "What say the Citizens?" Buckingham's response is deeply disappointing: "Now by the holy Mother of our Lord, / The Citizens are mum, say not a word." As Richard asks for details of the failure, Buckingham recites his new list of palpable devices against the children of Edward. Nowhere are his devices more preposterous than in his claims in favor of Richard: "Withall, I did inferre your Lineaments, / Being the right I*dea* of your Father, / Both in your forme, and Nobleness of Minde." Richard may have been a successful soldier and administrator in Scotland; since then he has shown little "Wisdome in Peace," even less "Bountie, Vertue, faire Humilitie" (2215–30; 3.2.2–17, passim). The reference to that crooked form as matching the father of the Plantagenets is possibly the most embarrassing of all these preposterous claims. And so Buckingham has failed. Shocked by the palpable slander of Edward's children and the equally palpable flattery of Richard, the Citizens are struck dumb:

> *Buck.* And when my Oratorie drew toward end,
> I bid them that did love their Countries good,
> Cry, God save R*ich*ard, Englands Royall King.
> *Rich.* And did they so?
> *Buck.* No, so God helpe me, they spake not a word,

But like dumbe Statues, or breathing Stones,
Star'd each on other, and look'd deadly pale. (2233-39; 3.7.20-26)

Less clever than the lords in council or the Mayor in conference, these simple Citizens are unable to hide their unbelief much less act out their part.

The Mayor, Buckingham's confederate planted in the midst of the Citizens, tries to soften the blow, but his answer, that "The people were not used / To be spoke to, but by the Recorder," deceives neither Richard nor his emissary. Nor does the Mayor's half-hearted recitation of what Buckingham "sayth" or "hath inferr'd" deceive the Citizens or fool Buckingham. Only "some followers of mine own" also planted "at lower end of the Hall, hurld up their Caps, / And some tenne voyces cry'd, God save King Richard." Buckingham "took the vantage of those few," to be sure. But the deception simply did not work.[10] Richard knows, and he is crestfallen: "What tongueless Blockes were they, would they not speake? / Will not the Mayor then, and his Brethren come?" (2245-57; 3.7.32-44). From what we have seen and heard, Richard's logic is inescapable; so is the logic of the dramatic sequence. The plot has failed. The Citizens will not come.

But of course, they do come, in Shakespeare and in Hall. Has Richard underestimated the cynicism and the opportunism of the Mayor and his Citizens, even as he has overestimated his own abilities to ingratiate, deceive, and persuade? We can only guess. But despite the absolute failure of Buckingham's playing, and the Scrivener's devastating review, they will have an audience for their finale. No one is fooled, yet still they come to Baynard's Castle. That the audience is bought and sold is a compelling explanation of such apparent discontinuities; it also fits comfortably with what we have been hearing of this rotten charade for the last three scenes. It must be all surface, this last little play of theirs, for form only. Richard will be proclaimed king by a handful of hired actors. Only with such a purchased audience could his histrionics possibly work. It is not to Richard's credit here that he congratulates himself and Buckingham for the artistic success of such a reception.

The Mayor has clearly hedged his political bets with his half-hearted recitation of what Buckingham "sayth" or "hath inferr'd." That he "nothing spoke in warrant from himself" can remind us in 3.7 of how little of their charade he has found convincing. Still, undeceived but self-serving, the Mayor comes to the aid of Richard and Buckingham during their last scene. He even hurries the plot along with such setups as "Marry God defend his Grace should say us nay"; "See where his Grace stands, tweene two Clergie men"; "Do good my Lord, your Citizens entreat you"; and "God blesse your Grace, we see it, and will say it" (2297–98, 2314–15, 2244, 2458–59; 3.7.81, 95, 31, 237). What a perfect audience. The only speaking role in the scene besides those of Richard and his confederates Catesby and Buckingham is that of this possible yes-man, the self-serving Mayor. The rest may be the hand-picked crowd of yesterday. The particulars of the dramatic sequence make it clear that the crowd was not fooled; yet they come to Baynard's Castle. What could make their cynicism and the falseness of the whole dramatic moment clearer than these details? The Mayor's hypocrisy is perfect. Of the four lines he speaks, three call Richard "his Grace," the fourth "my Lord." Like Macbeth trying to convince the desperadoes that they have true motives against Banquo, so Richard here is naive in assuming that the Mayor must believe in order to participate in the rotten charade: "In saying so, you shall but say the truth." "Whatever you say, my lord."

Worse, the two divines flanking Richard are in fact the corrupt and dishonored Friars Penker and Shaa, the latter the Mayor's brother.[11] How convincing can the pageant be with such a supporting cast? Shakespeare even names them: "Goe Lovell with all speed to Doctor *Shaw*, / Goe thou to Fryer *Penker*, bid them both / Meet me within this houre at Baynard's Castle" (2191–93; 3.5.103–5). This increases the likelihood that he intended for their tarnished reputations in the historical tradition to discredit Richard's charade in the play. The Scrivener has just told us that seeing is not believing in this bad world. The best lack all conviction; only the worst are full of passionate intensity. The cast and the audience are as rotten as the armor. On the surface the rotten armor is a symbol contrived by Richard and Buckingham to suggest their haste and their vulnerability to such arch-deceivers as Hastings. But with an irony that the theater audience can understand even if Richard's suborned audience ignores it, the surface of their armor represents the substance of their rotten moral and aesthetic being. False appearance has been Richard's ally throughout half of the play. Finally appearance is turning against him, for anyone who will see it and say it.

Nevertheless, we are left with Richard's apparent victory, in Hall and in Shakespeare. "Long live King *Richard*, Englands worthie King," says Buckingham, and all respond "Amen" (2462–63; 3.7.240–41). Of course, who they are and how they speak are everything, and the stage directions again give us nothing to go on. We can have a rapt audience, as in any production that is glorifying Richard at this moment of his supreme deceptiveness. The BBC videotape is a prime example, though it must contradict its more interesting treatment of 3.5 in the process. At the end of 3.7 the text favors neither the ravishing performance nor the rotten charade. From 3.4 through the beginning of 3.7, the words of Hastings, the Scrivener, and Richard and Buckingham formulate reviews that are decisively negative. Pure theatricality does not necessarily favor Richard's success here. In fact, many recent productions have taken their cues from these bad reviews in the play, rather than from the earlier theatrical tradition. A bogus assent concludes their representation of this bogus deception.

Hall treats the outcome of the charade in ways that deserve our careful attention, for they address again the central issues at dispute. For example, Hall's Richard sounds much more appealing than Shakespeare's at this crucial moment. He delivers a stirring, patriotic speech, which culminates in another promise to defeat the French and reunite the two realms. "By God his speciall providence" Richard has already controlled the affairs of England. Now he will to France, "by God his grace and youre good helpe to get again, subdue, and establishe for ever in dewe obedience unto this realme of Englande." "With this there was a greate cry and shoute, criyng kyng Richard, and so the lordes wente up to the kynge, and so he was after that daie called" (fol. xxiiii). Shakespeare does not give Richard this rousing moment anywhere in 3.7.

Finally, Hall's account ends not in triumph but in irony. Many left after the play dissatisfied with the performances:

> But the people departed talkynge dyversely of the matter, every man as his fantasye gave hym, but muche thei marveiled of this maner of dealyng, that the matter was on bothe partes [Richard's and Buckingham's] made so straunge as though never the one parte had communed with the other parte thereof before, when thei wiste that there was no manne so dull that hearde theim, but he perceyved well ynough that all the matter was made betwene them. (fol. xxiiii)

Even the people Hall has earlier called "the common people onely, whiche waver with the wynde" (fol. xiii), saw through their charade. Why, then, did they go along? Hall's analysis is so apposite to Shakespeare's vision that it could be the text for the scene:

> Howbeit, some excused that again, saiynge: all thynge muste bee doen in good ordre, and menne muste sometyme for the maner sake not bee aknowen what they knowe. For at the consecracion of a bishoppe, every manne perceiveth by paiment of his bulles that he

entendeth to bee one, yet when he is twise asked whether he will bee a bishop, he muste twise saye naie and at the thirde tyme take it upon hym as compelled thereto by his awne will. (fol. xxiiii, verso)

To the fearful, Richard's public ceremony is no more deceitful than the liturgical form prescribed for the ordination of a bishop. Or perhaps it is like a child's game, or a stage play:

And in a stage plaie, the people knowe right well that he that plaieth the sowdaine, is percase a souter, yet yf one of acquaintaunce perchaunce of litle nurture shoulde call hym by his name while he standeth in his majestie one of his tourmentours might fortune breke his hed for marryng the plaie. And so they saied, these matters bee kynges games, as it were staige playes, and for the moste parte plaied upon scaffoldes, in whiche poore men bee but lookers on, and they that wise bee, will medle no ferther, for they that steppe up with them when they cannot plaie their partes, they disorder the plaie and do theim selves no good. (fol. xxiiii, verso)

"Who is so grosse, that cannot see this palpable device? / Yet who so bold, but says he sees it not?" The rationalization that compares this rotten pageant to the consecration of a bishop, or a stage play, or a king's game explains how so bad a play could have worked so well. The best in this kind can be held in contempt by all manner of men, from Touchstone's "most faining" to Duke Theseus' "shadows." Even the most thoughtful Citizens of all ages may try to ignore the worst of times with such analogies. It is better than getting one's head broken, or losing all hope. Leave the scaffold for the actor, the child, the priest, and the politician.[12] Prudence, then, and custom, cynicism, not enthusiastic reviews, seem to have marked this performance of Richard and Buckingham in Hall. If this cautious response of the Citizens granted a superficial success to their rotten charade, it also marked its substantial failure. Like Pilates, they wash their hands of the performance; they do not applaud enthusiastically. The scaffold of the actor will soon be the stage for Richard's execution. The game, the play, the consecration as well, will be Richmond's.

We might end by asking if this competing version of the sequence with the Mayor and the Citizens can fit comfortably into the process of our involvement with Richard throughout the rest of the play. Richard obviously compels our attention and our allegiance as the play begins. By the end of the second scene we are enjoying his confidence and his early achievements with Anne and Clarence. He comes off witty, resourceful, light-hearted, brave, candid with himself, sly but engaging with his enemies, full of energy and vitality, a consummate ironist, an accomplished actor. He is vigorous in his vernacular speech, discerning about others, and contemptuous about God, providence, and those who believe in them. This initial impression is only momentarily threatened by Margaret's powerful presence in 1.3. But when Richard stops confiding in the audience through soliloquies at the end of the same scene, his own contemptuous disregard can quickly begin to chill our earlier relationship. When we next see Richard in soliloquy, in his coronation scene, he is wracked with confusion, fear, and superstition, and unaware that we are listening. Then we overhear his shattered soliloquy after the ghosts' visitation. But now we are eavesdropping, not sharing Richard's ravishing confidences; our ironic advantage over Richard lasts through most of the fourth and fifth acts. This changing relationship to Richard in soliloquy helps the audience communicate as surely with his disintegration at the end as we did with his strength at the start.

Even as Richard insinuates himself less and less into the confidence of the audience, so his powers to persuade the characters on the stage also begin to diminish after the second act. At first beguiling, Richard fools fewer and fewer characters in the play. He intimidates, and he exploits a growing cynicism that he also has nurtured. At the same time, Buckingham usurps more and more of Richard's manipulative plotting, which further distances us from the arch-deceiver. By 3.5–3.7, the putative culmination of his evil artistry, Richard may be alone deceived into thinking that his deception is working. In an aside in Legge's play, the Citizens point clearly to a decline that we can perceive in Shakespeare as well:

> O [his] stubborn impudence striving [to fool us] with [this] deceit, when he mocks [our intelligence] with this foreign outward appearance. Secure he fears nothing, and thinks that others do not recognize [his] concealed evil, but [his] villainy deceives [only] himself. (p. 368)

After these scenes, Richard's image suffers from the agonies and the mutual compassion of the chorus of wailing women, who know him as well as the Mayor and the Citizens in Legge. It suffers from Anne's comment about Richard's "timorous Dreames" (2564; 4.1.84) and his own confused commands to Catesby and Lovell. Then it must bear the moral superiority of a Buckingham, a Tyrrel, even the two murderers Dighton and Forrest, not to mention Richard's growing fears and superstitions. "If to have done the thing you gave in charge, / Beget your happinesse, be happy then, / For it is done" (2730–32; 4.3.25–27). These are devastating words from this discontented gentleman. Richard deflates himself further by the cowardly attempt to intimidate the ladies, stop their discomfiting words, with "the clamorous report of Warre" (2928; 4.4.153). I would argue that this script of his decline culminates in his defeats by Queen Elizabeth and Richmond in the last two acts. Such undertones are so consistent with one another and so often available to the audience that the music of disintegration can become the primary theme of the last half of the play.

In spite of these songs of death, many readers cling to the exciting tonalities of Richard's earliest portrayal, and ignore what can be seen as Shakespeare's carefully orchestrated decline. The theatrical tradition, omitting as it has for almost three centuries such important details of Richard's decline as the Scrivener's speech, and often oversimplifying the sequence with the Mayor and the Citizens, both embodies (and encourages) this competing perception. Admittedly, Richard's last soliloquy and his final desperate battle oration are exciting dramatic moments, and remind us of the bustling tempo and bright harmonies of the early Richard. They are at the same time the final crumbling of the inner keep of his castle walls, after an assault on his attractiveness that may have lasted for half of the play. Most of the remaining bubbles of his initial charisma can be decisively pricked during the three scenes with the Mayor and the Citizens, unless those scenes are dismissed with a farcical inattention. In Hall the Citizens even predict after the Pyrrhic victory of this rotten charade the outcome of Richard's last scene on earth. It will be played not on the boards of the theater but on the field of battle. His scaffold in that final act is also his place of execution. For Death comes at the last, and farewell king. Richard's rotten armor is no match for the music of that final adversary.

5

Perceptions of Providence in Richard III

✝ One of the most persistent criticisms of Olivier's film concerns its general loss of "the larger significance" of *Richard* III. Particularly disturbing has been its distortion of the force of providence. Griffin laments the sacrifice of "Margaret, who runs like a thread through Shakespeare's text, reminding Richard, his fellow sinners, and the audience, that retribution will come." Jorgens agrees that "cutting foreknowledge and Margaret's curses... shifted the emphasis away from history and the working out of Divine Justice." Nicholas Brooke, and others, regret the absence of an effectively dramatized ritual patterning. In Olivier's film, the ghosts are also severely truncated, and do not appear to Richmond at all. Thus they cannot function as a "sign that divine providence is guiding him." Roy Walker refers further to the "butchery of Richmond's part," and like Brown sees it as a part of Olivier's (and Cibber's) systematic elimination of attractive alternatives to Richard from family, church, state, or universe. Jorgens particularly complains that the supernatural forces of providence are emasculated along with the human representatives of the church. Hammond summarizes many of these complaints when he mentions that Olivier's extensive cuts "cannot fail to damage the play's internal structure, its patterns of imagery, rhetoric, and tone, and its moral and historical fabric." The refusal to give fair play to Richard's discovery and reversal in the closing minutes of the film is yet another example of this distortion. Many recent stage productions of *Richard* III have apparently done a much fairer job of clothing the force of providence, the "sense of structure and ritual," the "inexorable dramatic logic" of the conclusion in theatrical garments.[1]

Until recently, most critics essentially agreed with these reviewers of the Olivier film that the action of *Richard* III reveals, in addition to the intriguing malignity of Richard himself, "the working out of God's plan to restore England to prosperity." The words are Tillyard's, but there are many articulate representatives of such a view. Reese finds this theme "as elaborately patterned as the verse"; "curses are fulfilled, sometimes in the very language in which they were spoken." Jones sees in the play's characterization and structure a "conception of a supernatural order that surrounds and contains the main action and from which judgment will eventually come." Moody Prior calls the ghosts "ritual messengers of divine vengeance on Richard and of fulfillment of divine promise for Richmond." Hammond and C. A. Patrides think of *Richard* III as "providential ritual." Rossiter writes that it presents "a rigid Tudor scheme of retributive justice." Hunter has presented an arresting defense of these general assumptions.[2]

However, a significant countercurrent has been evident since the 1960s. Perhaps it has been quickened by the Olivier film; probably both are also symptoms of a deeper turmoil.[3] Frey argues at one point "that Shakespeare rejected the theme of divine providence as found in the sources." John Wilders distrusts "Richmond's claim to be the instrument of divine justice . . . because we have heard such claims before." Sanders argues similarly that the audience has been trained by the action of the play to have "a wary alertness about the invocation of moral sanctions." While Nicholas Brooke does not agree with the letter of their position, he revels in its spirit, conceding the divine pattern, but finding it "repulsive," and Richard "bolder than ourselves in resisting oppression." Wilbur Sanders also senses a heroism in this Richard, admiring in his last words "an intransigent naturalism that will yield no ground to the supernatural." For these last two critics, so many kneel to affirm the chastising hand of providence that the one who remains standing seems heroic by default.[4]

Can we find some concord of this discord? The second half of this chapter will seek it by investigating the theological context of some of the most persistent interpretive issues. More critics than characters have questioned providence in *Richard* III by asking about unanswered prayers, unfulfilled curses, "external providence," and the "wicked wills of wicked men." I think a more likely area of harmony is anticipated in the willingness of several members of the Tillyard school to suggest that some of the complexities that bother their opponents are woven into the fabric of the play. Rossiter, for example, knows that Shakespeare is not merely dramatizing the Tudor myth: "This historic myth offered absolutes, certainties.

Shakespeare in the histories always leaves us with relatives, ambiguities, irony, a process thoroughly dialectical." Hunter and Prior also discuss the ways in which "the mystery of God's judgment" enriches the experience of Richard III. Hunter argues that complexities of characterization and theme abound in Richard III; but in the final analysis, "evil is done but good comes of it. Divine providence is necessarily among Shakespeare's subjects." Prior writes, "Shakespeare, like all his contemporaries of whatever intellectual bias, approached Richard III through the providential idea of history, but he left the idea more complex, less rigid, more humane than he found it in any of his sources. He was thus liberated of its conventional pieties and mechanistic rigor."[5]

The first half of this chapter will investigate such complexity in the words and actions of the play itself. It will argue that the play's movement toward affirming a providential hand in the individual and the national experience can be seen as both joyful and consistent because it is not usually imposed from without but generated from within. In most of the characters in Richard III belief is achieved, not coerced; and skepticism, like Elizabeth's, is not always eliminated and does not necessarily guarantee humiliation and defeat. The result is not a single, homogeneous "belief" but a complex of individual responses to the mysteries and the miseries of human life. Only on the extreme edges of this world do we find Richmond's consistent faith and Richard's outspoken naturalism, to be absolutely rewarded and punished by the hand of God at the play's conclusion. I will argue that even Richard wavers in his disbelief, from beginning to end. In this world, Richmond suffers more in theatrical appeal from the stability of his faith than from the deficiency of his rhetoric in act 5. This problem is real, but it may also be unavoidable in a genre like drama in which spiritual agonists are so compelling to watch.

Omens, dreams, prophecies, prayers, curses, ghosts, and their relationship to the enveloping question of divine providence—these matters are vigorously debated throughout Richard III. Characters often engage the issues with one another and alone. The structure of the play itself encourages an ongoing scrutiny of such issues by the audience as well. The resulting dialectic, as both Rossiter and Sanders call it, deserves our close attention.[6] So does the resultant response to this dialectic—a ritualized pattern within the dramatic sequence in which character after character vigorously affirms the activity of divine providence in his own life and death, and prays for its continued operation in English history. Such affirmations derive much of their theatrical excitement from the uncertainties out of which they have been forged. Looking carefully, systematically, at most of the relevant testimony in the play should clear away some smoke, even if it also stirs up a few more sparks.

Perceptions of Providence

In one sense, every incidental reference to these matters in Richard III forms a part of the debate. Richard and Clarence are both scornful of "Prophesies and Dreams" in the first scene (35, 58; 1.1.33, 54). Their cynicism, set against King Edward's gullibility, is the prelude to the debate. Richard has nothing but disdain for prophets, dreamers, and those who listen to them:

> Plots have I laide, Inductions dangerous,
> By drunken Prophesies, Libels, and Dreames,
> To set my brother *Clarence* and the King
> In deadly hate, the one against the other:
> And if King *Edward* be as true and just,
> As I am Subtle, False, and Treacherous,
> This day should *Clarence* closely be mew'd up:
> About a Prophesie, which sayes that G,
> Of Edwards heyres the murtherer shall be. (34–43; 1.1.32–41)

Richard will merely use their credulity to his own advantage. Beneath this cynical façade, however, lurks an ironic affirmation. Edward's heirs will be murdered by "G," not George but Gloucester (Richard). That prophecies and dreams can be both misused and misinterpreted is therefore not our only impression during this first encounter; they may also be true.

Clarence seems equally disdainful of prophecies and dreams when he meets Richard on the way to the Tower. Of Edward he complains:

> He hearkens after Prophesies and Dreames,
> And from the Crosse-row pluckes the letter G:
> And sayes, a Wizard told him, that by G,
> His issue disinherited should be.
> And for my name of *George* begins with G,
> It followes in his thought, that I am he.
> These (as I learne) and such like toyes as these,
> Hath moov'd his Highnesse to commit me now. (58–65; 1.1.54–61)

Clarence's anger is understandable. However, the letter "G" has not been plucked from the "Crosse-row" by the wandering hand of some idle compositor, though it is now being misset in the "forme." In time, Clarence, like Richard, will come to know the folly of his skepticism and suffer the consequences.

Anne's belief in ghosts, curses, prayers, and omens in scene 2 is similarly rebutted by Richard's preemptive disbelief. This keen encounter of wits is in some measure a clash of world-views, a debate within a debate early in the play. Curiously, Richard himself, even this soon, betrays fascinating inconsistencies in his own views. Like Anne's, his phrases are full of images of supernatural agency; "Angels," "the Divell," "Saints," including John and Paul, "Heaven," and an immortal "Soule" all inhabit the universe of his devious mind, however vigorously he would deny them. His skeptical looks dissemble a complexity of mind, conscience rather, that will later return to haunt him.

As these incidental details of belief and assumption begin to set a dialectical tone at the beginning of the play, so does a debate of sorts occur in each scene of the first act. Richard and Brakenbury debate the questions of "private Conference" and Richard's loyalty in scene 1. Richard even challenges the lieutenant to rebut him: "Can you deny all this?" Scene 2 is full of the "keene encounter" (90, 100, 301; 1.1.86, 96; 1.2.115) of wits between Anne and Richard. In scene 3 the queen and Rivers try to counter Richard's preposterous claims and insults, and Margaret more effectively rebuts his lies in her asides to the audience. Scene 4 contains not only the Murderers' debates about conscience and damnation, but also their debate with Clarence about "God's dreadfull Law" and the "vengeance in his hand, / To hurle upon their heads that break it" (1040, 1031; 1.4.209, 200). Debate, vigorous argument, is unusually prominent in act 1 of *Richard III*.

More particularly, divine providence is itself subject for debate among these disputatious characters. Near the end of 1.3, the quarrel seems to concern who has been visited most harshly and most appropriately by divine vengeance. Richard opines that his father's curses have fallen flush upon Margaret:

His Curses, then, from bitternesse of Soule,
Denounc'd against thee, are all falne upon thee:
And God, not we, hath plagu'd thy bloody deed.
(648–50; 1.3.178–80)

This ironic affirmation of divine providence, however spiteful its motivation, is followed by Elizabeth's equally spiteful support: "So just is God, to right the innocent." She will live to regret this comment. For Margaret, however, these taunts become a bridge from agnosticism to belief, a moment of epiphany and release. In five brief lines she asks, "Did Yorkes dread Curse prevaile so much with Heaven?"; "Can Curses pierce the Clouds, and enter Heaven?" Her answer is implicit in the deluge of curses that follows: "Why then give way dull Clouds to my quick Curses" (660-65; 1.3.190-95, passim). Then she curses King Edward, and his son, and his queen, and Rivers, Dorset, and Hastings, and finally, for almost twenty delicious lines, Richard himself. Even more curses follow, leading finally to Margaret's crucial exchange with Buckingham.

Because his "Garments are not spotted with our blood," Margaret would leave him out; "Nor thou within the compasse of my curse." But Buckingham does not believe in the efficacy of curses, and he says so flatly: "Nor no one heere: for Curses never passe / The lips of those that breath them in the ayre." Margaret, having apparently just discovered the efficacy even of those curses against herself, is loath to let go of this new belief: "I will not thinke but they ascend the sky, / And there awake Gods gentle sleeping peace" (757-60; 1.3.284-87, passim). But Buckingham will not relent, will not "respect" her curses; so he too is finally cursed.

Even Richard betrays a belief in supernatural agency in three telling ways during the scene. In an aside just after the Margaret-Buckingham exchange, he confides in us: "For had I curst now, I had curst my selfe" (793; 1.3.318). Before, his attempts to gag Margaret before she had a chance to deliver any of his curse, then to name her in his place, betray a similar nervousness. Still earlier, when Richard avers that "God, not we, hath plagu'd thy bloody deed," there is yet another indication of his belief in the efficacy of curses and God's agency in their fulfillment. Though some of these lines are tinged also with cynicism, they may express more of Richard's beliefs than he or some of his champions would acknowledge. These are dangerous beliefs for a Machiavel.

The tempo of the debate increases in 1.4. Clarence, who once scorned the "toyes" of his brother's superstitions, has through his own premonitory dream been convinced of providential agency in his death: "thou wilt be aveng'd on my misdeeds." He has also seen beyond the bank and shoal of time. While Clarence sleeps the Murderers turn several theological issues topsy-turvy in their own little debate. Both apparently believe in "the great Judgment day." But conscience becomes a "passionate humor," "certaine dregges" of the wine of life, coins in a purse, and then, the urging of cowardly impulses. It mutinies; it beggars; it would destroy a "tall man's" reputation. Even to these desperadoes, the alternative good to this insinuating evil, conscience, is a supernatural force: "Take the divell in thy minde, and beleeve him [conscience] not" (941-84; 1.4.105-52, passim). For all their upside-downing, conscience therefore remains supernatural too. When Clarence awakes, the debate intensifies. Prior has already suggested the relevancy of the subsequent arguments about damnation, divine vengeance, broken vows to God and broken laws. We even hear of a "bloudy minister" of God's providence, sent "To cut off those that have offended him."[7] But though both Murderers apparently believe with Clarence in this avenging providence, only one is moved to "Relent, and save" his soul (1050-51, 1090; 1.4.219-20, 256). The other does his deed, and the first part of Clarence's prophetic dream is confirmed. Of its eschatological validity, we can only guess.

The first act, then, begins with some interesting if incidental references to such issues as the efficacy of curses, prophecies, and prayers, the validity of premonitory dreams, and the supernatural agency of God's providence. It concludes with two scenes in which such issues are frequently the subject of vigorous debate. A moment of equal intensity, to which we will quickly move, occurs from scene 2 to scene 4 of act 3. Hastings's agonistic experience in the middle of *Richard* III establishes a pattern of response to supernatural agency that will become familiar by the end of the play. In the first scene of this sequence, he is, like Buckingham in 1.3, a confirmed skeptic. Margaret's curses are "false bodings"; Stanley's dream "mock'ry" (1823; 3.2.27). By the third he has been converted to more traditional beliefs. Poised between these two scenes, the three nobles die at Pomfret, acknowledging God's hand in the potency of past curses and prophesying future divine retribution. As accentuated scenes in the play's developing dialectic of supernatural agency in human affairs, they demand a careful look.

The shape of Hastings's experience is clear enough. Stanley's messenger "certifies your Lordship, that this Night / He dreamt, the Bore had rased off his Helme." Stanley also fears the two councils. Therefore, he urges Hastings to "post with him toward the North, / To shun the danger that his Soule divines." We have recently heard the Citizens testify that it is "by a divine instinct" that "mens mindes mistrust" (1479; 2.3.42). Hastings has not heard, and he does not believe. He finds the political concerns "shallow, without instance";

And for his Dreames, I wonder hee's so simple,
To trust the mock'ry of unquiet slumbers. (1806-23; 3.2.10-27)

Like Chaucer's Chauntecleer after Pertelote has worked him over, Hastings assumes natural, second causes for Stanley's premonitory dream. So he naively rejects its warning. Our foreknowledge of Richard's plot against

Hastings and the princes heightens our perception of Hastings's error and defines it for us. The parallels to Clarence's premonitory dream and our foreknowledge of his fate are inescapable. Heavy dramatic irony further intensifies our sense of Hastings's mistake: "But I shall laugh at this a twelvemonth hence," or "Thinke you, but that I know our state secure, / I would be so triumphant as I am?" (1857–82; 3.2.57–82, passim). This motif goes on and on, and each time it reminds us of a future that few besides Hastings do not already foresee.

That future becomes Hastings's present soon enough. But first we see "*Sir Richard Ratcliffe, with Halberds, carrying the Nobles to death at Pomfret.*" Juxtaposed as it is against Hastings's jaunty skepticism about premonitory dreams, this scene speaks persuasively in the debate over supernatural agency. Rivers, Grey, and Vaughan all pray for God's protection of the prince and his mother, or invoke God's vengeance upon their enemies. All expect to "meet againe in Heaven." Even more impressive to an audience still responding to the ironies of Hastings's skepticism is their mutual, ritualistic confirmation of God's providential hand in the efficacy of prayers and curses. Grey says, "Now *Margarets* Curse is falne upon our Heads, / When shee exclaim'd on *Hastings*, you, and I, / For standing by, when *Richard* stab'd her Sonne." Rivers: "Then curs'd shee *Richard*, / Then curs'd shee *Buckingham*, / Then curs'd shee *Hastings*. Oh remember God, / To heare her prayer for them, as now for us" (1933–55; 3.3.1–20, passim). There are complexities of motivation that we will consider in a moment. But the central thrust of the scene is to confirm the supernatural agency of curses, prayers, and prophecies in God's providential universe. No voice says it nay.

Immediately afterward Hastings, just cursed by the lords at Pomfret, meets the fate that Stanley's dream also presaged. He remains the theological skeptic and the political naif as late as two lines before his death sentence. But in his response to his sudden, unexpected political reversal, the skeptic is converted to belief. Hastings acknowledges the folly of his hubris and his disbelief. He acknowledges the validity of Stanley's dreams and Margaret's prophecies. This is just the sort of thing that Olivier so persistently cuts from his film. The moment is so powerful and so obvious a part of Hastings's own personal dialectic and the play's patterning of such internal debates that it deserves to be quoted in full:

Woe, woe for England, not a whit for me,
For I, too fond, might have prevented this:
Stanley did dreame, the Bore did rowse our Helmes,
And I did scorne it, and disdaine to flye:

Three times to day my Foot-Cloth-Horse did stumble,
And started, when he look'd upon the Tower,
As loth to beare me to the slaughter-house.
O now I need the Priest, that spake to me:
I now repent I told the Pursuivant,
As too triumphing, how mine Enemies
To day at Pomfret bloodily were butcher'd,
And I my selfe secure, in grace and favour.
O *Margaret, Margaret*, now thy heavie Curse
Is lighted on poore *Hastings* wretched Head.
(2053–66; 3.4.80–93)

There follows as impressive a piece of traditional moral wisdom as occurs in Shakespeare; its last lines, "Lives like a drunken Sayler on a Mast, / Readie with every Nod to tumble downe, / Into the fatall Bowels of the Deepe" (2072–74; 3.4.99–101), contain overtones of Clarence's premonitory dream. This one-time skeptic, convinced at last of supernatural agency in human affairs, himself prophesies and goes to his death. Hastings's debate is over, its conclusion clear. To save his life it may be "bootlesse to exclaime" (2075; 3.4.102). But as another affirmative in the play's debate over supernatural agency, Hastings's words are anything but bootless. Five lords have now died convinced of a supernatural agency in their death, and invoking that same divine providence to continued activity in human affairs. At least two of the five were initially skeptical but ultimately converted by the inescapable evidence of their own experience.

Complexities of characterization keep the dialectic alive, however, even at this affirmative moment. The lords at Pomfret have every reason to hope at their death that Margaret's curse was effective; that hope will be their only means of revenge against Hastings, Buckingham, and Richard. They are also downplaying their own guilt; few men die guiltless deaths. Further, at least half of their prayer for "my Sister and her Princely Sonnes" (1956; 3.3.21), will be answered "No," if at all. For converts, the lords at Pomfret pray poorly. Clarence's prayer is somewhat more deserving, but the state of his soul is similarly parlous in his last hours. After all, though he sincerely believes that his dream presages betrayal and death, and quickly learns this to be true, he spends most of his scene with the Murderers arguing divine providence in an attempt to save his own skin. Only Hastings's conversion is free of such complexity.

Further, there is no question that belief in supernatural agency can be abused by clever men like Richard and Buckingham. If Edward believes in wizards and prophecies, he can be gulled to execute his brother Clarence. If the lords at council believe in witchcraft, even if they demand some plausible excuse for an execution without that belief, a withered arm can become Hastings's death warrant. These complexities make us look more carefully at the testimonies of all of these characters. They do not necessarily convince us that all such testimonies are false. Hastings, Clarence, Rivers, Vaughan, and Grey all die affirming supernatural agency in human affairs and attributing it to divine providence. Unlike Richard, they are not trying to fool anyone. They have seen, and they believe. That is the overwhelming impression of scenes 2 through 4. The complexities that Frey and others harp on are interesting undercurrents in this sea of faith. They are not its melancholy, long, withdrawing roar.

At first glance act 4, scene 1 would seem strongly to affirm the activity of divine providence in human affairs. The queen, hearing of Richard's impending coronation, feels the cold embrace of Margaret's curse about her diminishing family. Anne, remembering her own curses against Richard's wife, now recites their ironic visitation upon herself. But these affirmatives are countered by some provocative ambiguity. In the first place, Elizabeth is not yet conceding the absolute efficacy of Margaret's curses. She is no Hastings in this scene, nor was meant to be. Dorset is sent across the seas "from this slaughter-house" (2523; 4.1.43); Elizabeth would not die the thrall of Margaret's curse. She is still a mother, and she wants to remain one. Further, like the prayers of Clarence and the nobles at Pomfret, many of the prayers at the end of this scene are also answered "No," if at all. Elizabeth is guided to Richmond and better fortune, but Anne is hardly tended by good angels, unless death is preferable to life with Richard. Most obviously, the "ancient Stones" of the Tower apparently do not take pity on "those tender Babes," or "use [her] Babies well" (2580-85; 4.1.98-103, passim). Elizabeth fears the futility of her final prayer even as she utters it: "So foolish Sorrowes bids your Stones farewell." She is as skeptical about the efficacy of her prayer as she is about Margaret's curses. Though Elizabeth will waver in this skepticism as Margaret's curses increasingly come true, her stubborn agnosticism, forged in agony, will never be completely burned or blasted away. Elizabeth may have believed "So just is God, to right the innocent" (651; 1.3.81) early in the play. By her next scene, this belief too is shattered in the crucible of experience. Hastings and Clarence, then, are converted by experience from skeptics to believers in providence; Elizabeth's experience becomes the first serious negative to their affirmative.

The behavior of Richard in relation to supernatural agency becomes more complex during his coronation scene. At the height of his power he seems increasingly subject to the very "babling Dreames" (3778; 5.3.308) and prophetic voices he scorned and exploited in others. His fears about Richmond stick deep, in considerable measure because "*Henry* the Sixt / Did prophecie, that *Richmond* should be King, / When *Richmond* was a little peevish Boy" (2694-96; 4.2.95-97). In fact, Richard, distracted by these "meditations," as he calls them, goes on to recall "when last I was at Exeter, / The Maior in curtesie showd me the Castle, / And called it Rugemount, at which name I started, / Because a Bard of Ireland told me once / I should not live long after I saw Richmond" (2697+5-9; 4.2.103-7).[8] To my eye, Richard has never been totally skeptical of supernatural agency. He has been manipulative when others' superstitions are of use. He has also been nervous when curses or prophecies touched him too closely. It is the new degree of vulnerability that is troublesome here. Richard once spurred his religious hypocrisy like a courser; now he is cowering from the hooves of superstition. The puppeteer may be too suddenly a puppet; if so the hands of providence are paradoxically implicated along with Shakespeare's in this crude manipulation. This giant step toward Richard's discovery of the truth of that divine providence which will finally destroy him finds many subtle parallels at this point of the play. It works like imitative polyphony in a musical score. Still, so much new vulnerability seems imposed upon Richard. While that imposition is hardly morally repulsive, it is aesthetically disappointing.

In two consecutive scenes, then, prayers and prophecies provoke complex reactions in the audience. This complexity increases as the women try to understand their personal tragedies in terms of providence in 4.4. As R. G. Hunter suggests, their responses add dignity and complexity to the tragic experience.[9] Margaret's gloating asides are a case in point. On the one hand they affirm the workings of divine providence. She has cursed her curses; now she watches them come true, watches the "waining of [her] enemies." But her catalogue of "right for right" and "dying debt" is both so spiteful and so simplistic that it probably provokes discomfort rather than joyful affirmation. Similarly, it provokes the queen and the Duchess, in the midst of Margaret's gloating affirmatives, to sing out their pained negatives, their Job-like questioning of the very providence to which they have themselves appealed before: "why art thou dead?" "Wilt thou, O God, flye from such gentle Lambs, / And throw them in the intrailes of the Wolfe?"; "When didst thou sleepe, when such a deed was done?" (2774-95; 4.4.1-24, passim). Such questions are provoked by their increasing grief, to be sure; they are also a natural response to Margaret's ruthless, literalistic scheme of providence.

Margaret's ready answers to each of their questions only intensify the discomfort of these characters and the audience. For their questions are more than rhetorical, and her answers are less than comforting. We are perhaps most uncomfortable when Margaret delights that the Duchess's own son Richard has served her curses so faithfully: "O upright, just, and true-disposing God, / How do I thanke thee, that this carnall Curre / Prayes on the issue of his Mothers body, / And makes her Pue-fellow with others mone" (2826-29; 4.4.55-58). Margaret has clearly created a vicious God of vengeance to suit her own hunger for revenge, her own sense of immeasurable wrong. Her confusion is highlighted a few lines earlier when she also calls Richard "That foule defacer of Gods handy worke" (2822; 4.4.51). Providence is what she says it is; when Richard kills her kith and kin he serves the Devil, not God. Far from the "mouthpiece of a Christian deity," as Frey calls her, Margaret is another individual in Richard III grappling desperately with disasters that would challenge anyone's mind and faith.[10] Like Clarence with the Murderers, like Rivers and Grey and Vaughan before their death, Margaret offers a biased testimony, a warped vision. She would be pitiable were she not still so powerful, and apparently so prescient too. For she has the knack of cursing effectively. Even the skeptical Elizabeth knows this to be true, though she never knows quite what to make of it. Theologically, we may know that we should separate the wicked will of Margaret from the providence of God. Aesthetically, the connection is harder to break. A repulsive Margaret is much more vivid than an inscrutable God.

More coherent, and less ambiguous, is her recitation of the curses that have been fulfilled during the play. Edward IV and his son have died; so have Hastings, Rivers, Vaughan, Grey. Richard still lives. "But at hand, at hand / Insues his pittious and unpittied end." After this "proof," her curse against Richard is a sure thing: "Cancell his bond of life, deere God I pray, / That I may live and say, The Dogge is dead" (2834-49; 4.4.63-78, passim). Then Margaret recapitulates her curses against Elizabeth, so many of which have also come true. Elizabeth has lost husband, brothers, children, and the crown. For a moment she actually concedes that Margaret is "well skill'd" in curses. Yet ten lines later, neither Elizabeth nor the Duchess of York is convinced of the supernatural efficacy of her words. Curses are good therapy; beyond that they may be just so much wind: "Windy Atturnies," "Ayery succeeders," "Poore breathing Orators of miseries."

"Let them have scope, though what they will impart, / Helpe nothing els, yet do they ease the hart." At least this is true of the words of Elizabeth and the Duchess. Of Margaret's Elizabeth is not sure. Subject as she is to calamity, she will not "dye the thrall of Margarets Curse" (2525; 4.1.47). One has desperation in faith; the other desperation in skepticism. The audience is suspended intriguingly between Margaret and Elizabeth as they grapple with the complexities of divine providence and supernatural agency at this point in the play.

Suspended thus, we hear Richard cursed by his own mother. At least, she gives it a try. Like Elizabeth, she is not sure about curses. The Duchess does not deny Elizabeth's negative judgment about curses as therapy, or mere words. What she affirms is more difficult to say:

If so then, be not Tongue-ty'd: go with me,
And in the breath of bitter words, let's smother
My damned Son, that thy two sweet Sonnes smother'd.
The Trumpet sounds, be copious in exclaimes.
(2904–7; 4.4.132–35).

She would like to kill this son; that much is certain. But she has only copious words as her weapons, and Richard has little patience to hear them. What is clearer is Richard's continuing superstition. He nervously tries to drown out their smothering words: "Let not the Heavens hear these Tell-tale women / Raile on the Lords Annointed" (2924–25; 4.4.150–51). The audacity is still there, of course. He is Christ-like; they are gossips. But so is that nervousness, that curious streak of belief that is one of Richard's abiding flaws. Characteristically, the queen says only "Amen." She has little "spirit to curse" (2976–77; 4.4.197–98), though much cause, much cause. Her silence is more richly motivated than by grief; it stems also from her own continuing agnosticism. The long debate which follows between Elizabeth and Richard reminds us again of the centricity of debate in the play. It also continually touches on the question of supernatural agency. Richard has "promises" for Elizabeth, but not prophecies. He will not win, not beget children for Elizabeth. Further, he can swear no better than he can prophesy. There is nothing left for him to swear by that he has "not wrong'd" (3159; 4.4.373).

Elizabeth's brutally effective exposure of Richard's isolation of himself from all things worth swearing by is, of course, better than her curse. It is his curse upon himself, upon his kingship, upon his immortal soul. Her ironies work against him precisely because he has created for himself a kingdom of ironies. He is all irony; he is therefore nothing, even as his words are nothing. If they always have double meaning, then they can have no meaning at all. Richard is smothered not in the curses of his mother but in his own words. He is eaten quick by his own verbal quickness.

Then Richard, desperate, ends by cursing himself:

> As I entend to prosper, and repent:
> So thrive I in my dangerous Affayres
> Of hostile Armes: My selfe, my selfe confound:
> Heaven, and Fortune barre me happy houres:
> Day, yeeld me not thy light; nor Night, thy Rest.
> Be opposite all Planets of good lucke
> To my proceeding, if with deere hearts love,
> Immaculate devotion, holy thoughts,
> I tender not thy beautious Princely daughter.
> (3188–96; 4.4.397–405).

He does not intend to repent, nor does he "with deere hearts love, immaculate devotion, holy thoughts" "tender" her "beautious Princely daughter." Therefore, by the terms of his own pledge, he will not "thrive." He will confound himself with fear and despair, coward conscience, and desperate heroics; he will be barred from the "happy houres" of fortune here and Heaven hereafter. He will continue to sleep poorly. He will awake at last to a sun that "disdaines to shine" on his cause, a "blacke day" to "somebody" (3746–48; 5.3.278–80). And finally he will die and be damned. Margaret knows it; his own mother prays for it. Now Richard too curses himself with death and damnation: "Heaven, and Fortune barre me happy houres." They do. They will. The ultimate irony of this scene may be this self-directed curse, which will probably be visited against Richard just as surely as the sins Elizabeth has so eloquently catalogued.

The debate over divine providence swings radically though not simplistically toward the affirmative from this moment through the end of the final act. First, with cyclic formality, we see "*Buckingham with Halberds, led to Execution.*" Like Hastings near the end of his life, this worldly, confirmed skeptic is much changed. Once he averred that "Curses never passe / The lips of those that breath them in the air" (757–58; 1.3.284–85). Now he recalls his own ironic self-curse, his false vows to his king, in God's name, and attributes his fall to God's providence: "That high All-seer, which I dallied with, / Hath turn'd my fained Prayer on my head, / And given in earnest, what I begg'd in jest" (3392–94; 5.1.20–22). His fall is a "determin'd respit" of his "wrongs," not bad luck or clever statecraft. Second causes would never explain this calculated, preordained repayment of his sins. "That high All-seer" has taken his pledge and his prayer literally, just as he will take Richard's ironic curses against himself. With Clarence and Hastings, then, this clever king-maker has been converted to a belief in supernatural agency. Divine providence has justly paid him back, and he accepts its fair sentence: "Wrong hath but wrong, and blame the due of blame" (3401; 4.5.29). In act 4 Elizabeth and the Duchess are not sure about supernatural agency; Margaret is, but her affirmative comes out of blatant self-justification, even despair, and it is stated in grotesquely simplistic, judgmental terms. Richard, never sure, wavers toward the affirmative, and begins to be overwhelmed by it will he nill he. After this complexity, we are probably impressed by Buckingham's straightforward testimony, though it is not the last word in the debate. He has little reason to deceive himself. And Buckingham is not a man easily deceived.

As the final battle looms, Richmond and Richard both look for omens of their victory. Richmond finds in the bright sunset "token of a goodly day to morrow." Richard the next morning sees the sky "frowne, and lowre upon our Army" (3457, 3751; 5.3.21, 283). Both are correct in their immediate interpretations, though Richard then tries to reject his with the rationalization that "the selfe-same Heaven / That frownes on me, lookes sadly upon him" (3754–55; 5.3.286–87). He fails on two counts to escape this providential token. First, Richard slips again into remembered belief: Heaven is frowning, not the clouds of act 1. Second, frowning and sadness are not the same thing. Try as he might, Richard cannot erase Heaven's hand. Before the ghosts arrive, Richmond utters one of the only completely efficacious prayers in the play. In victory, he is true to the terms of his prayer. It is God's victory that he finally celebrates; he is merely God's minister. Richard does not pray, though the ghosts force a call to "Jesu" out of his tormented soul (3640; 5.3.178).

The ghosts are themselves obviously crucial late participants in the play's debate over supernatural agency, though their testimony is not quite as unequivocally affirmative as it might first seem. They are apparently supernatural beings, though both Richard and Richmond refer to them as dreams.[11] They announce again and again a retributive justice that is gathering head for a final distribution of rewards and punishments. All of Richard's sins against them are recounted and set in the balance against him as they will be on Judgment Day. All of Richmond's virtues are set in the opposite tray. On this side Richard and on that side Richmond. The ghosts manifest supernatural agency; they believe unequivocally in divine providence; they mirror the last judgment in their activity in act 5. And they, of all the characters in the play, ought to know the truth about the outer mystery.[12] Like the many confirmed curses, prophecies, dreams, and omens, they have, then, a powerful affirmative voice in the debate. They say the truth and they predict the future, with great accuracy. Richard does "dispaire, and dye," acting out a ninefold refrain of the ghosts' prophecy.

Still, the debate continues. Richard tries to counter the prophetic and persuasive power of the ghosts with "I did but dreame." Ratcliffe supports his skepticism by calling them "shadows." Of course, Richard has every reason not to believe. He has defied all laws of God and man, broken most of society's taboos, and alienated most of his allies. Only in a purely natural universe does he have any chance at all. But Richard has never been entirely sure of that purely natural universe. He has been haunted throughout the play with intimations of immortality, and the experience with the ghosts is therefore all the more terrifying to him. If "the Soules of all that I had murther'd / Came to my Tent, and every one did threat / To morrowes vengeance on the head of Richard," if they were not dreams, shadows, but souls, then the worst is confirmed for Richard at the worst possible time. These ghostly manifestations of supernatural agency activate Richard's coward conscience in the sequence that follows. In fact, R. M. Frye has pointed out that the promptings of conscience were themselves considered manifestations of divine agency in the Renaissance: "for Catholic and Protestant alike, conscience was not autonomous, being subject to the judgment and will of God."[13] Richard's conscience prompts the same misgivings as those expressed by the first Murderer before the murder of Clarence. It provokes the kind of confession that Hastings and Buckingham and Clarence uttered at similar moments in their souls' lives. It leads to the despair the ghosts prophesied for him. It creates waking images for Richard of that sleeping vision of Judgment. All tongues, all tales bear witness to his murders. All several sins cry "Guilty" (3640–75; 5.3.178–214, passim). This is not "perjury," and Richard knows it. These shadows, and Richard's response to them, have a terrifying substance to them, for all of Richard's desperate attempts at denial.

Though political rhetoric rather than introspection characterizes most of the rest of the play, the question of supernatural agency remains before us to the end. Richard explains away the premonitory omens and ghostly visitations as "babling Dreames." "For Conscience is a word that Cowards use." But he cannot completely escape their spell: "If not to

"Dispaire and dye," frontispiece (dated 1617) from Rowe's 1709 edition. Courtesy of the Folger Shakespeare Library, Washington, D.C. PR 2752, 1709a, c.1, v.4, Sh. Coll., frontis. to Richard III.

heaven, then hand in hand to Hell." At the end he invokes Saint George, but only to ask him to "Inspire us with the spleene of fiery Dragons" (3778–79, 3783, 3821–22; 5.3.308–9, 313, 349–50). There is a sulphurous smell about this Richard, in spite of his final energy and will, and because of them too.[14]

Richmond remains convinced that "God, and our good cause, fight upon our side." "The Prayers of holy Saints and wronged soules" are his "Bulwarkes." Richard "hath ever beene Gods Enemy. / Then if you fight against Gods Enemy, / God will in justice ward you as his Soldiers." "God, and Saint George" (3706–36; 5.3.240–270, passim) are allied in his final invocations. And then Richard is slain. The thankful references to divine providence bathe the play's conclusion in some impressively unambiguous affirmations of supernatural agency. The play ends, in fact, with a celebration steeped in its articulation of God's victory and God's providential plan for Tudor England. Richmond, who has been portrayed throughout as an honest and pious man, proclaims repeatedly God's agency in their victory: "God, and your Armes be prais'd, Victorious Friends." Then, promising to take the sacrament, and unite in marriage "the White Rose, and the Red," he prays, "Smile Heaven upon this faire Conjunction, / That long have frown'd upon their Enmity." If peace and prosperity come, it will be only by "Gods faire ordinance," God's providence. "Abate the edge of Traitors, Gracious Lord," Richmond prays, and adds, "That [peace] may long live heere, God say, Amen" (3866–87; 5.5.20–41, passim). To an audience which had long been led to understand that a providential hand orchestrated the Tudor succession, those last words, like the whole last act, would probably have closed the debate pretty conclusively.

The final act testifies so persuasively to the benevolent operation of divine providence in the overthrow of Richard and the victory of Richmond that even the most skeptical of the critics grudgingly concede its ringing affirmative. That is not to say that they like it, however. Sanders and Frey, unable to dismiss Richmond's words as hypocrisy, though they flirt with the possibility, dismiss them instead as "pious platitudes," aesthetically unattractive utterances that leave "the closing minutes of the play sadly contracted to the stature of Tudor propaganda." Nicholas Brooke grouses, "The divine pattern [in act 5] is explicitly Christian; one cannot help reflecting that it is, at the same time, repulsive." Even some of the apologists for a complex providential pattern remain unimpressed by what they call Richmond's "repeated pieties" or his "flat, unimpassioned utterance."[15] Because I like both symbolic utterance and knights in shining armor, the idealized human portraiture so common to the art of the high Renaissance, and because I respond positively to most final assertions of order in Renaissance drama, I find Richmond much more attractive than this. Comparing his portrait to that in the historical sources, and considering his oratory in light of many of the military manuals on battle oratory has made him even more attractive to me. Still, we walk to different drummers, dance to different tunes. Such is the complexity of Shakespeare and his critics.

The pattern of the debate over divine providence in *Richard* III would also seem to contribute to the complex experience of affirmation at play's end. Act 1 establishes the debate motif in general, as in Richard's scene with Anne, and dramatizes some direct discussion of divine providence. Clarence, the Murderers, Margaret, Richard, Elizabeth, and Buckingham all participate in the debate, singly or in concert. It balances belief and skepticism among its participants. The next cluster of relevant scenes, 3.2–3.4, comes down squarely on the affirmative, particularly in the scenes of the death of Hastings and the nobles at Pomfret. All die affirming the potency of curses, dreams, and their place in a providentially ordered universe. In contrast, ambiguity in the fourth act outweighs either a positive or a negative position. Richard, Elizabeth, Margaret, and the Duchess of York engage in the debate with their complex attitudes and motivations. Finally, act 5 presents what I hear as its ringing affirmatives, in the last words of Buckingham, Richmond, and the ghosts, but also paradoxically in Richard's anxiety. From dispute in act 1 to affirmation in act 3; from ambiguity again in act 4 to affirmation in act 5: we move through two complete cycles, both of them ending affirmatively.

But the complex motives of some of the affirmative voices, and the prominence of several of the negatives, particularly Elizabeth's searching intellect and the intense will and aesthetic power of Richard, make the final balance far from uninteresting, even at the play's ritualistic, celebratory conclusion. As overwhelming as the providential presence can become in *Richard* III, it remains the servant of the drama, not its master. The play's dialectic strategy deserves much of the credit for this unusual achievement.

Questions of Providence

According to the majority of witnesses in *Richard* III, divine providence, working through various curses, prophecies, omens, prayers, and dreams, is instrumental in the system of rewards and punishments leading finally to the victory of Richmond over Richard at Bosworth Field. As they are about to die, the victims of these premonitory instruments almost universally acknowledge divine agency in their own destruction, and invoke its assistance against their enemies. The most impressive of these witnesses, Clarence, Hastings, and Buckingham, confess and repent their former misdeeds, acknowledge the justice of their punishments, and testify to God's providential hand in their experience. All three are converted skeptics. The ghosts of Clarence, Anne, Hastings, Rivers, Vaughan, Grey, Buckingham, Henry VI, his son Prince Edward, and Richard's nephews the two princes in the Tower all apparently affirm their faith in providence. So does Margaret. After the battle, Richmond asserts a joyous concert of divine and human agency: "God and your Armes / Be prais'd Victorious Friends" (3845–46; 5.5.1). The audience is therefore filled to the brim and even over the brim with such evidence and such testimony.

Paradoxically, despite this overwhelming evidence and also because of it, questions continue to be raised about the operation of divine providence in the play. Why are there so many unanswered prayers? Why is there no direct divine intervention? Why are the hands of the agents of providence, if that is what they are, so often dirty? Is the divine pattern therefore "repulsive"?[16] Finally, if some of the curses and prophecies are not fulfilled, is their failure frequent or significant enough to challenge our sense of the operation of divine providence in the play? These questions gain some currency because the play itself dramatizes an ongoing debate about supernatural agency in human affairs. Because the questions are theological as well as critical, some background in their theological implications should help us address the critical issues. Since this is obviously not all virgin ground, I will only sift through the soil that has already been turned and tilled. I will plough deeper when the field seems to lie relatively untouched.[17]

External Providence

Frey, the most outspoken opponent of what he calls "the Christianizing firm of Tillyard, Reese, [Irving] Ribner, and Rossiter," is disturbed that they "all seem to know that God had directly intervened to end the bloody reign of the butcher of England." He disagrees: "Shakespeare's plays, although they do not specifically rule out that interpretation, certainly do not lend themselves to it." In support, Frey refers to Sanders's position that in *Richard* III an "external, meddlesome providence is at times transmuted into a natural providence." Without adducing theological evidence, Frey insists again and again that the "usual sense" of divine providence is God's direct intervention in human affairs: "No such pattern is found in the play, in the usual sense of an external providence, a divine providence which takes vengeance on the guilty and rewards the righteous." Sanders's argument, though more sophisticated, is on this point essentially the same. This is the heart of their argument. It is also their Achilles' heel, having as it does no basis in the Christian theology of any age.[18] Because their position is so precarious here, and also because this ground has been often touched before, I will look only briefly at the theologians. Even that most cursory glance should demonstrate the naiveté of this first objection.

A repeated theological formula established three ways in which providence operates in human affairs. According to John Calvin, "sometyme it woorketh by meanes, somtyme without meanes, and somtyme agaynst all meanes." In his *treatise of Gods providence*, the Calvinist Ralph Walker explains that the first, "without meanes" refers to God's direct action, as in the life of Christ on earth, the creation of Adam and Eve, the giving of the Ten Commandments to Moses, Noah's flood, and the like. Such examples of God's direct intervention in human history are quite rare. God's action "agaynst all meanes" is equally unusual. This refers to God's direct intervention "contrarie to the nature of second causes," or against the normal operation of nature. Examples would include the virgin birth of Christ, stopping the sun at Jericho, turning water into wine, raising the dead. Direct intervention of divine providence can occur without natural causes, or against natural causes. But as Walker makes clear, "The third and usuall way of God's governing, is by second means appointed in his heavenly wisedome for that purpose," Calvin's "by meanes."[19]

Because this is not a controversial theological position but basic theology, it severely undermines the position of Frey and Sanders. "Natural providence," the "usual sense" of divine intervention, the very phrases Frey and Sanders use to challenge the operation of providence in *Richard III*, could actually confirm that operation for the Renaissance audience. As Bishop John Jewell says, "natural causes are only the instruments of God's will." Or Calvin himself: "all chaunces are governed by the secrete councell of God"; "nothing can chaunce but that which is decreed by hym both witting and willing it so to be."[20] John Veron's treatise on divine providence makes it clear that this operation of divine providence through second causation is no less real because man cannot always accept or understand it:

Because that [our] weakenesse & imbecillity can not well understand or comprehend such hygh misteries, ... thoughe al thynges be governed by the devine providence of almighty God, yet they be unto us fortuite & casual.

The true causes, the first causes, "are hidden in the secreates of God, & in hys unsearchable and incomprehensyble judgements."[21] Calvin also explains that we assume chance or fate or natural causation only because of our limited wisdom: "men do not atteine to see the first cause which is farre hidden from them." "God by the pure lyghte of his ryghteousnesse and wysedome, dooeth in well framed order governe and dispose even those very troublesome motions themselves to a ryght ende."[22]

Hunter offers the best recent clarification I have seen of the possible confusion of first and second causation in *Richard* III:

> The actions of the play must take place within a dramatic version of what we may call the world of second causes. What happens in that imagined world must be clearly the result of acceptable artistic imitations of those emotional and political forces with which, as creatures who inhabit the real world of second causes, we are altogether too familiar. But because the world in which the action of the play unfolds is proclaimed to be providentially ordered, the play must also make us aware that those very psychological and political forces are themselves caused and that their first cause is the nature and will of the God who has created and now governs that world— or Shakespeare's imitation of it.[23]

Characters in the play may grotesquely misunderstand or distort these matters. Margaret believes them far too simplistically, and far too vengefully; Richard tries with all of his considerable will (and fails) to deny them altogether; Elizabeth's attitude is an agnosticism about them born of bitter experience and desperate hope. Most of the other characters in the play finally affirm the operation of divine providence in their individual lives and in the life of their country. But whatever their precise final beliefs about the operation of providence in their lives, none of them even thinks to question the operation of this providence through second causes or natural means. Since that is the "usual way," why should they? Most of the play's characters can be described as Frey describes the critics he attacks: "they all seem to know that God had directly intervened to end the bloody reign of the butcher of England."[24] Given this overwhelming community of belief and testimony in the world of the play, and given this elementary course in the "usual sense" of the operation of providence in human affairs, even the contemporary audience is under considerable pressure to suspend its disbelief and celebrate with Richmond and his troops a miraculous, providential victory. The play lends itself very nicely, overwhelmingly in fact, to such an interpretation.

Unanswered Prayers
As Rivers dies he asks that his sister and her two sons be spared:

> Oh remember God,
> To heare her prayer for them, as now for us:
> And for my Sister, and her Princely Sonnes,
> Be satisfy'd, deare God, with our true blood,
> Which, as thou know'st, unjustly must be spilt.
> (1954–58; 3.3.19–23)

Elizabeth also prays before the Tower that her children be spared from Richard's fell hand:

> Pitty, you ancient Stones, those tender Babes,
> Whom Envie hath immur'd within your Walls,
> Rough Cradle for such little prettie ones,
> Rude ragged Nurse, old sullen Play-fellow,
> For tender Princes: use my Babies well;
> So foolish Sorrowes bids your Stones farewell. (2580–85; 4.1.98–103)

The apparent failure of these two prayers is another objection raised by the demythologizers of the Tudors and of Shakespeare in *Richard III*. Wilders is particularly concerned: "In these plays not all well-deserving prayers are answered." Frey and A. L. French raise similar questions about unfulfilled curses. All three imply that such details indict an undependable if not a nonexistent providence.[25] The matter demands closer attention.

Do these unanswered prayers for innocents seriously challenge the operation of divine providence in the play? Are they, as Wilders argues, "well-deserving prayers"?[26] One could respond by referring to the theological commonplace that God sometimes answers even well-deserving prayers with "No" to serve His own inscrutable will.[27] But simple logic also suggests that these are not well-deserving prayers. If we evaluate them by the theological standards of the day, their undeserving status becomes still more obvious. First, concerning the most unsuccessful prayer, the queen's for her two sons, John Marbeck makes it clear that the prayer must be addressed to God for it to have any chance to work: "whosoever doth praye ... to any other then to God onely ... without doubt ... be ... against the promise of God, and doth sinne grievously in Gods sight." So does Lancelot Andrewes: "First, prayer must be made to God, and to none other."[28] Obviously, then, Elizabeth's prayer to the Tower's stones hardly qualifies as prayer at all. It is certainly not a prayer to God.

Her reticence about addressing a deity or otherwise accepting supernatural agency also indicts her faith, however interesting it makes her as a character. Faith, of course, is a related requisite to successful prayer. As John Marbeck says, "The true and acceptable prayer consisteth ... in the stedfastnesse of our beleefe," as well as "the beautie of our desires, and in the pure intentive thought of our hearts fixed on God's divine mercie at such time as we doe pray." Calvin says, "We never shall be heard while in doubt." To Alexander Nowell, "Such as pray doubting ... do without fruit pour out vain and bootless words."[29] Elizabeth's desires are beautiful enough here. She wants to save her children. Her belief is not so surely fixed on God's mercy.

Unlike Elizabeth's prayer, Rivers's for his sister and her sons is offered to God. However, it is sorely lacking in humility, repentance, and forgiveness. Thomas Becon quotes Saint Paul: "I will that men pray in every place, lifting up pure hands without wrath and contention." Only the faithful and charitable heart "is fit to pray in the sight of God." Nowell adds, "unless other do find us ready to forgive them ... he plainly warneth us to look for nothing else at his hands but extreme severity of punishment." Andrewes specifies "forgiving all injuries"; for "if we be uncharitable, our prayers wilbe barren and unfruitfull." Further, the prayer, to be successful, must "acknowledge the impurity of our soules, and confesse our selves wicked."[30] Rivers asks for vengeance, and proclaims himself innocent. He may be innocent of crimes against the state; but as his plea for vengeance indicates, he cannot be innocent before God. On both counts, his prayer too is undeserving.

Both Rivers and the queen also fail to make the most basic of Christian petitions, a sure mark of humility and faith: "not my will but thine be done." Becon advises, "whatsoever we ask we must refer it unto the will of God." "The will of God above all things is to be considered in our prayers; or else we pray in vain." Marbeck writes that the prayer must involve "the seeking of his glorye and doing his will."[31] Every gloss on the Lord's Prayer contains these commonplaces. Such failures as are in evidence

113   Perceptions of Providence

in Rivers's prayer and the queen's are not legal technicalities. They are fundamental, obvious flaws that could threaten the efficacy of their prayers.

In contrast, Clarence's prayer for his innocent wife and children is more deserving:

> O God! if my deepe prayres cannot appease thee,
> But thou wilt be aveng'd on my misdeeds,
> Yet execute thy wrath in me alone:
> O spare my guiltlesse Wife, and my poore children.
> (905-8; 1.4.68-71)

Clarence is humble, expecting God's wrath and admitting that he deserves it. If he must die, Clarence asks only that his innocent wife and children be spared. He asks no vengeance on his enemies. He prays to God in faith and fear, though never quite with the faith of "Thy will be done." Clarence's is thus as close to a deserving prayer as will be found in *Richard* III, until Richmond's prayer before he sleeps in act 5. Interestingly, Clarence's prayer is also the closest to being fulfilled until Richmond's. Richard transplants his brother's children into an inconspicuous corner of his garden kingdom (2646-49; 4.2.52-55). He does not pluck them up root and all. Though I am not trying to argue that the play dramatizes the difference, it is clear that the most deserving of these three prayers is also the most successful.

Richmond prays too. His prayer comes last, and is fulfilled almost to the letter. This is our last impression of the efficacy of prayer in the play, and quite obviously the most impressive:

> O thou, whose Captaine I account my selfe,
> Looke on my Forces with a gracious eye:
> Put in their hands thy bruising Irons of wrath,
> That they may crush downe with a heavy fall,
> Th'usurping Helmets of our Adversaries:
> Make us thy ministers of Chasticement,
> That we may praise thee in thy victory:
> To thee I do commend my watchfull soule,
> Ere I let fall the windowes of mine eyes:
> Sleeping, and waking, oh defend me still. (3551-60; 5.3.108-17)

The prayer is addressed to God, in intense faith in His providence. It is rich in humility; God's is the victory, here in prayer and later in praise. Its desire is beautiful: the elimination of this "noisome weed," this hideous enemy of God and man. Commending his watchful soul to God illustrates not only Richmond's abiding faith but also his abiding trust in God's providence; it is akin to "Thy will be done." To be fair, though, the prayer is not perfect. There is nothing of repentance, though there is little in Richmond's portrayal to be repented. There is much of vengeance, though Richmond's is a minister's righteous vengeance that he and most of the audience might well associate with God's will. In fact, such phrases in the prayer as "thy bruising Irons of wrath" and "thy ministers of Chasticement" reveal Richmond's understanding that he is the agent of God's will, not his own, and that God's will directs the bruising chastisement of this grievous offender.[32]

One other cluster of "deserving prayers" must be mentioned before we go on. As Richmond glosses his own prayer in his battle oration, so he reminds us there that "The Prayers of holy Saints and wronged soules, / Like high rear'd Bulwarkes, stand before our Faces" (3707–8; 5.3.241–42). There is a host praying against Richard and for Richmond in the final battle. Apparently their prayers are heard and answered as completely as Richmond's. Together, in God's cause and with God's help, they "reape the Harvest of perpetuall peace." If such an accounting is required, it reveals that most of the truly deserving prayers in *Richard III* are apparently heard and answered "Yes."

Providence and "the Wicked Wills of Wicked Men"
A related problem concerns the apparent efficacy of Margaret's prayers and curses. Few of them conform to most of these requirements, yet her prayers for vengeance seem overwhelmingly successful. She obviously has faith, at least after she realizes in 1.3 the efficacy of the curses that have been directed against her. But by her own admission she is "hungry for revenge," insatiate in fact for the blood of innocent and guilty alike, so long as they are associated with the house of York. She lessons God in lavish particulars of vengeance as well, and assumes without humility that her will, her view of justice, her sense of her own innocence are also God's. She is unrepentant; her desires are almost as ugly as Richard's. Yet her prayers and curses apparently prosper. What do we make theologically of these apparent contradictions?

Frey deals with this puzzle by calling Margaret the image and the "mouthpiece" of a vengeful and capricious God. Sanders apparently initiates this unpleasant if clever conceit when he calls Margaret's God a "supernatural agency under contractual obligation to exterminate the house of York."³³ Murder Inc. Though most readers would not confuse God with some movie-mafia don ordering executions and needing a hired gun and a good mouthpiece, Margaret's uncharitable prayers and curses are apparently answered "Yes" so often and so exactly that we might all feel uncomfortable about the relationship of her will and God's. Does her accuracy in foretelling God's providential activities not indict God himself in her vindictiveness, as Frey and Sanders suggest?

From a theological perspective there are several reasons to answer "No." First, to attack providence through Margaret is the classic straw person fallacy. She invokes but flattens the mystery. She clings to a notion of cycle and a pattern of restitution that serves her own revenge rather than a higher and inscrutable purpose. Calvin confronts this sort of question by reminding his reader of the limitations of all perceptions of God in the image of man. Margaret might be among the "vessels of wrath," ordained for the service of providence. So, of course, is the scourge Richard. Hamlet talks about this concept, and implies its complexity in the individual conscience. But God's wrath is not Margaret's, any more than it is Richard's. As Calvin says, "as he hymselfe is without all moving of a troubled minde, he yet testifieth that he is angry with synners" so that we might fear and understand his law and his judgment: "We should always fear God's justice." We should "not come to imagine [as Frey, Sanders, and Brooke do] that He uses any tyranny or cruelty." That would be another mistake of accommodation, of anthropomorphism, that Margaret herself makes in her neurotic human fierceness. God may be "framed lowe to our capacitie," described "after the maner of men," for our limited understandings. But one should never confuse that accommodation with God's inscrutable nature or his divine providence.³⁴

More crucial is the distinction of God's will and man's in such matters. As Ralph Walker explains, the violence that is done to others, innocent and guilty, in God's name is not necessarily "man's will agreeing with God's will": "God wils a voluntarie permission; man a willful effecting." To illustrate, God may will the death of a holy man as the blessing of eternal life and the end of earthly tribulation; he may will the death of the wicked as punishment and "to cut him off." In other words, "God willes his own glorie in the execution of justice, and in shewing mercie to his children: but the manslaier regards neither, but whollie the satisfying of his bloudie desire." As a result, the same act can display "both yᵉ fault of man ... and also the righteousnesse of God" ("the criminality of man and the justice of God").³⁵ What this suggests in *Richard* III is that God's will should not be understood to coincide with either that of Richard the bloody manslayer or Margaret the neurotic prophetess, though both may serve that will. God wills justice and mercy, both in death and in the sparing from death. Reprobates will the "satisfying of bloody desires."

Further, free will itself demands God's "permission" of such creatures as Margaret and Richard. Walker writes, "Gods permission of the sin is the meanes of his glorie . . . because God respects not the purpose of man in sinning, but his owne purpose in permitting. . . . In suffering sinne, he no way approves of it, for he punisheth him that commits it"; "it is not God's permission which is evill," for that allows free will in all men. Rather, it is "the sinne it selfe."[36]

Calvin, Martin Luther, indeed most sixteenth-century theologians, would affirm this difficult paradox. It is essential to the treatment of evil in any monotheistic theology. In at least two ways "theves and murtherers & other evill doers are the instruments of God's providence." God makes "a lawful use of their evilnesse" to exercise His own inscrutable will to reward and punish righteously. He also permits their free choice as a good greater than their destructiveness in evil. God uses reprobates, but contracts "no spot of their fault" ("no defilement from their criminality"). "For those thynges whiche God willeth well he bringeth to passe by the evill willes of evyl men" ("the wicked wills of wicked men").[37]

This issue is discussed so often in the sixteenth century and before that it is obviously an enduring theological problem, with solutions that are not universally satisfying. Its solution to the theologian always lies in God's inscrutable will. He permits the scourge, the Richard, and yet uses his destructive evil for a greater good; He apparently answers the prayers and curses of a Margaret, only because they coincide with His "unsearchable and incomprehensible judgments." The first cause "is far hidden from them." As Calvin quotes Saint Paul in Romans 11:33–34: "howe unsearchable are his judgementes, and his waies paste fyndyng out?"[38] William Elton calls this bafflingly inscrutable providence a traditional view of the latter half of the sixteenth century, one that can be attributed to both Montaignian and Reformist writers. Calvin and Montaigne share "comparable views regarding not only *debilitas rationis*, the limitation of human reason, but also *Deus abscondus*, the hidden God."[39] To the rationalist, Calvin's answer may be no answer at all. To the Christian apologist, it is as much bedrock as man's free will and God's justice and mercy. Between such poles there is room for much attraction and repulsion. However, knowing something of the theological information available to Shakespeare and his contemporaries may help us position ourselves more intelligently on this ground.

Fulfilled and Unfulfilled Curses

French asks those who would demonstrate the operation of divine providence in *Richard* III to explain why some of the curses and prophecies are not "fulfilled in the minutest detail." Frey exults the few times the curses of Anne or Margaret are not immediately or literally fulfilled. "But providence failed to arrive on cue" is a characteristic comment.[40] Without question, some curses in *Richard* III are fulfilled neither literally nor immediately. That they are fulfilled in God's own time and in God's own way, rather than exactly as the women prescribe, would seem to offer the very evidence of providence that Frey and French demand. As it is traditionally understood by informed theologians and laypeople of any age, providence is inscrutable. It is faith in a coherence which is beyond understanding "in the minutest detail." Independent of these human agents, it can yet mysteriously use them. If a deserving prayer appears to have been ignored, in whole or in part, the outcome has merely coincided with God's inscrutable will.[41] If an evil curse or prayer is apparently fulfilled, the imperfect will of the curser does not impugn the perfect will of God. God is not tainted by the wicked agents who providentially do or ask His will. Neither is He restricted from carrying out the letter of improper petitions for His own good ends, or bending them to His will. According to Luther, cursing is itself against the will of God; yet in *Richard* III, this cursing apparently serves His will.[42] Such is the power and mystery of divine providence. Once again we can address the objections of Frey and French with basic theology.

But do their objections stand scrutiny even outside this theological framework? Most of the curses and prophecies in *Richard* III are almost literally fulfilled, and then formally confirmed by their victims and other witnesses. The play recounts them for us, as one of its most impressive assertions of supernatural agency. Further, after these curses and prophecies begin to be fulfilled, no voice says them nay. Even Richard's early skepticism is almost as short-lived as his kingship. Clarence's skepticism flickers even more briefly. Then he announces his conversion. Rivers, Vaughan, Grey, Hastings, and Buckingham follow his lead. Their assertions are also never seriously challenged. Presumably, this is because they are thought to be true, by all who hear them. The executioners are sometimes impatient during their victims' little homilies; they do not deny their truth. Only Elizabeth moves from belief to skepticism during the progress of the play. Yet even she understands Richard's evil in terms of grace and providence during their debate. With the occasional exception of Elizabeth, affirmation of the accuracy of curses, not denial, is the overwhelming experience of the play. How frequent, and how significant, are the few inaccurate curses?

Anne lavishly curses Richard in 1.2 (188–202; 1.2.14–28). Since this is the curse that so amuses Frey in its impotence ("but unfortunately no lightning strikes, no earth opens up"), it must be looked at closely. What does Anne ask and how is she answered? She asks that Richard be cursed in hand, heart, and blood, to start with. If he is not already so cursed, he is well on the way. He will know in his heart by the play's end that he is unloved, unpitied, even by himself. He will himself spill most of the noble but cursed Yorkist blood, "manure the ground" with it. Like Macbeth, he will have no children to perpetuate his blood after it is spilt at Bosworth Field. In that battle his hand will carry an "edgelesse Sword" (3583, 3620; 5.3.135, 163). Then, his ultimate "hap" could hardly be more "direfull" (191; 1.2.17). First, the loss of personal power with Elizabeth; next, the loss of self-control and political power in the scenes which follow; finally despair, defeat, death, and almost certain damnation. Anne herself becomes "the subject of mine owne Soules Curse" (2560; 4.1.80) as Richard's cursed wife. So far, she is batting 1000.

Frey questions the literal success of the last of her curses against Richard: "Either Heav'n with Lightning strike the murth'rer dead: / Or Earth gape open wide, and eate him quicke" (241–42; 1.2.64–65). Literally, neither thing happens. But in substance rather than shadow, this curse works too. Since Richard is "Hell-govern'd," goes Anne's thinking, he should be Heaven-punished, that is, damned. The overwhelming opinion among characters in the play is that he will be. If Richard is not literally buried alive by earth or struck dead by lightning, he is buried under the weight of his own sins, the visitation of eleven wronged spirits, and possibly under swarms of Richmond's troops. He is also struck down by an avenging God through the hand of his "minister" Richmond. Nothing is clearer at the end of the play than its celebration of Richard's deserved damnation and Richmond's victory "in the name of God and all these rights" that Richard has wronged.

Margaret reinforces our sense of the ultimate accuracy of even this part of Anne's curse with a final curse of her own:

> Richard yet lives, Hels blacke Intelligencer,
> Onely reserv'd their Factor, to buy soules,
> And send them thither: But at hand, at hand
> Insues his pittious and unpittied end.
> Earth gapes, Hell burnes, Fiends roare, Saints pray,
> To have him sodainly convey'd from hence. (2842–47; 4.4.71–76)

Most of her other prophecies have been fulfilled and affirmed by their victims. "Th'adulterate Hastings, Rivers, Vaughan, Gray" (2840; 4.4.69) have already met their death. So have two young Yorks, and two old ones, Clarence and Edward. Now earth gapes for Richard's deformed body, and Hell burns for his depraved soul. God will soon "Cancell his bond of life" and "send [him] thither" (2848, 2844; 4.4.77, 73). With their supportive images of an earth gaping for his body, Anne's curse and Margaret's are in harmony. Richard's mother joins their chorus. She too calls him "my damned Son" (2906; 4.4.134). Hell's mouth is ready for another victim. If death and damnation were ever a certainty in Shakespeare, this is the time. Richard's "glorious Summer" is providentially reaching an early fall of leaf.

Margaret's curses are extraordinarily accurate, but there are significant exceptions. Edward IV dies "by Surfet," his son by Richard's "untimely violence." Elizabeth "live[s], to wayle" her children's death, and to "see another" queen. "Unlook'd accident" cuts off Rivers and Hastings; Buckingham, only cursed as an afterthought in 1.3, is also subject to Richard's hate (666–83, passim; 775; 1.3.196–213, 301). Son Dorset, however, and daughter Elizabeth both escape Margaret's scythe. In fact, Elizabeth works hard throughout act 4 to frustrate as many of Margaret's curses as she can. Though hers is a compelling voice of dissent, the primary effect of her resistance is rather to affirm Elizabeth's fierce will than to challenge the operation of divine providence. It may even clarify the ambiguous relationship of providence to vengeful Margaret. The survival of these ancestors of Elizabeth and the Tudor dynasty was certainly used to argue the providential basis of their reign. For in this instance, the good will of providence would seem to have countermanded the wicked will of Margaret's curses.

Unlike the rest of Margaret's victims, Richard does not testify to the accuracy of her curses or Anne's as he approaches death. His experience reeks of it, however, and he increasingly credits things which presage, dreams, prophecies, omens, and the like. "The Worme of Conscience" assaults his soul after his "tormenting Dreame." Margaret predicted both correctly, though the "ougly Devills" become the ghosts of his tormented victims (691–96, passim). Richard will wrongly suspect Surrey and Northumberland before the battle, and trust Stanley to his utter destruction. Also, Richard sleeps poorly. We see it at Bosworth Field; Anne was "still awak'd" "with his timorous Dreames" (694, 2564; 1.3.224; 4.1.84). Most crucially, Heaven has a "grievous plague in store" for him more literal and more frightening than lightning or the gaping earth (686, 692–93; 1.3.216, 222–23). The ghosts all prophesy it too. In the most resounding ostinato of the play, he will "dispaire and dye." This worst of all punishments fulfills

Anne's and Margaret's curses as well as those of the ghosts. It exceeds all those that Margaret can wish upon Richard. It is God's ultimate punishment, and it lasts forever.

This reaching beyond life into the outer mystery is unusual in Shakespeare. The afterworld of God's judgment, of eternal reward and eternal punishment, is made real, even tactile, in Clarence's vivid dream, as it is later in Richard's and Richmond's. Clarence's argument with the Murderers, "as you hope to have redemption, / By Christs deare bloud shed for our grievous sinnes" (1021–1021+1; 1.4.189–90), is another vivid description of the supernatural universe all of these characters know they inhabit. Incidentally, during Clarence's argument with the Murderers, the question again arises about the relationship of the hand of God and the hand of His scourge. So does the question of first and second causation, as Clarence tries to convince them that God will directly intervene if He wills Clarence's death. The Murderers may be morally depraved, but they are not so theologically naive as to accept his obviously spurious argument.[43]

Confirmations of the accuracy of premonitions, dreams, curses, and prophecies run like a leitmotif through the play. Questions of their accuracy are almost nonexistent. The dissent and the questioning seem to lie almost exclusively in the mind of Elizabeth. We have already seen several interesting examples. Another occurs during her debate with Richard, when Elizabeth confirms providentialism with a vengeance. Richard initiates her "argument" when he tries to invoke the idea of an inscrutable and unavoidable fate to evade his moral responsibility in the death of her two sons: "All unavoyded is the doome of Destiny." Elizabeth won't let him escape so easily, from her or from God: "True: when avoyded grace makes Destiny" (2997–98; 4.4.218–19). Destiny may be a secular complex of human psychology and political necessity. It is also man's ultimate relationship to God. Richard has made his own "destiny" by avoiding the grace of God. In the process he has lopped away lots of superfluous branches, innocent and guilty alike. Free will can exist only if a man like Richard can choose to avoid grace, choose evil over good. In so choosing, Richard has hacked a bloody trail through "miserable England." He has also, in his own words, chosen the shape of his eternity.

Richmond's heroic piety at the end of the play, set against Richard's heroic despair, becomes particularly attractive when we highlight the play's relentless focus on the fulfillment of prophecies, dreams, curses, premonitions, and deserving prayers. There is an inevitability about Richard's overthrow that is intensely dramatic precisely because it culminates this pervasive pattern. Fulfilled in this finale are Richmond's prayer;

the curses of Margaret, his mother, and his wife; the prayers and prophecies of all of the ghosts; and even Richard's ironic curses against himself. After the excruciating uncertainties of seemingly random destiny, of chance and change, that have been vividly dramatized in this world of time, God's providence has finally been manifested and vindicated. "Peace lives agen; / That she may long live heere, God say, Amen" (3886–87; 5.5.40–41). Such peace as this, which passes all understanding, is joyfully invoked by Godly men who believe in a providential universe. This final harmony of Richard III is amply precedented by everything that has gone before. In no way is it grafted onto the rest of the play, as Sanders suggests.[44] If such extraordinary men as Richmond are more readily found in art than in nature, so much the worse for nature. It is both meet and right that this Richmond, the idealized but still human Richmond of Shakespeare's art, should prevail in God's name. And so, finally, he does.

6

"Odde Old Ends":
Textual Cruxes and
Interpretive Problems

✝ The text of *Richard* III is particularly crucial to our acts of interpretation, on the stage or in the study. Think, for example, of the interpretive implications of Olivier's cutting all of Margaret's lines and those of the Scrivener, of his eliminating the attempted seduction of Queen Elizabeth, of his severe truncation of the play's measured rhetoric, the speeches of the ghosts, the many affirmations of the hand of providence. Consider what Roy Walker called his "butchery" of the role of Richmond in act 5, or his elimination of Richard's last soliloquy.[1] The entire recorded stage history of *Richard* III from Cibber to Olivier has been subjected to such gross (but successful) manipulations of the theatrical text. While variations in the literary text have hardly been so radical as these, they have been extraordinary as well. Neither literary nor theater people can afford to ignore their interpretive implications. This is particularly true in an age that is finally performing Shakespeare's text with theatrical success.

Shakespeare's text is itself, however, a model of instability. More than 2,000 substantive and semi-substantive variants exist among the major editions of *Richard* III. Most of them are heirs of the two pretenders to textual authority, the first Quarto of 1597 and the first Folio of 1623. While a lively debate continues over which of these editions should hold sway, their 2,000 descendants grapple individually or in small groups for authority. The chair is not so much empty as it is overpopulated. As frustrating as such uncertain lineage must be to today's informed textual editor of *Richard* III, it is a boon to any serious reader who is also interested in problems of interpretation.[2] For each of the major interpretive issues in the play can be colored in various ways by scores of legitimate textual cruxes. This chapter, which is addressed primarily to the general reader rather than the textual scholar, will consider the range of possible meaning in the most interesting and important of them.

The Orations of Richard and Richmond

Several of the textual cruxes that appear in the orations of Richard and Richmond in act 5 could affect our response to these adversaries as the play concludes. Many intensify the claims for and against legitimacy and power that each makes to his men. An editor or a director inclined to brighten or darken either character could therefore do so rather decisively with some systematic choices. Every serious reader needs to be alert to these possibilities. Though the general interpretive question concerns the relative attractiveness of Richard and Richmond throughout act 5, I shall look now only at those textual cruxes which might affect their public utterances, and therefore their public appearance.[3]

Richmond's first speech to his leaders begins to assert just cause by establishing Richard as the illegitimate king, the usurper, and Richmond as true successor to the throne. The most important crux in this first oration comes in Blunt's lines, interestingly appropriated from Richmond's speech in Hall's history. Richard's men will "flye" from him in the Folio (3426; 5.2.21); they will "shrinke" from him in the Quarto and several later editions.[4] The words are almost equally unpleasant. The first possibly stresses Richard's repugnance more than the second, which would seem to underline his friends' treachery more than their horror. Three other textual variants in the oration might also affect our sense of the relative attractiveness of Richmond and Richard. First, Richard is called either "wretched" (F1, Q1) (3412; 5.2.7) or "reckless" (COL3). Both are obviously pejorative. The first would seem to focus our attention more on Richard's personal worthlessness and spiritual agonies; the second would stress rather his potential and already-realized violence. Second, the immediacy of Richard's "wretched" violence, its present tense, is emphasized more in the Folio's "Swilles" (3414; 5.2.9) and "makes" than in Pope's grammatically consistent past tenses.[5] In the same line with "spoyl'd," Richmond calls the field "your" in the Folio (3413; 5.2.7). Rowe's emendation to "our" would seem to strengthen his legitimacy; no other editors have followed it.[6]

In Richard's following scene occur two more cruxes that could alter the effectiveness of his description of his enemies. In the Folio he calls them "Traitors" and a "Faction" (3443, 3447; 5.3.9, 13); in the Quarto "foe" and "partie." According to the OED, "faction" feels more negative than "partie." It can mean "a party in the state . . . always with opprobrious sense, conveying the imputation of selfish or mischievous ends or turbulent or unscrupulous methods" (1 *Faction* 3).[7] Richard will spell out precisely these imputations when he later describes Richmond and his men to his troops. They engage in "desperate Adventures, and assur'd Destruction"; they "bring you to [or 'to you' (Q1)] unrest" (3789, 90; 5.3.319, 320). They would "enjoy our Lands? lye with our Wives? / Ravish our daughters?" (3806–7; 5.3.336–37). More simply, in the second variant, "Traitors" elevates Richard's cause by lowering Richmond's; "foes" in contrast serves neither cause.

The choice between "token" and "signall" (3457; 5.3.21) in Richmond's next public utterance seems to bear both on the questions of providence in the play and on that of their relative attractiveness in act 5. "Token," the Folio word, can have a distinctively theological meaning: it is "in a biblical sense, an act serving to demonstrate divine power or authority" (1 *Token* 4). "Signall," on the other hand, does not carry that connotation. Richmond's claim to just cause and his direct invocation of divine providence are both, therefore, clearer with "token" than with "signall." Two-thirds of the major editors have followed the Folio reading. At the end of Richmond's scene occurs a second choice between "our" and "my" (3483; 5.3.46). This time the Quarto has the word that implies legitimacy; interestingly, Rowe does not follow it. To compound this inconsistency, at least from an interpretive perspective, the same editors who reject "token" for "signall" choose "our" over "my." But of course, their principle of choice, in many cases at least, may be a preferred copy text, not interpretive consistency.[8]

The battle orations after the ghosts' appearance contain some of the most interesting textual cruxes in the play. In Richmond's speech, Richard is called in all four Folios and Quartos 3–6 (1602–22) "A base foule Stone, made precious by the soyle / Of Englands Chaire, where he is falsely set" (3716–17; 5.3.250–51). In the first and second Quartos, Rowe's editions, and all following, "soyle" becomes "foile." The preferred reading is much richer. "Foil" can mean "a thin leaf of some metal placed under some transparent substance to give it the appearance of a precious stone" (1 *Foil* 5a). Richard is less precious stone than transparent substance, falsely set in his "foil" the throne of England. We might also understand the phrase with OED 2 *Foil* 1: "the fact of being thrown," as in wrestling; 2 *Foil* 2: "a repulse, defeat"; 2 *Foil* 2b: "a disgrace, stigma." Among the meanings of "foil" as a verb are other apposite definitions: 5 *Foil* 1: "to tread under foot, trample down"; 5 *Foil* 6: "to foul, defile, pollute"; 5 *Foil* 7: "to dishonor"; 5

Foil 8: "to cause filth, drop excrement." "Foil" can even refer "by allusion to the annual fall of the leaf" (1 Foil 1b). With this wealth of disgusting interpretive possibilities, "soil" can hardly compete.⁹

Another important cluster of textual cruxes occurs in Richard's public words before battle, first those to his leaders, then those to his assembled troops. First, who reads the puzzling riddle: *"Jockey of Norfolke, be not so bold, / For Dickon thy maister is bought and sold"* (3774–75; 5.3.304–5)? Most editors after Capell give the lines to Richard; the Folio and Quarto have Norfolk. In either mouth the warning of overconfidence and betrayal, even preordained defeat, undermines Richard's upcoming oration. In Richard's mouth this undercutting might be more obvious. Also interesting is the marking of Richard's lines 3778–81 (5.3.309–12) as an aside:

> Let not our babling Dreames affright our soules;
> For Conscience is a word that Cowards use,
> Devis'd at first to keep the strong in awe,
> Our strong armes be our Conscience, Swords our Law.

On the one hand, such an emendation is only an editorial curiosity; it has neither Folio nor Quarto authority, and only two editions I have seen use it.¹⁰ On the other, the lines contain an embarrassing revelation of Richard's uncertainty and his pathetic rationalizing just before the battle, an implicit denial of just cause, and a loss of his vaunted control and attractiveness. His leaders may be less afraid of bad dreams and bad conscience than he is. Betraying these weaknesses aloud, as both authoritative texts have Richard do, further weakens him here, both politically and aesthetically. Richard cannot keep his doubts to himself; yet any good military orator, not to mention any Machiavellian worth his salt, should certainly be able to do so. Is Richard trying to bluff it out publicly? If he is, the tactic is unsuccessful. The leaders hear the desperate misgivings of a doomed man. Despairing, Richard is about to die.

In the king's oration to his troops, does Richard say "they bring you to unrest" (F1) or is it "they bring to you unrest" (Q1) (3790; 5.3.320)?¹¹ The former reading plants the unrest within Richard's troops; the latter, followed by many nineteenth- and early twentieth-century editions, implies rather that it is imposed from without by Richmond's men. The former therefore implies an emotional state, the latter political disruption. Two lines later "distraine" (3792; 5.3.322) is introduced by Hanmer (HAN) to replace the "restraine" of both the Quarto and the Folio. It has been the choice of many subsequent editors, probably because of its wealth of applicable meanings.[12] Besides "to confine, bind" (1 *Distraine* 1b), "to control by force," "to restrain" (1 *Distraine* 3), its common meaning with the original, we have the following possibilities: "to squeeze, to clasp [or] grasp tightly" (1 *Distraine* 1a); "to rend or tear asunder" (1 *Distraine* 6); "to constrain a person to pay for damages" (1 *Distrain* 7), a legal meaning. Richmond's vagabonds would ravish, destroy, and impoverish their wives if they should lose the battle. Richard is more persuasive, Richmond less attractive, in the Hanmer reading. But can that reading stand on textual grounds?

At the peroration of Richard's speech we are confronted with the intriguing choice between "Right Gentlemen of England" and "Fight gentlemen of England" (3809; 5.3.338). Though every editor since Pope has gone with the second, Quarto reading, the potential force of "Right" in that passage is worth a closer look. It can mean "direct, legitimate," pertaining to lineage or descent (3 *Right* 1d); it can mean "disposed to do what is just or good; upright, righteous" (3 *Right* 5); "mentally normal or sound; sane" (3 *Right* 13). It can mean "judging, thinking, or acting in accordance with truth . . . ; correct in opinion, judgement, or procedure" (3 *Right* 14); "having due title or right; rightful, legitimate, lawful" (3 *Right* 16); "justly entitled to the name: true, real, verifiable" (3 *Right* 17). Is this merely another Q3 misprint, or does it correct a prominent Q1 error? We cannot know. But Richard is going down with all his argumentative guns blazing if he uses "Right" here. He is claiming his cause and his men rightful, legitimate, lawful; himself legitimate, mentally normal, correct in opinion, judgment, and procedure. However, the terrible irony that neither he nor his cause is any of these things brutally undermines this oration at its conclusion. Elizabeth has already deprived Richard of all he might swear by. Richard himself now reveals the desperate absurdity of his position through these preposterous claims that neither friend nor foe could possibly credit.

Good, just, upright, righteous, justly entitled to the name of king? There is no way. He has no name, no title; neither do his followers. He is as dispossessed as Richard II was of his throne; he is also apparently possessed at last even to dispossess himself. Richard is not even literally "right," that is "straight; not bent, curved, or crooked in any way" (3 *Right* 1a). "Fight" brings none of these ironies to the surface at this crucial moment. It makes the conclusion of Richard's battle oration much more attractive than it is in the Folio text. The Quarto variant, almost universally adopted, has helped lead interpreters and performers of this last speech and this last scene to miss the ultimate desperation, the ultimate loss of inventiveness, the ultimate irony of Richard's "Right." "Right" is so wrong in Richard's mouth that no one could believe it. That may be what makes it so appropriate.

G. Blakemore Evans asks his college reader in the excellent Pelican text to "note how Shakespeare is moved imaginatively by Richard in these lines." He contrasts them to "the comparative flatness" of Richmond's oration.[33] The Sher-Alexander production that we will discuss in the epilogue vividly illustrates that the question is still very much up in the air. These textual cruxes that we have considered, especially the last of them, suggest how much our impressions of their relative attractiveness might be altered from text to text. In the most extreme case the preposterousness of the Folio's "Right" might have led every editor since Pope to prefer the Quarto's much more rousing "Fight." But "Right" might be right precisely because it is so preposterous. It certainly deserves more light than it has received since Pope preferred the Quarto variant.

The Wooing of Elizabeth

Does Richard seduce Queen Elizabeth to his will in 4.4, as he apparently thinks he does, or does he fail not only to change her mind but even to perceive his failure?[14] More than forty substantive and semi-substantive variants that occur during their exchange may have a bearing on this question. We will consider here only the most important.

First, Richard may refer to his adventure against Richmond as "my enterprize / And dangerous successe of bloody warres," or as "my dangerous attempt of hostile armes" (3015-16; 4.4.236-37). In the latter, Quarto reading, Richard seems less sure of himself and his cause. Gone is the positive "enterprize"; "successe" is replaced by the more tentative "attempt." The Folio's "bloody warres" seems more brutal than the blander "hostile armes" of the Quarto. On the other hand, "attempt of hostile armes" has an inherent ambiguity that may call into question Richard's cause. His arms may be those hostile to his own country's good enterprise. Just after this, Richard may refer to Elizabeth either as "gentle" (F) or "mightie" (Q) lady (3021; 4.4.242).[15] The latter raises the level either of his flattery or his regard. In either case, Richard's confidence seems less sure in the Quarto. At the same time, since the Quarto also omits Elizabeth's whole speech preceeding this exchange (3002-3014; 4.4.223-35), her resolve is also lessened. Characteristically, neither edition can be inferred to be Elizabeth's or Richard's ally here. Few later editors have followed the Quarto's omission of all these lines, though Pope and Hanmer do omit the first two.

Skipping about twenty textual cruxes of slighter interest (including the Quarto omission of 3073–3127, Richard's longest and least successful speech in the scene), we come to their best stichomythic exchange. To Richard's ploy, "say she shall be a High and Mighty Queene," Elizabeth counters, "To vaile the Title, as her Mother doth" (3132–33; 4.4.347–48). "Waile," the Quarto variant used by every editor from Pope to Sisson, is certainly the more immediate choice. However, the Folio "vaile" has possibilities too. First, it can mean "to be of use or service" (3 *Vail* 2). Elizabeth may lament in her sadness that she has served the title, been its slave, as her daughter would be as Richard's queen. "To cause or allow to descend or sink" (4 *Vail* 1a) is another possibility. Does she lament another lost title, another fall from power, with all its attendant pain, for her child? "Small joy have I in being Englands Queene" (575; 1.3.109). "To throw down, give up or surrender" (4 *Vail* 1d) is a similar definition. Finally, "vaile" can mean "to abase, humble, lower" (4 *Vail* 4a). Elizabeth has spent such a vailed queenship, "bated, scorn'd and stormed at" (574; 1.3.108). Even when Elizabeth's happiness was at its height, she feared its overthrow. What, then, can another such position "avail" her daughter? "Vaile" makes both Elizabeth's resolve and her sadness much more vivid than the merely pathetic "waile." It is a formidable word against Richard at this moment.

Such fascinating textual cruxes continue throughout the exchange. Does Elizabeth intellectually challenge Richard's word when she asks "How long shall that title 'ever,' last?" (3135; 4.4.350). Or is she more pathetically wondering how long her young daughter will ever last as queen ("how long shall that title ever last")? Most editors after Theobald go against both the Folio and the Quarto to achieve the first distinction. Does Richard vow to be her "subject love" or her "subject low" (3140; 4.4.355)? The Folio "low" may exaggerate Richard's humility before Elizabeth; it may also contain an ironic self-indictment. Elizabeth's pun in the next line, "lothes such Soveraignty," plays better to the ear against "low" than against the Quarto's "love." To the mind, though, it more appropriately opposes "love." The editors are about evenly split on this curious toss-up.[16]

A related pair of cruxes occurs just seven lines later: "Too deepe and dead (poore Infants) in their graves" (3148; 4.4.363). First, is it "Too," the Quarto and Folio 1–3 reading, or "Two," that of Folio 4 and most of the eighteenth-century editors? "Two" is the right number, and an ugly enough fact. "Too" intensifies "dead," and therefore possibly Elizabeth's fury, even more. "Their graves" versus "their grave" (Q1) raises the question of burial. Renovation in the Tower in the seventeenth century may have confirmed a common burial in an unsanctified pit, one grave, rather than two. "Grave" may therefore be more pointed emotionally and more accurate too. It would further Elizabeth's advantage over Richard at this moment in their debate.[17] Does Richard respond to the next challenge by Elizabeth "I swear" (F1, 3153), or is it "I sweare by nothing" (Q1, RID)? The latter seems to put more self-defeating (if still stubborn) words into his mouth, and may thereby emphasize Elizabeth's continuing leverage against him.

Near the end of Elizabeth's relentless recitation of what Richard cannot swear by, she comes to the phrase "times ill-us'd repast" (3187; 4.4.396). This is one of the most famous cruxes in the play. Almost every editor has emended the phrase to read either the Quarto's "time misused orepast" or "times ill-used o'erpast." Both options make more immediate sense. But the Folio "repast" is not without possibility. Richard has "slaughter'd" and "butcher'd" fathers and children to stock his grisly banquet as king. Now his "funeral bak'd meats / [Do] coldly furnish forth the marriage tables." "Repast" may work better than the traditional emendations to complete this horrible conceit that Elizabeth directs against him.

In Richard's last, blustering speech to Elizabeth, to which she responds "Shall I be tempted of the Divel thus?" (3209; 4.4.418), there are several other vital textual variants. Richard's early line, "Heaven, and Fortune barre me happy houres" (3191; 4.4.400) is omitted from Q1 and GLO. This is a key moment for Richard, audacious in its disdain of both heaven and fortune. Whether Richard's world is governed by God's providence or blind chance, he is forfeiting their aid if he is lying. Of course, he is. Death and damnation are the consequence. "Deserts" instead of "desires" (F4, ROWE), would further the theological undertones here. Richard is alluding, however cynically, to the doctrinal controversy of salvation by grace or salvation by merit, faith versus works. He concedes no good works in his past, no deserts, when he says, "Not by deserts, but what I will deserve" (3206; 4.4.414). But he also promises that he will earn Elizabeth's love and forgiveness by his good works to come. From what we see of these good works, Richard of all men would need extraordinary grace to be loved or forgiven, by man, woman or God. He is playing with fire again. Neither "that nest of spicery" nor the balm of Gilead will be his if "desert" is his plea. Appointing Queen Elizabeth as his attorney heightens the irony. With such an advocate, who needs a prosecutor, much less an eternal auditor at compt? That Shakespeare was playing lavishly with the same controversy in *Love's Labour's Lost* increases the likelihood of such an informed allusion.[18] Most of the editors have preferred this theological word to the less interesting "Not my desires." The Q1 "Not by desertes" may add brighter theological color. It is, after all, "by merit" or "by grace" that we are saved in the traditional phraseology.

Fittingly, the exchange ends on two more textual cruxes with interpretive significance. Does Richard kiss Elizabeth at the end of their interview? Does he merely salute her? What are we to make of the curious line, "Beare her my true loves kisse, and so farewell"? (3221; 4.4.430). Almost one hundred years of editors from Johnson through Halliwell all add something like *"kissing her"* as a stage direction to the silent Quarto and Folio texts. Some contemporary editions still include it.[19] Aside from the question of its textual authority, what does this kiss imply? Richard may still be deluding himself, kissing a reluctant but clever adversary who knows that her very life may at this moment depend upon her successful dissimulation. The actress could reveal to us a revulsion that Richard never imagines, or one that he enjoys. Richard himself could betray his own uncertainty, kiss or no kiss; he may know that he has not won, or he may fear loss, regardless of the testimony of his words. Those words have been systematically undercut throughout most of the scene. Elizabeth's pointed rejection of the proffered kiss would demolish his presumption of victory here. The silence of Q and F is pregnant with that possibility.

Finally, Elizabeth has revealed through most of the scene that she is neither shallow nor changing. She has devastated most of Richard's arguments. She has beaten him in quickness and in strength. There is little evidence in the text to convince us that she has changed her mind at the end of the scene. There is even less likelihood that she would become suddenly shallow after so much depth. We may know, then, even if Richard will not, that Elizabeth is not a "shallow, changing" (3222; 4.4.431) woman, the choice, incidentally, of a lot of editors.[20] Is she, then, the Folio's "shallow-changing"? Is she too easily changed, even in Richard's reeling brain, precisely because she has won all of the skirmishes and yet apparently loses the war? Or does he mean this in his self-deception, and yet convey to us in spite of himself that she was merely shallow-changing, pretending to change on the surface only, but firm within? The dramatic irony of this last possibility works strongly against Richard as their exchange comes to an end.

This brief selection of textual cruxes illustrates their intricate involvement in important interpretive issues in 4.4 of *Richard* III. That each of us would prefer a slightly different coloring is both natural and perplexing. For if our interpretive preferences were to translate themselves into hard textual decisions, we would each produce a different text of the play. Even if all of these choices weighed against Richard or Elizabeth, the interpretive problem would not go away. But its evidence would be substantially altered.

The Questions of Providence

Scores of substantive and semi-substantive variants can also influence our response to the questions of divine providence in Richard III.[21] Scenes 3 and 4 of act 1 both establish central theological issues and illustrate the dialectic approach to those issues that runs through the play. We will look at them first. Then our focus will move to the shifting attitudes of the characters who participate in the debate, through the same textual lens. Richard will receive our closest attention among the men, Elizabeth among the women. But most of the characters who debate the issue of divine providence will be included in our scrutiny. To the obvious danger that such a microscopic perspective might distort or reduce our vision, there is a corresponding advantage. Looking closely at the most important of the "wild and whirling words" of Richard III might improve our understanding of its largest and most elusive interpretive issue.

ACT 1, SCENE 3

Margaret's prophecies touch most of the characters in 1.3. The responses they provoke help establish those characters' earliest attitudes toward the efficacy of curses and prayers, the accuracy of prophecies and dreams, and the relationship of all of this to divine providence. They also initiate the motif of debate about those issues that characterizes much of the rest of the play. Intriguing textual cruxes thread their way throughout the scene.

The first occurs in Richard's ironic vindication of his father's curses in III Henry VI: "His Curses then, from bitternesse of Soule, / Denounc'd against thee, are all falne upon thee: / And God, not we, hath plagu'd thy bloody deed" (648–50; 1.3.178–80). Richard enjoys rationalizing his misdeeds with another piece of religious hypocrisy, but two ironies stick to these remnants of holy writ. One lies in the accuracy of the prophecy of his own forthcoming doom; the other in his own continuously ambiguous stance toward supernatural agency throughout the play. We are never quite sure just where his hypocrisy stops and his belief begins; neither is Richard. The Folio "all falne" would seem to confirm a more literal, direct intervention of God than the later "now falne." In both, however, Richard attests to God's agency in fulfilled prophecies more forcefully than if the "all" and the "now" were both omitted, as they are in Q3 and F2–F4.[22] Most of the other characters in the play will eventually affirm the just operation of providence at their own moments of doom. As we have just seen, even Richard conforms at the last to that pattern, though briefly and with characteristic complexity. Only Elizabeth will not.

Who responds, "So just is God, to right the innocent" (651; 1.3.181)? If it is Margaret, as ROWE1 through THEO2 have it, this represents a rigorous consistency in her view of curses, even those against herself. If Elizabeth, we may hear petty sniping at her erstwhile rival and continuing enemy, as much a taunt as an affirmation of belief.[23] But Elizabeth does begin *Richard III* with a fairly conventional belief in divine providence. Giving her this line, as both the Folio and the Quarto do, would emphasize that early belief. The rubbing of chance and change will have worn it pretty thin by 4.4.

Several notable cruxes mark Margaret's next speech. "Though not by Warre, by Surfet dye your King" (666; 1.3.196), the Folio reading, is a much more accurate and confident prophecy than the Quarto's "If. . . ." The latter implies only that Edward will die, one way or the other. In the Folio Margaret foretells both how he will die and how he will not. Two semi-substantive cruxes follow: "Long may'st thou live, to wayle thy Childrens death," and "Long dye thy happie dayes, before thy death" (673, 676; 1.3.203, 206). In the former, the Folio's comma suggests first a prayer, long life, and then the sinister reason: "to wail." Without the comma there is only the suggestion that long life will equal long wailing. In the second line the Folio comma again establishes a rue with a difference. Each of Elizabeth's happy days should die a long, slow death, before her own death. The protracted pain of this suggestion is lessened by the Quarto's omitted comma that every editor since Pope has followed. It asks simply that Elizabeth's happiness should die long before she does. It is odd that more editors have not stuck with the more vicious comma of the Folio.[24]

Later in the scene, Margaret may predict or she may simply describe her own fate when she says, "And in that shame, still live my sorrowes rage" (750; 1.3.277). The Quarto and Folio "live" articulates an accurate prophecy; "lives," an infrequent emendation from the mid-nineteenth century, is merely a statement of fact. Next, is Margaret's speech to Buckingham an aside from lines 761–66 (1.3.288–93) ("O Buckingham, take heede . . . attend on him")? The audience hears it in any event. The rest of the assemblage does not if it is an aside, and thus Richard's "What doth she say" is more curious, more vulnerable to the power of her words. On the other hand, Buckingham's response, "Nothing that I respect my gracious Lord," would be more likely to prompt Margaret's curse against him if her warning were public.²⁵ For then Buckingham's rejection of it would be a public repudiation of her prophecies.

Three other particularly interesting cruxes pertain to Buckingham's skeptical attitudes toward Margaret's curses in 1.3. First, he avers in the Folio that "Curses never passe / The lips of those that breath them in the ayre" (757–58; 1.3.284–85). The Quarto also has "breath." Yet almost every editor since Rowe has accepted his emendation to "breathe." I would revert to the two early texts. "Breath" emphasizes Buckingham's disbelief better than "breathe." It sounds harsher, more abrupt, more insulting. It also stresses the insubstantiality of Margaret's words better than the neutral "breathe." Cleopatra's "He words me, girls" is a similar insult with similar cleverness of diction (*Antony and Cleopatra*, 5.2.191). Elizabeth in 4.4 also reduces curses and lamentings to mere air, breath. Second, does Buckingham "soothe" the devil Richard, or does he "sooth" him (771; 1.3.297)? The former, nineteenth-century emendation also has no Quarto or Folio precedent, yet almost every edition since COL2 has used it. "Soothing" Richard, affirming his truth against Margaret's falsehood, seems again much more effective than the change. True, "soothe" can mean "to prove or show (a statement) to be true"; "to verify, to support, back up"; even "to maintain (a lie) as being true" (OED 1 *Sooth* 1, 2b, 3). And "breath" is listed in the OED as a spelling variant for "breathe." But two more powerful meanings would come across better today with the spellings "sooth" and "breath." All the popular emendations are likely to suggest are the blander "to tranquilize or calm, mitigate," or "to exhale."

Finally, does Buckingham or Hastings say "My haire doth stand [on] end to heare her curses" (777; 1.3.303)? Capell replaces the Folio and Quarto "Buckingham" with "Hastings." The line seems an unexpected response from either of these worldly, skeptical politicians. Buckingham has earlier said, "Curses never passe / The lips of those that breath them in the ayre" (757–58; 1.3.284–85). Hastings has earlier called Margaret a "False boding Woman" (718; 1.3.246). Why would her curses make either's hair stand on end? Do they grate like scratching on a blackboard? Or does one of the men feel in his crawling skin intimations of last things? Then, which one? Since there is little interpretive reason to prefer Hastings, the Quarto and Folio precedent would seem the better choice. Once again, most of the editors since Capell have disagreed and given the line to Hastings.²⁶

Our perceptions could often be altered by these selected textual cruxes in 1.3. The beliefs of Richard, Margaret, Elizabeth, Buckingham, and Hastings about curses, prophecies, and providence could all take on slightly different shadings. So could our exact understanding of two of Margaret's curses against Elizabeth, and our response to the dynamics of the Margaret-Buckingham exchanges. Buckingham's attitude toward divine providence may be as ambiguous as Richard's by the end of the scene; it may be consistently skeptical throughout if the hair on end is Hastings's. The dialectic itself, within characters like Richard and Elizabeth and Buckingham and between other characters, can also be altered by various cuts of this textual cloth.

ACT 1, SCENE 4

Clarence, thrust by his dreams "into the tumbling billowes of the maine" (856; 1.4.20), is also thrust in 1.4 into the midst of the theological debate. Its issues are quite literally a matter of life and death. He learns when Richard's men drown him in the malmsey butt that dreams are not always the "toyes" he once called them (64; 1.1.60). But first he disputes several theological questions with the Murderers. They also debate issues of conscience and salvation with one another, and evidence quite distinct beliefs and attitudes through that debate. As in 1.3, the questions these characters discuss and the strategy of dialectic which their discussion establishes are both affected by textual cruxes.

For example, as Clarence fights rhetorically for his life, among the most potent weapons in his arsenal are the "wilts," "arts," and "thous" of biblical rhetoric. At least this is true in the Quarto version of several key speeches:

> Hast thou that holy feeling in thy soule,
> To counsell me to make my peace with God;
> And art thou yet to thy owne soule so blinde,
> That thou wilt war with God, by murdring me?
> (1083–86; 1.4.250–53)

The Folio lacks six of these peculiarly biblical words, and therefore lacks their persuasive weight as well.[27] Did a careless actor drop this distinctive diction as the play evolved over the thirty years between the Quarto and the Folio texts? Did an insightful actor add the distinction to the Quarto's possibly memorial reconstruction? Did Shakespeare himself intensify the moment with these altered details? Does either alternative suggest an evolution from Folio to Quarto that reverses the chronology of their two publication dates? Or was one of the compositors merely careless when he set the Quarto or the Folio text? We can only speculate today. But six such variants in four lines would be noticed by the Murderer whose conscience is already bedeviling him.

In the Folio as well as the Quarto, Clarence begins using these biblical words just as he refers to the tablets that Moses received at God's hand on Mount Sinai: "Erroneous Vassals, the great King of Kings / Hath in the Table of his Law commanded / That thou shalt do no murther" (1026-28; 1.4.195-97). The Murderers may have suggested this strategy to him with their own words, "command" and "commanded" in the previous two lines, particularly, "And he that hath commanded, is our King" (1025; 1.4.194). Clarence's "thou shalt" strongly echoes this rare moment when divine providence directly intervened in human affairs. The Quarto reads "wilt thou then" at the end of 1028 (1.4.197), intensifying the theological overtones over the Folio's "will." Further, the second Folio has "shall" instead of "shalt," a variant that forfeits more of this associative power.[28]

As Clarence begins to explore the consciences of the two Murderers, he says in the Folio: "I charge you, as you hope for any goodnesse" (1021; 1.4.189). The Quarto has again the more explicitly theological, "I charge you as you hope to have redemption, / By Christs deare bloud shed for our grievous sinnes." "Redemption" replaces "goodnesse" and the reason for that redemption, Christ's sacrifice for man's sins, follows. In each of these cases the Quarto's Clarence is more "well spoken" than the Folio's.[29]

In the midst of the theological debate, Clarence, desperate, tries to make a good argument out of bad theology: "If God will be avenged for the deed, / O know you yet, he doth it publiquely, / . . . He needs no indirect, or lawlesse course, / To cut off those that have offended him" (1146-50; 2.1.23-26). It's worth a try, but neither Murderer is buying. Even their relatively unsophisticated theological minds know that God's normal operation is through second causes like themselves, however flawed those agents might be: "Who made thee then a bloudy minister, / When gallant springing brave *Plantagenet*, / That Princely Novice was strucke dead by thee?" (1051-53; 1.4.220-22). Sinai's are rare events in human history. Clarence's own actions as God's scourge argue against him here. "My Brothers love, the Divell, and my Rage" (1054; 1.4.223) might be psychologically and even theologically valid, but it does not rule out God's operation through second causes. If the crucial line, "O know you yet, he doth it publiquely," is left out, as in the Quarto, or degraded, as in Pope and Hanmer, Clarence's desperation and the clear theological point are both diminished. God usually neither rewards nor punishes "publiquely." Thus emerges a work like *The Book of Job*, and endless theological arguments about inscrutable providence, as in *Richard* III.

But if the fabric of Clarence's theological argument is more intricately woven in the Quarto, the crucial distinction between the two Murderers is blurred almost beyond recognition. In the Folio they are distinct. *One* is obdurate in evil, cynical about religion, and sadistic in his pretended solicitousness toward Clarence. His accomplice, *Two*, has more compassion, more conscience, and more religious faith, despite his all-too-human wavering between better and worse, belief and disbelief. However, Quarto-influenced texts blur these distinctions. Who, for example, says "Strike" (991; 1.4.159), and how does he say it? If *One*, it is business as usual; if *Two*, hasty action before reason, the warder of the brain, can intervene. Who says "No, wee'l reason with him" (992; 1.4.160)? If it is callous *One*, the motives must be largely sadistic; if *Two*, read indecision, even a need, however dimly realized, for the long theological disputation with Clarence. "You shall have Wine enough, my Lord" (994; 1.4.162) is similar.[30] *One* would speak the line with heartless sarcasm, *Two* full of pity and the beginnings of remorse. Still, with such altered attribution, the lines, not the speakers, would be the chameleons. Compassion, indecision, remorse would become sadism or sarcasm. The speakers would, or could, remain distinctive, their debate intact.

However, other choices would more definitely muddle the dialectic so clearly implied in the Folio's attribution of lines. Who stammers "To, to, to" (1004; 1.4.172)? If both, as half the editors have it against the Folio, the distinction between *One* and *Two* is blurred; if *Two*, the sharp edge of debate continues to operate. The "CAM group" follows Q1 in giving *One* the crucial line, "Make peace with God, for you must die my Lord" (1082; 1.4.249). Piety and compassion seem strange in *One's* profane mouth. Two earlier uncharacteristic lines are similarly given to *Two*: "Why so he doth, when he delivers you / From this earths thraldome, to the joyes of heaven" (1080–81; 1.4.247–48). The desire to pain Clarence with his brother's treachery is so clearly sarcastic, even sadistic, that the lines seem right only for *One*, unless there is no distinction between the two. Likewise odd, if *One* and *Two* are distinct personalities, or at least distinctly illustrative characters, is the CAM group's decision to give the uncertain "What shall we do" (1089; 1.4.256) to *One*. In the Folio and most other editions, it belongs to the more humane, indecisive second Murderer. Finally, Neilson (NLSN) goes so far as to give the long, comically confused speech about conscience to *One*, and the lines around it to *Two* (979–91; 1.4.145–59). The effect? Briefly, it changes *Two* into an advocate for the Devil against this insinuating conscience, at least until Clarence wakes up and begins to speak. This change has no Quarto precedent. Most of the rest do. A handful of editors even follow Q in omitting or degrading Two's warning, "Looke behinde you, my Lord" (1102; 1.4.268). Each of these choices dulls the edge of debate that is so sharp in the Folio.[31] Critics have used that edge to carve for themselves the dialectical basis of this scene and to imply its use throughout the play. Their case would be more difficult to establish with a predominantly Quarto attribution of these lines.

One final cluster of textual variants in 1.4 bears upon the issue of providence. The moment: Two's grappling with his conscience. Just after the speech, "strong fram'd" and "strong in fraud" (983; 1.4.151) are the two mock-heroic choices describing Two's (or One's) resistance to the force that is still with him. The first suggests physical confrontation with the potent adversary, good conscience; the second implies moral commitment to its opposite, evil, or "the devil" to use their words. Within the speech about conscience, "(by chance)" is omitted in Q1 from the line "It made me once restore a Pursse of Gold that (by chance) I found" (973–74; 1.4.139–40). Was it by chance? As we have seen in the theologians, nothing occurs by chance in a providential world. The speaker's injection of this little parenthesis would thus seem a nice piece of willed self-deception, especially since Two so clearly believes in a providential, Christian universe where one can "make peace with God," struggle with an insinuating conscience, suffer God's vengeance, and also "repent me that the Duke is slaine" (1113; 1.4.278). One can, that is, if one will. Two will; One will not. So it goes. Incidentally, Two tries earlier to deceive himself, calling his conscience either a "passionate," a "compassionate" or a "holy" humour (954; 1.4.117–18). It is finally more than a humor to Murderer Two, at least the compassionate and holy Two of the Folio.[32]

RICHARD

Determining Richard's attitude toward divine providence and supernatural agency is made even more complicated by a number of textual cruxes scattered throughout *Richard III*. As early as the third line of Richard's first soliloquy, the textual editor finds a crux. The clouds either "lowered" or "loured upon our house." The Folio and the Quarto both read "lowr'd," which could be either; later editors have had to take one road or the other.[33] "Louring" clouds suggest more clearly than "lowering" ones the angry glances of God. On Bosworth Field there is less confusion. The skies there "frowne, and lowre upon [Richard's] Army" (3751; 5.3.283). Change the second word to "lower" and there remains the personification of a frowning heaven in the first. But at the beginning of the play, when patterns are being established, "lowered" diminishes that first impression of heaven's angry opposition to Richard's cause. It may eliminate it completely.

From divine to individual judgment, does Richard claim in 2.1 that he has committed offenses against the queen and her friends "unwillingly" or "unwittingly" (1181; 2.1.56–57)? The second, Quarto version has been chosen by every editor since Pope, and it does make more immediate sense. Richard did not know he was harming anyone. "Unwillingly," however, could suggest the subtler self-justification of the reprobate, his lack of free will ("Our will became the servant to defect, / Which else should free have wrought"). If Richard erred "unwillingly," who could blame him, God or man? Paradoxically, of course, the second word actually admits a profounder guilt than the first. Richard knew that he was doing wrong, but he could not, or would not, help it. A related crux occurs just two lines later. Has Richard "ought committed that is hardly borne / To any in this presence" or is it "By any in this presence"?[34] No mere slip of a preposition, this "committed to" versus "borne by." "By," another Quarto reading taken by most editors since Pope, shifts the blame from the offender to the offended. If Richard has committed any sins to be forgiven, his victims still bear them with anger. "Ought," the "anything/nothing" pun that Richard is so fond of, further intensifies this shifting of blame. He may even have committed nothing, ought, against these arbitrary judges. The irony of Richard's feigned reconciliation with them is accentuated by the slickness of "By" and "unwillingly." Whether one wants to intensify that irony is obviously an interpretive rather than a textual decision. Textually, grammatically too, one way is "just as fair" as the other.

Richard's exchange with Catesby, Buckingham, and the Mayor and Citizens in 3.7 contains another series of textual cruxes, the choice of which can also exaggerate or minimize their mutual disdain of God's judgment as well as man's. Does Richard proclaim himself "earnest in the service of my God" or is it "th' high God" (2326; 3.7.106)? Only Folios 3 and 4 and ROWE1 and 2 have this more unctuous second reading. Had it slipped into the acting tradition by 1663? The Mayor's "Do good my lord" (2422; 3.7.201), the Quarto and Folio 1–3 reading, is likewise more audaciously hypocritical than the merely polite "Do, good my lord." Nevertheless, all editions since Folio 4 and ROWE have added the apparently innocuous comma. If a blatant disregard of man's judgment and God's justice is one point of the scene, this traditional emendation might be in error. Buckingham's "Zounds ile intreat no more (2440; 3.7.219), a Quarto reading, is a similar byway. It sets up Gloucester's unctuous "O do not sweare my Lord of Buckingham"; after the Folio's unswearing "we will entreat," the line is omitted. Both conspirators are playing fast and loose with their Creator and the Citizens in the Quarto sequence. Finally, do all say "Amen" (2463; 3.7.241) (F) to this rotten charade, or only the Mayor? (Q) Is this whole city a ship of fools or cynics? Is the city rather one with either a gull or a hypocrite at the helm? The disdain of Richard and his cronies for man and God can be trodden blacker or lighter by each crux in this little sequence.[35]

The best cluster of textual cruxes bearing on Richard's attitudes toward divine providence occurs during and after his experience with the ghosts in act 5. First, these ghosts, all eleven of them, obviously believe in divine providence and invoke its intervention against Richard, and for Richmond and England. Two cruxes in their lines could give more emphasis to their belief. Early in the Folio sequence, the Ghost of Vaughan curses Richard: "Let fall thy Lance, dispaire and dye" (3592; 5.3.143). Capell reads "hurtless lance"; several other editions have "pointless lance." Later, the Ghost of Anne in the Folio curses: "And fall thy edgelesse Sword, dispaire and dye" (3620; 5.3.169). COL 2 and 3 change the phrase to "powerless arm."[36] Clearly, the first changes are metrically inspired. Just as clearly, none has Quarto precedent. Still, knowing how way leads on to way, a pointless or a hurtless lance, like an edgeless sword, suggests divine intervention far more directly than its textual alternative. As an editor, I would not follow the road of emendation here. But such an emendation would brighten and clarify the reader's sense of the operation of providence at this moment of *Richard* III.

The choice between "I and I" and "I am I" (3645; 5.3.183) may be even more important to our understanding of Richard's mind at this crucial moment of discovery. "Richard is Richard" may be a new insight provoked by the ghost's testimony of things past and their prophecy of things to come. "Richard, the self I love, is also Richard, the self they cannot forgive." Worse, goes Richard's reasoning, "I have myself been provoked by this dream to see another Richard, their Richard, so engrained with sin that even I would act against that self. I am a murderer; I am a villain. I have done deeds so hateful that I might even revenge that shattering of my charming, clever, Machiavellian self-image by killing myself." "I and I" may be awkward; it is also very relevant. It is curious that so few textual editors have preferred it.[37]

If we look at the sequence of Richard's thoughts here, we could even argue that "I am I" contradicts the insights, theological and psychological, that Richard is now grappling with:

> What? do I feare my Selfe? There's none else by,
> Richard loves Richard, that is, I am I.
> Is there a Murtherer heere? No; Yes, I am:
> Then flye; What from my Selfe? Great reason: why?
> Lest I Revenge. What? my Selfe upon my Selfe?
> Alacke, I love my Selfe. Wherefore? For any good
> That I my Selfe have done unto my Selfe?
> O no. Alas, I rather hate my Selfe,
> For hatefull Deeds committed by my Selfe.
> I am a Villaine: yet I Lye, I am not.
> Foole, of thy Selfe speake well: Foole, do not flatter.
> (3644–54; 5.3.182–92).

The crux follows, and hinges upon "Richard loves Richard." "That is, I am I" supports this desired self-deception. "I and I" rejects it. For then there are two Richards, two I's, two selves, one attractive and the other disgusting. So is it always in the audience's response to this character; so is it in the critical and theatrical traditions. Our aesthetic response, for a time at least, conflicts with our moral response. But for Richard to begin to judge himself morally as well as aesthetically is devastating indeed to his self-image. In fact, Richard will never be reconciled to his simply aesthetic self again. He will never again be one. The capitalized "Selfes" of the Folio accentuate this discovery.

"I and I" articulates a truth of two-ness that Richard has discovered through the ghosts. But in the theater of God's judgments, there is only one Richard, the moral one. So finally, "I am I" is also true. It sings out the truth about himself that Richard will have to live with for eternity. This is the discovery that leads to Richard's despair. Having tried to gull God and man, having disdained the judgment of his fellows and the justice of God, he finds both judgment and justice visited upon him. He must listen to all voices, finally even his own, crying "Guilty." The Quarto "and" is a potent word here, a connector that disconnects Richard from self-deception and shackles him to truth, personal and universal. But "I am I" is that truth, only one Richard, with all that guilt, forever. One would therefore like to travel both these roads, each having perhaps the better claim. In an essay, such double-going is possible; in a text or a production, it is not.

Pope and Hanmer omit the whole line "Richard loves Richard, that is I am [and] I." They also degrade most of the lines of self-examination just quoted. While these two manipulations of the text are consistent with one another, they almost eliminate our sense of the objective scrutiny of self by self that is the heart of the dramatic moment. Without these lines, Richard's sense of despair, of inevitable judgment, here and hereafter, has far less point and far less power. Conversely, the Quarto addition of Richard's frightened words to Ratcliffe, "Zoundes, who is there?" intensifies the psychological and the theological moment.[38] Since Richard has just involuntarily called on "Jesu," this reference to Christ's wounds may be more than an idle curse. Much as Elizabeth's irony in 4.4 hoists this engineer on his own petard, so his audacious hypocrisy with Buckingham in 3.7 returns to plague the inventor Richard. He will soon be taught bloody instructions. "O do not sweare my Lord of Buckingham" was better advice than either realized at the time.

Richard's last description by Catesby is also affected by a textual crux that may emphasize or diminish our sense of his despair, and therefore our final response to his last burst of energy. Is Richard "Daring an opposite to every danger" (3828; 5.4.3)?[39] This suggests wild fury, the desperate heroics of a doomed man intent upon death, Macbeth against the world. So Catesby seems to interpret the line: "Rescue faire Lord, or else the day is lost." If, on the other hand, we read with the Folio "Daring, and opposite . . . ," or with other editions "A daring opposite," the point about desperation is muted or lost. The latter feels more like Olivier's Richard, or Cibber's. These late cruxes, like the choice between "Fight" and "Right" in Richard's final speech, can significantly modify our understanding of Richard's life and death. Desperation, personal and theological, is not an attractive way to exit.

Finally, is Richard slain on or off the stage?[40] If on, is it by Richmond in a clean, heroic stroke or two as God's minister against God's scourge, or is it by a pack of jackals, closer to history and the historical world-view than to Tudor myth and the sacramental understanding of history? Editors and directors have divided almost evenly on this question, which also has a direct bearing on our idea of providence at the play's end. In both the Folio and the Quarto, Richmond slays "the bloudy Dogge" in single combat. Cleanly. Providentially. At least from my interpretive bias.

THE OTHER CHARACTERS: A FEW LAST WORDS

Chosen for their direct and varied relationship to interpretive problems in *Richard* III, these examples already illustrate how closely textual and interpretive sophistication must be connected in this play. However, a few more cruxes that could influence our understandings of Queen Elizabeth, Margaret, Buckingham, Hastings, and Richmond are too significant for us to omit them completely.

Elizabeth, still talking about her husband's "swift-winged" soul in 2.1, still apparently believing therefore in the kingdom of heaven, calls the afterlife in the Folio "the Kingdome of nere-changing night" (1320; 2.2.46). This dismal image is directly contradicted by the Quarto's "perpetuall rest." The editors have split almost evenly on the crux, which bears directly on Elizabeth's attitude toward divine providence in this hour of grief. The afterlife seems dark indeed in her Folio line, peaceful in the Quarto. The rest can be silence without being darkness. Collier was apparently so shaken by her darkness that he gratuitously changed it to "perpetual light." No one has followed this lead.[41] No one is likely to resolve the crux either. It depends too much on critical predilection, too little on textual evidence. But a textual choice could hardly be more crucial.

Three cruxes in 4.4 can bear just as impressively upon Margaret's understanding of providence. Is this play they are watching "franticke" or "tragicke" (2839; 4.4.68)? The latter implies more meaning, more order, than the Folio "franticke." Later in the same speech, Margaret predicts again Richard's "pittious and unpittied end": "Earth gapes, Hell burnes, Fiends roare, Saints pray, / To have him sodainly convey'd from hence" (2845–47; 4.4.74–76). POPE1–JOHN2 replace the second line with "for vengeance." Hieronimo's mad again. The Folio and Quarto join the voices of saints and fiends in a concerted plea for Richard's damnation, his conveyance "from hence" or "away" (Q1), from earth to hell. Pope's reading is more earthbound, less precise about Richard's eternal punishment in hell. In Margaret's next speech, has the course of justice "whirl'd about" or has it "whe'eld about" (2876; 4.4.105)?[42] The second, Quarto, reading, like "tragicke" over "franticke" earlier, has a plan, an order to it that the Folio alternative lacks. "Whe'eld" is constrained, providential; "whirl'd" is arbitrary, capricious. Interpretive predilection would almost certainly have to determine textual choice in such cases, unless an overriding textual principle, like the Globe's Quarto preference, is all-dominant. Such a theory seldom overrides interpretive preference in such interesting choices as these.

Among the men, Buckingham and Hastings are the major skeptical voices early in the play. Of Margaret's curses Buckingham allows, "Curses never passe / The lips of those that breath them in the ayre" (757–58; 1.3.284–85). Hastings calls Margaret a "false boding Woman" (718; 1.3.246). Their parallel conversions to belief in providence and prophecy are more impressive because of this early skepticism. Pope oddly omits two of Buckingham's most pious utterings just before death. Both are allusions to

All Souls Day: "Why then Al-soules day, is my bodies doomsday," and "This, this All-soules day to my fearfull Soule" (3384, 3390; 5.1.12, 18). Lost in the shuffle are the precise theological words "doomsday" and "soul." Buckingham's final repentance is more vivid and more traditionally Christian with these two lines than without them. The hand of providence is also more visible. Even the church year participates in a punishment that the victim acknowledges as just, deserved, determined, and directed by the "high All-seer" (3392; 5.1.20). Further, in the Folio this "All-seer" forces "the swords of wicked men / To turne their owne points in their Masters bosomes" (3395–96; 5.1.23–24).[43] This seems a particularly cruel punishment, death and sadistic torture, though Buckingham does not quarrel with it. "On their Masters bosomes," the Q1 reading and choice of about half the subsequent editors, is just as providential but not sadistic. God is less eager for pain in the Quarto reading. But like Margaret, the cruel Buckingham might be expected to imagine a cruel God when he becomes a God-perceiving character in the play.

Finally, does Richmond ask his "Gracious Lord" to "abate" or "rebate" the "edge of Traitors" (3881; 5.5.35)?[44] Both work well. "Abate," the Folio and Quarto choice, may suggest somewhat more physical force in its first two meanings: "to beat down, demolish, destroy" or "to do away with" (OED 1 A*bate* 1, 2). However, both words can mean direct divine intervention: "to beat back the edge or point of anything; to turn the edge, to blunt" (1 A*bate* 8); "to reduce the force or effect of . . . a blow, stroke, etc."; "to make dull, to blunt the edge or point of a weapon" (3 R*ebate* 3b, 4a). Such direct intervention was already invoked against Richard by the ghosts of his wife and his brother ("edgelesse Sword") (3583, 3620; 5.3.135, 163). Now Richmond asks it against all future traitors. It is appropriate that the last two significant textual cruxes in R*ichard* III, like the "louring" clouds in Richard's first soliloquy, pertain so directly to the attitudes of Richmond and Richard toward divine providence. At the last, Richmond, with either word, believes literally in its protective and punitive agency in human affairs.

Our perceptions could often be altered by these and other textual cruxes in R*ichard* III. The beliefs of Richard, Margaret, Elizabeth, Buckingham, Clarence, and Hastings could all take on slightly different shadings. So could our exact understanding of two of Margaret's curses against Elizabeth, our response to the dynamics of the Richard-Elizabeth exchange in 4.4, and the Richmond-Richard opposition in act 5. Buckingham's attitude toward divine providence may be as ambiguous as Richard's by the end of 1.3; it may be consistently skeptical until his final soliloquy if the hair on end is Hastings's. The dialectic itself, within characters like Richard, Elizabeth, and Buckingham and between such adversaries as Richmond or Elizabeth versus Richard, can also be altered by various cuts of this textual cloth. Clarence's argument to the Murderers would be much more persuasive with the distinctly biblical "wilts" and "shalts" of the Quarto, and also with its more explicitly theological reference to their hope of "redemption / By Christs deare bloud...." On the other hand, the Quarto-influenced texts, like the Quarto itself, tend to blur the sharp Folio distinctions between the first Murderer and the second Murderer. Such distinctions were crucial to Rossiter and Prior in their attempts to establish the dialectic strategy of the play.[45] As these last two examples illustrate, the issues of providence are not consistently "debated" by the opposed Quarto and Folio readings, but there are clusters of readings more in alliance with one side or the other.

Such an array of textual variants at moments of interpretive disagreement raises some important questions for textual and historical scholars, interpreters in the study and the classroom, actors and directors, indeed any serious readers of Shakespeare. Can the editors of a text of *Richard* III completely avoid interpretive biases as they select the best text? Should they? Has such objectivity ever been practiced in the textual or the theatrical traditions? Should directors or interpreters, on the other hand, use their knowledge of this smorgasbord of choices and set their own table? Olivier certainly did. Should readers abstain from readings that might help their cause, knowing as they do that in fact they have no prior literary or theatrical text without some interpretive bias? We have seen how radically an altered theatrical text may have changed representations and understandings of Shakespeare's *Richard* III. A similar manipulation of the most important of these textual variants could have a similar though subtler impact on the "literary" text, which is increasingly today's theatrical text as well. The burden of fairness rests on each editor, interpreter, and director of the play. The burden of basic textual sophistication is the more general responsibility of every serious reader. From a literary, a scholarly, or a theatrical standpoint, the text of *Richard* III is a feast of languages; its digestion is another matter entirely.

Epilogue

And for all this,
Richard is never spent

✝ As we have seen, a conflict between aesthetic and moral responses has often marked the theatrical and the interpretive traditions of *Richard* III. To an extraordinary degree, Bill Alexander's 1984–85 Royal Shakespeare Company production makes the intensely charismatic Richard played by Antony Sher consonant with the strong religious overtones of a morality play. The resultant production is as theatrically powerful as Olivier's, but without the corresponding loss of significance. Crucially, it is also Shakespeare's *Richard* III, not Cibber's. Though Sher's Richard has his impressive day, he is matched throughout by well-played male and female adversaries, an imposing, pervasive Gothic set, and the "pageant-like, religious and morally straightforward" tones of Alexander's "clear and forthright" production.[1] When Richard's day ends, he is dispatched with a clean, quick act of ritual sacrifice. As much as Sher's Richard has captivated us with his physical drive, his imaginative fire, his intense intellect, and his ingratiating wit, we are as relieved as Richmond at his surcease. In fact, this Richard is himself not loath to die; he has supped too full of horrors for us, or for him, to regret this preordained and prophesied end.

Antony Sher will almost certainly be remembered as the most impressive Richard since Olivier. The reviews are nearly unanimous in their praise of his "amazing, outstanding, bravura" performance. Jack Tinker writes that Sher's performance has "scorched its mark in the annals of Stratford like a thunderbolt." He is the "master of the role, the stage, . . . an era."[2] Michael Ratcliffe celebrates his "sheer joy of acting," "eyes shining, curly head alert."[3] Michael Billington calls him a "vigorous, compelling, totally deformed and yet astonishingly mobile Richard."[4] Anthony Masters focuses on the shocking athleticism of Sher's opening soliloquy. Until "But I," the crutches support him in a languishing posture"; then, he "hurtles manically" toward us.[5] To Ratcliffe, "The speed with which . . . Sher rises on crutches and reaches the front of the stage, apparently on six legs . . . has the audience drawing back in alarm."[6] This stunning opening gambit sets a standard for excitement, for "relentless theatricality,"[7] that the rest of the production consistently maintains.

Besides using the crutches to spring across the stage, how else does Sher use these sinister extensions of his deformity and his energy? They are effective weapons against the guard of Henry's corpse. They punctuate obscene innuendo, as when they grind together on the line "Naught to do with Mistress Shore?" They find their seductive way between Lady Anne's legs, and crash with intimidating power on the table as Sher pronounces Hastings's sentence of death. Two mandibles, they saw back and forth on Hastings's doomed neck. They bully Margaret, "frighten recalcitrant children,"[8] and direct the "York, York" chant against Margaret. Smashed together, they express violent anger at little York's insults; crossed before Sher, they become a protective crucifix against sinister opponents. Naseem Kahn suggests that the crutches embody and symbolize the "anarchic energy that takes him to the crown."[9] Abandoning those crutches deprives him of much of that energy after the coronation. To Michael Coveney, after the crutches are abandoned, so are "all those outward signs of rash authority, sexual goading, and tolerated eccentricity" that led him to power.[10]

Another dimension of the mobility of Sher's Richard is his "illusion of metamorphosis." Tinker refers to Sher's "almost supernatural . . . ability to shed [his] skin at will."[11] The crutches contribute to this illusionist's repertoire. He uses them to accentuate his deformity and to overcome it, whatever serves his turn. At times he is acrobatic, at times grotesquely feeble. So consummate is Sher's metamorphosis that we hardly notice the contradictions. He is also completely convincing in all the roles he has to play, even though we know that he is playing, and loving it. Weeping lover to Anne, devoted brother to Clarence and Edward, pious convert, intimidating political manipulator, master ironist, reluctant maid to Buckingham's suit, exultant king at the coronation, then a "cornered, sweating rat"[12] after the visit of the ghosts. Perhaps best is his role of innocent. So convincing is Sher in this frequent posture that Masters wonders if there is not another Richard lurking beneath the cynical facade: "Such is Mr. Sher's sensitivity that all Richard's innocent roles in fact, give [us] a tragic glimpse

Antony Sher as Richard, from the 1984–85 RSC production. Courtesy of the Royal Shakespeare Theatre, Stratford-upon-Avon.

of the person he might have been instead of a... perverted genius, desperate and ultimately damned." As Tinker says of all this incredibly quick and convincing pantomime: "Seldom have I seen an actor switch mood with such speed."[13]

Coveney nicely captures the energy of Sher's bravura style during the first scene with Margaret:

> He proceeds with a series of slithering genuflections—the knees swivel to the left and buckle under him to the ground—furtive images and cackling commands interspersed with dangerously pious intonations. His speed is genuine and frightening and for once you really believe the court is half mesmerized and half indulgently suspicious of this extroverted cripple with the bizarre manners of a capering beetle. Stunned momentarily by Queen Margaret's... curses, he springs onto a pew and settles, stock still, like a frog on a stone, idly flicking his tongue around his cheeks. The crutches then levitate like magnetic antennae to remove the old crone's crown.

That serpent's tongue, as Stanley Wells describes it, is as ubiquitous as the crutches.[14] Excitedly moving behind his lower lip as he plans his next move, it darts out whenever he is threatened or on attack.

Appropriately provoking more mixed reviews was the comic side of Sher's extraordinary portrayal of Richard. Francis King calls Richard's role one of Shakespeare's "finest comic creations," and notices how Sher evokes "titter after titter" throughout the play. His saying "the most outrageous things in the most matter-of-fact of tones and so making them doubly funny and offensive" is one cause of this effect.[15] Tinker agrees that his "matter-of-fact delivery makes his most monstrous remarks breathtakingly funny." With his extrapolated "hmms?" ending such lines as "Was ever woman in such humour won?"—"Hmmmm?"—he even challenges the audience to extra laughter.[16] His "Yummm" after the famous strawberry line is another example of this playing for laughs. Sher's antic mobility also contributes to this comic effect. J. C. Trewin is less than captivated by all the dexterity and humor, though he calls Sher's acrobatic and comic turn a "relishingly macabre experiment."[17] Two other reviewers illustrate the excitement and the liability of Sher's experiment. To Ratcliffe, he's "a daddy-long-legs on speed." To Peter McGarry, "He's wicked but he's fun."[18]

Billington identifies the risks involved in such a comic Richard as Sher's, carried too far, too long. Richard delivers the line "Men shall deal unadvisedly sometimes," broad and joking, to get a laugh "after having murdered half his relatives." Billington responds, "For my money Mr. Sher keeps up his sardonic mask almost too long, so that the final scenes lose tragic weight."[19] An excellent illustration of the problem occurs after the intermission. "I wish the bastards dead" is sinister enough in its delivery, and one can hardly imagine its evoking a laugh. Yet that was precisely the response of almost half the audience both nights I saw the production. Giles Gordon blamed the giggling, which carried even into act 5, on "less seasoned theatregoers," "mostly American tourists and schoolgirls."[20] As one of those American tourists surrounded both nights by attentive schoolboys and schoolgirls, and a variety of other sorts who responded similarly, I think the "wrong" response could have been avoided by playing down the comedy by the end of act 2, and by making Richard more sinister than silly thereafter. It might have served Alexander's straightforward moral and religious vision better to begin to wean us half an act earlier from Sher's ravishing villainy. As Billington says, "It is still a superb Richard, both fleet and demonic."[21] I think it would have been even more superb, the Richard and the production, had the playing for laughs been curtailed before the death of Hastings. One could even argue that such control is a vital theatrical point of the last half of act 3.

Of course, there is ample theatrical precedent for a farcical interpretation of 3.5–7, the sequence with the Mayor and the Citizens. In such a coherent and thoughtful production as Alexander's, however, it comes as something of a shock to witness here the evening's culminating comic moment. At the beginning of 3.5, Hastings's hideous head is tossed around the stage like a rugby ball. At the end, seduced by this death's head, Richard almost kisses it, or licks its blood. But then he looks up at us, smiles, and implies that it is all theatrical make-believe. That is not a bad way to set up the farcical scenes to follow, but it makes it difficult for the audience to take the vampire seriously.[22] The Scrivener's moral address can also have little impact, no matter how well it is done, in this farcical world. Near the end of 3.7 Buckingham so overplays his peroration that "More bitterly could I expostulate" draws an inevitable laugh. Then the scene degenerates into total farce. The Mayor, the two Aldermen, Buckingham all crawl about the stage in slithering pursuit of a Richard now playing the maid's part as a reluctant lizard. Richard pipes later, in the highest comic pitch, "Call them again." It is hilarious business, all of it, and the audience loves it. It also evades the possible complexity of the scenes. None of these characters, none of these actions, can possibly be taken seriously here. The scenes can therefore have little psychological or political or moral validity.

Undertones of the rotten charade still surface, despite this generally farcical interpretation. In 3.5, when the head is passed all around, the Mayor does not faint, but he is clearly horrified, unlike Richard and his cronies. Intimidation increases when Richard and Buckingham begin to crowd the Mayor several times near his exit. Once they grab his hands until he winces, then abruptly separate, a pointed reminder of Hastings's severed head. At the start of 3.7, we listen with a despondant Richard to all the details of Buckingham's failure with the people of London, and we sense how devastating these details can be to Richard's aura of invincibility. However, farce again intervenes too quickly for this effect to become established. Buckingham laughs; it has all been a little joke at Richard's expense, nothing more serious. Unamused, Richard raises his crutch to strike Buckingham, only to have it wrested away by a quicker, stronger opponent. But Richard does realize that success, not failure, is the thrust of Buckingham's sadistic little message. Such a reading, however clever, eliminates the possibility that this sequence dramatizes an initial tearing of their intricate web.

As 3.7 continues, we see Richard's false but convincing piety aloft through the Gothic tracery. Actually, several in the audience mock it with laughter, but all know that it is convincing on stage, as a charade. Buckingham crowds the Mayor again, who backs off, frightened and clearly out of his depth. More than once, the audience is addressed directly as the Citizens, each time to Richard's disadvantage. With "To move your Grace" all five of the supplicants look directly at us for affirmation. Without a recorder, we, like the Citizens in Holinshed and Hall, say nothing. We sit as still as stones, except that some in our number inevitably laugh as we did at the hypocritical piety earlier. Their silent wait onstage is long and embarrassing. It appropriately deflates Richard and undermines the whole charade. When Richard later raises the prayerbook and the crucifix, some audience-citizens also greet these gestures with scornful laughter, thus rejecting another cynical detail of their charade.

But there is too little of this, however much it points up the possibility of playing the scene to Richard's disadvantage. Generally farce predominates in this sequence over seriousness, and success over failure. As co-conspirators, the audience may become cynics too. We are amazed at the gullible Mayor and Aldermen, not ourselves gullible. We amorally approve of Richard's theatrical effectiveness, even in this morally coherent production. One can see why farce is so often the theatrical recourse here. It plays very well, and it absolves Richard of his first serious failure, or even a muted success. But in a production that is seriously dedicated to the overriding power of providence and Richard's inevitable decline, a good chance to begin that decline is missed. Other recent productions have done more with the possible ambiguities of these scenes.[23]

The attempted seduction of Elizabeth is handled with more integrity. Throughout, Frances Tomelty plays Elizabeth as a tough, smart, skeptical, worldly woman. From her first appearance in 1.3, she has consistently scoffed at the references to God and providence. When Margaret and the Duchess of York kneel to pray at the beginning of 4.4, it is therefore completely consistent that Elizabeth be pointedly apart from them—slouched irreverently on a stone pew above both their prayers and their curses. She once laughs out loud at Margaret's gloating recitation of her curses; she will not credit their efficacy, or their inevitability.

Sher's Richard is physically brutal with Elizabeth from the start. Twice he forces her to face him, first by roughly turning her cheek with his scepter, then by seizing the bodice of her gown and spinning her around. Once he throws her to the ground. But she is not without her own weapons against this intimidation. She has those withering words of irony of course, and this production gives them fair play. She also has a venomous kiss for Richard at the end, from which he recoils as from an adder's sting. Just earlier, his mother had sealed her curses with a similar kiss, from which he similarly recoiled. He spits, in fact, her cursing kiss away.

Masters suggests that Elizabeth finally yields, despite her obvious discomfiture, to his "grossly sexual approach." King describes her yielding at the end of the scene as that of a "harsh, imperious Elizabeth, at once fascinated and disgusted by the cacodemon who fumbles with her while demanding her daughter's hand."[24] Tomelty's Elizabeth can also be seen as so eager for power and position that she puts up with this repulsive snake for her own motives. Alexander essentially confirmed this perception when we discussed the scene: "She is a bourgeois, a *parvenu* opportunist and no saint either. She is dressed in the clothes of outraged morality, but she is basically as corrupt as the rest of the members of the court." Both nights I saw an Elizabeth more horrified than fascinated by Sher's clumsy sexuality. For once her lips moved in silent prayers and exorcisms, something we had not seen them do since that first startling appearance of Margaret forced prayers even out of Richard's profane mouth. Richard is so hideous that he has almost driven this strong, skeptical woman to prayer, or collapse. Though Richard acknowledges neither perception, he is all warts and scales; she is all revulsion. Throughout Alexander's production the women were all impressively played. Here the strongest and smartest of them becomes a potent adversary for Sher's Richard, and spells the beginning of his end in this deceptive, Pyrrhic victory. Because her changing is on the

Antony Sher with Frances Tomelty as Queen Elizabeth, from the 1984–85 RSC production. Courtesy of the Royal Shakespeare Theatre, Stratford-upon-Avon.

surface only, it is Richard who comes off shallow here. He has fared just as badly in other recent productions.[25]

Though it begins a bit late for my taste, Richard's decline is impressively handled, its continuity with the rest of the production thoroughly convincing. Coveney notices that "Richard's life seeps away, together with his alacrity of mind, long before the emblematic staging of the Bosworth Field shadows." Kahn points to one effective signal of this decline: "Interestingly, once king, he more or less abandons his crutches" for a sceptre, and therefore forfeits much of the "anarchic energy that takes him to the crown."[26] This loss of energy and mobility is most vivid when Richard must confront Elizabeth and his mother in 4.4. Now carried about on the throne by four bearers, Richard can only move by commanding them with two sharp raps of the scepter. Such unwieldy power is no match for the quick, stichomythic thrusts of these two embittered ladies. Sher's Richard tries again and again to turn and face them, but before the scepter has commanded and the servants responded, he is facing the wrong woman. Only the noise of drums and trumpets can drown out their penetrating word-thrusts. We sense last things in this brilliant moment, and the inscrutable hand of providence. Seldom has stichomythia been more effectively staged.

Even in the splendid coronation pageant that precedes the intermission, "the ghosts are already arriving with the trumpeters to herald the decline even at the apex." Their prophetic and apocalyptic shadows ironically darken Richard's bright, loud celebration. The coronation itself, though grand, is also "so monstrous that the flesh creeps, a fitting climax to the passage before and a foundation for the open savagery to come."[27] We may be fascinated with the hideous hump that finally becomes flesh when the scarlet and ermine robe falls from kneeling Richard's shoulders. We may be gripped by Sher's grotesque slithering, alone, into the seat of power. We are also repulsed. Then, after the interval, we see the "drained and moving figure"[28] of Penny Downie's fine Lady Anne, Ophelia-like, distracted if not mad, cowering next to Richard while he plots her death. Mumbling silent prayers and counting her rosary, she asserts the rising "theme of guilt, . . . which sounds through the play like a leit-motif."[29] Richard is not oblivious to its ominous music.

Coveney suggests that we are most alienated from Sher's Richard "when fear of defeat tears away his outer shell." Alexander glosses this experience similarly when he says that "the ballast of Richard's heroism is removed by his inner doubt." Ratcliffe describes the resultant Richard: "Terrified by his nightmare before Bosworth that after all there may be a

God above, his face seems to shrink and the spider is briefly transformed into a cornered, sweating rat." Gordon similarly refers to him as a "Kafkaesque bug, eyes glittering like search lights, but static, dead."[30] Even before the ghosts condemn him to despair and death, we hear Sher's Richard try (and fail) to make "But where tomorrow?" a gag line. Reverence replacing irreverence is a repeated motif of the production; here it sounds in Richard's soliloquy and his failure of wit and will. The soliloquy is played with real fear, real tears after all those false ones. Wells rightly calls its "grim self-knowledge" "a strength of his performance and of Alexander's production."[31] In response, we feel some pity; we feel more justice. How much can we pity a sweating rat, an adder who has stung himself? Sher's Richard tries to play "A black day" as another gag; again he fails to carry it off. The ditty about "Jockey of Norfolk" has the same effect. Failing to play invulnerability to such "toyes" as these, Richard creeps guilty and fetal into the womblike throne.

The finest touch of decline is Sher's rendition of the battle oration. It is marked not by confidence but by uncertainty, a loss of alacrity and cheer. Long, embarrassing pauses precede and follow a pathetic "What shall I say?" His voice breaks on "Runagates" and again on "paltry fellow." By "distains" it has risen to a clearly false bombast. Wells calls the speech "at first hesitant, then rhetorically hectoring."[32] The faltering heart yields faulty inspiration. The words just will not come. When Richard tries to disguise his growing fear of Richmond, death, and damnation, he overacts. "Let's whip . . . themselves" is unconvincing bravado, not bravery, certainly not effective rhetoric. Only at the very end of the oration does Sher's Richard find the right words and the right delivery. By then it is too late to fool anyone. Norfolk and the others try to menace us in the audience with threatening, intimidating stares, which makes them all the more unattractive. So does the now bankrupt chant "York, York, York." It has been used to intimidate throughout; now it merely disgusts.[33]

Christopher Ravenscroft's Richmond presents an interesting contrast to this Richard. Alexander wanted to embody in Richmond a decent, intentionally underplayed heroism which "replaces the charismatic but corrupt power-maniac Richard." As a result, Ravenscroft's Richmond is attractive from the first, but never really charismatic, never even very "theatrical."[34] Witness the crew cut in contrast to Sher's flamboyant curls. Ravenscroft is humane, thoughtful, reaching out with love and respect to his men. Their smiles and embraces, though a trifle awkward, are always sincere. In contrast to Richard's thought-police, Richmond's attractive followers look attentively at Richmond during his composed but inspiring oration; they never try to intimidate the audience. Like Richmond they are also somber, serious, neither falsely heroic nor callous and brutal. There is lots of energy in Richard's camp; there is no such attractiveness, love, or respect. In fact, Tyrrel and the two Murderers compose almost half his band.

When Richmond prays, we see an example of his scrupulous conscience and his true piety. First he raises his sword up to God; then he realizes the incongruity of this proffered violence, lays it down, folds his hands, and devoutly crosses himself. Neither God's minister nor God's providence will be "repulsive" in this production. Richmond's oration is animated and confident, even rousing at times. But he and his men are never unaware of the grave task at hand, or the sorry state of England under Richard. The execution of Richard is similarly done, somberly, ritually, balletically as Hammond has suggested, with more reluctance than joy.[35] Ravenscroft portrays a man immediately overcome with the horror of killing another man, however horrible that man. He is also burdened immediately by the enormity of the job to come. The bright back-lighting of the kneeling Richard and Richmond's ritualistic act all accentuate the hand of providence in Richard's death. I like the concept very much; it eliminates a lot of the interpretive problems concerning the force of providence and the thrust of the final act. However, I find it difficult to respond to on stage.[36] A more manly, more relaxed, somewhat more charismatic and less somber Richmond might have made a similar point with more theatrical appeal.[37] But no one can call Ravenscroft's Richmond, or Alexander's conception of the character, "vacuous." If anything, it is almost too thoughtful, almost too still.

Actually, the idea of pious stillness is established early in the production as an effective contrast to Richard's deceptive and destructive energy. We see it first when Clarence tells his apocalyptic dream. Roger Allam's still profundity and honesty are in stark contrast to the deceptive mobility and charisma we have just enjoyed in Richard. At their discoveries and deaths Grey, Vaughan, Hastings, and Buckingham are similarly still and truthful. So is Queen Elizabeth, before the old bricks, contemplating first the vulnerability, then the deaths of her two sons. The solitary Scrivener is spotlighted stage-center while he tells his "round unvarnished tale" of Richard's cunning and the fear and cynicism of the Mayor and the Citizens. Even Richard is stone still during his soliloquy of self-discovery. By the time we see Richmond kneeling in prayer before and after the battle, we have thus been conditioned to equate that stillness with truth. With all his kneeling followers at play's end, we respond quietly, thoughtfully, to the

Richmond's avenging sword, from the 1984–85 RSC production. Courtesy of the Royal Shakespeare Theatre, Stratford-upon-Avon.

present victory and the awesome task to come. A quivering, pianissimo Gloria sounds "Amen." Richard's coronation was all noise and brilliant color and movement. It was accompanied by another Gloria, fortissimo but false. Richmond's prayer, God's providence, and our "amen" sound soft but true against this noisy, intimidating bustle.

As these details of Richard's decline already suggest, Alexander's control of this "full-blooded classic" was rightly called "immaculate."[38] The production has a "relentless theatricality"[39] about it, to be sure. Tinker is representative in calling it "extraordinary, exciting, and tumultuously successful."[40] That success obviously embraces Sher's extraordinary Richard. It just as obviously subsumes that Richard into the larger political, moral, and religious significance of Shakespeare's action. Billington represents the general response when he praises it as a "fundamentalist production ... that sees the play squarely in terms of sin and redemption, good and evil." Trewin calls it "clear and forthright" in this respect, Billington "pageant-like, religious, and morally straightforward."[41] Alexander uses Antony Hammond's commentary in the program notes, and acknowledges the striking consonance of Hammond's vision of providential ritual and his own vision of the play. The resultant production shows how effectively the ritualistic, providential, apocalyptic overtones of Shakespeare's *Richard* III can be translated to the stage.

This straightforward moral and religious vision is given particular emphasis by William Dudley's impressive set of "red brick and limestone perpendicular walls."[42] Coveney calls this set "entirely appropriate" to the play's vision, an "imposing design of plasterwork and arches, screens and wooden panelling, with heraldic shields and four huge tombs.... Throughout the play we are in an evocative medieval world with scenic hints of York Minster and the Westminster Council Chamber."[43] Our first and lasting visual impression is of these "decorated ecclesiastical buildings, with fine window tracery and mullions."[44] The audience settles down before the play even begins with an enormous perpendicular screen before them, intriguing the attentive with its "Knights, ladies, praying in dumb orat'ries," not to mention its "twilight saints, and dim emblazonings."[45] With the Tudor rose and the griffins, we could be sitting in the chapel at King's College, Cambridge.

Gordon calls the set "monumental," a visual metaphor for the "hallowed ground" Richard will soon begin to bustle in, and desecrate. The four massive tombs are particularly effective as backdrops for the mourning queens, for the prophecies of Margaret, and for her many dying enemies. They subtly frame Clarence's apocalyptic dream, his theological debate with the Murderers, and his death. They accompany the execution of Rivers, Grey, and Hastings, Buckingham's fine valedictory, and Richard's dream and the shattered soliloquy that follows it. The tombs, like the sanctuary in which they would normally be set, constantly represent the force of providence. This symbolism is most potent when the prophesying ghosts seem to emerge from these graves between the tents at Bosworth Field. At the end, Richard and then Richmond move between them, eerily lit by a providential beam, to their appointed destinies. Along with Guy Woolfenden's impressive religious music, these tombs and the perpendicular sidewalls work together from the start of the play to counterbalance Sher's enormously compelling Richard. By the final scene, these "stupendous" Gothic trappings lend a relentless inevitability to Richard's despair and death.[46]

Other details of the production also emphasize the ritual nature of the action and make attractive the force of providence that lies behind so much of it. Kneeling is a good example. At first, it occurs to Richard's advantage. He subdues Anne while both are on their knees, charms Clarence's children from a similar posture, and leads the Mayor and Aldermen on that merry and ultimately successful chase in 3.7. But by 4.4, the scene with Queen Elizabeth, his kneeling has begun to signify his vulnerability and his ultimate destiny. The Duchess of York controls Richard morally and physically in front of the throne by pulling him to his knees. After he dreams of the ghosts, he falls to his knees during his soliloquy and after it as well, with Ratcliffe. Fear of the despair and death the ghosts prophesied, like his mother's bitter curse and her strong old arm, drive him into this posture of humility and reverence. Finally, Sher's Richard dies kneeling, having crawled to the front of the stage at the end of the battle. As he kneels for this one last time, he may even try to pray. Antony Sher said that he considered this Richard's most disgusting moment, so inconsistent, so cowardly at the end.[47] His Richard yearns for death. It looms behind him in the majestic but impersonal figure of the completely armed and vizarded Richmond, bearing his sword of righteousness.

Alexander has also directed a procession of perfunctory, hypocritical, and sincere crossings. At the beginning, characters often cross themselves, hurried and insincere. As the play goes on, a transition from perfunctory to sincere crossing marks the dawning on various characters of the providential dimensions of their common experience. This change becomes a powerful emblem of the rising acknowledgment of the force of providence in the play. No one is more impressive in this light than the

Falstaffian Hastings of Brian Blessed. At court with Richard he is untroubled by Margaret's curses. At home just before his death, he snorts and cavorts about the stage, flamboyantly splashing himself with cold water, dressing, flirting with his two women, clowning with his friends (and enemies), all with delicious naiveté about God and man. His slow, solemn crossing after the reversal of all that fleshly exuberance and worldly skepticism sets the tone for the other conversions in the play. The parallel experience of Malcolm Storry's inscrutable Buckingham is equally impressive.

Crossings are particularly important in the scene of Clarence's murder. First, Alexander's text and his production both maintain the Folio's distinction between the two Murderers, and it is effective on stage. The first Murderer crosses himself again and again, and he is clearly devout in it. The second Murderer is ugly and cynical throughout, a nonbeliever comfortable in Richard's political world. Clarence holds a large crucifix before him through most of the debate with the Murderers. After Clarence is stabbed and drowned in the butt of wine, the first Murderer takes up the crucifix and places it tenderly on Clarence's pillow. In the context of the theological debate that runs through the scene, this suggestive business helps set the religious tone of the production.

The ghosts are also effective representatives of the force of providence and the pervasiveness of last things. Each holds a single candle. Smoke swirls around their feet. Most appear from behind the tombs that loom increasingly large as the play goes on. Some, of course, have been buried there since Tewkesbury. Each prophesies with the stillness of truth; each remains on stage as the others appear. Occasionally all echo key words of prayer and prophecy, like participants in a supernatural ritual. Though I thought the 1982 BBC television version of the ghosts more exciting, more imaginatively blocked out, this sequence worked well within Alexander's concept of understated truthfulness.

It is finally its rich blend of the force of providence and the magnetism of Sher's Richard that marks the rich integrity of Alexander's production. By giving fair play to the women, the prophecies, the dying acknowledgments of God's just hand, the ghosts, and Richmond's noble if restrained ministry, the production presents a ravishing, often comic Richard without sacrificing the significance of the whole. The Gothic tracery, the looming tombs, the haunting Glorias, the carefully orchestrated decline and discovery of Richard and those around him, the halting oration and the ritual death justly end an action that began eighty years earlier, with another Richard at Pomfret. Those stones are here too, held together by the mortar of history and cut and placed by the hand of providence.

Though I might want to move an inch of air here, a blade of grass there, Alexander's production is so theatrically exciting and so often consonant with my own vision of *Richard* III that I never expect to see its equal. Were I to inject a more serious sequence with the Mayor and the Citizens, a more rousing Richmond, a richer ghost sequence, I would surely break something far more exquisite than the minor annoyances I was trying to fix. No production "proves" an interpretive position, of course. This one certainly shows something about interpretive possibility. The Tillyard-Hammond conception of the play's intricate balancing of a brilliant theatrical role and an overriding scheme of providential ritual not only makes sense; it also plays very well. Equally important, its theatricality establishes beyond doubt the viability of Shakespeare's own *Richard* III as a stunning theatrical occasion. Aficionado and moralist alike will applaud the theatricality and the significance of the Alexander production. Like the Olivier film with which we began this book, I suspect that Bill Alexander's *Richard* III will become the touchstone against which future productions of the play are judged, at least into the next century. It is that good.

Notes

Introduction

1. William Shakespeare, *The Tragedy of Richard the Third*, in *Mr. William Shakespeares Comedies, Histories, & Tragedies*. Throughout, quotations from *Richard III* will always follow this first Folio, or passages that are only available in the first Quarto of 1597 (marked with a +). All the old-spelling quotations will silently modernize long s, i for j, j for i, u for v, and v for u. Through line numbering (hereafter TLN), editor Charlton Hinman's numbering system described on p. xxiv of *The Norton Facsimile of The First Folio of Shakespeare* (New York: Norton and Co., 1968), and used throughout that edition, will be used for all references to *Richard III*. In the parentheses the TLN's are followed by act, scene, and line references. These refer throughout to *The Riverside Shakespeare*, ed. G. Blakemore Evans, as do all the other references to Shakespeare's works. Kristian Smidt's parallel text edition of *The Tragedy of King Richard the Third* is an accurate and useful edition of the Folio and Quarto texts. See Julie Hankey, ed., *Richard III*, pp. 33-40, 47-50. The editors of one of Kean's acting copies (London, John Cumberland, n.d.), sig. A3-A5, note his unusual "energy and heroism," his "art and cunning," his "elegant and insinuating manner." They were eyewitnesses to his unusually attractive portrayal.

2. Hammond, ed., *King Richard III*, p. 71; Roy Walker, "Bottled Spider," pp. 58, 66-68; Jorgens, *Shakespeare on Film*, p. 147; Schein, "A Magnificent Fiasco?" p. 407; Phillips, "Some Glories and Some Discontents," pp. 399-400. See also Griffin, "Shakespeare Through the Camera's Eye," p. 434; and Graham, "Cinema," p. 841.

3. Roy Walker, "Bottled Spider," p. 59; Speaight, "The Old Vic and Stratford-upon-Avon, 1960-61" p. 434; Hammond, ed., *King Richard III*, pp. 71-72; Berry, "Stratford Festival Canada," p. 223.

4. Brooke, "Reflecting Gems and Dead Bones," p. 123.

5. Wells, "Television Shakespeare," pp. 261-73.

6. Berry, "Stratford Festival Canada," p. 223; see also Speaight, "The Old Vic

and Stratford-upon-Avon, 1961–62," p. 434; Kilfoil, "Current Theater Notes, 1960–61," p. 112.

7. See chapter 1, notes 15, 21, 25, 33.

8. In light of what has recently been called a "crisis of confidence" in Shakespeare studies, I have tried throughout *Songs of Death* to remain open to the range of possible meanings in *Richard III* while I argue my own interpretive perspectives, and thus to present my case forcefully but also fairly. Though I agree that reading and performing a text are always accompanied by certain interpretive conditions, I am disinclined to accept the most radical "indeterminacy" which asserts that a text has no inherent meaning. And though I acknowledge with the "new historicists" the complexity of cultural context and the difficulty of applying it to interpretation, I remain convinced that there are "continuities" of belief and assumption in every age that we can use with care in our "readings" of that age's artifacts. I am less comfortable with the general though not universal assumption of both "schools" of the inevitable "clash between moral and dramatic values and virtues," and with their general aesthetic preference for turbulence over order and for the relative over the absolute. In fact, I would suggest that such preferences are as culturally conditioned as the more conservative world-views they often question, and not as characteristic of a period like the Renaissance as they imply.

Using a variety of Renaissance documents, including Hamlet's advice to the players, R. M. Frye has persuasively argued that the "form and pressure of the time" can be profitably reconstructed, and that most Renaissance writers and readers still assumed that there was truth as well as beauty, instruction, and delight, in their literature. I suspect that most twentieth-century readers still share that assumption, refined as it must be within the crucible of time. Provocative discussions and illustrations of "indeterminacy" in Shakespeare criticism include Levin, *New Readings of Old Plays*; Rabkin, *Shakespeare and the Problem of Meaning*; Hawkins, *Poetic Freedom and Poetic Truth* and *The Devil's Party*; Adelman, *The Common Liar*; and Frye, *The Renaissance Hamlet*, esp. pp. 3–10 and 281–92. Three varied examples of "new historicism" are Dollimore, *Radical Tragedy*; Greenblatt, *Renaissance Self-Fashioning*; and Goldberg, *James I and the Politics of Literature*. Shakespeareans will have to rethink some of their most basic assumptions as a result of these works.

Chapter 1

1. Hankey, ed., *Richard III*, p. 60. Rabkin, *Shakespeare and the Problem of Meaning*, has suggested that looking closely at performances, as I propose to do in this chapter and again in the epilogue, can enhance our discussion of "the process of our involvement" in interpretive issues. Levin, *New Readings of Old Plays*, adds that a careful study of stage productions helps us pay attention to "the literal sequential structure in all its particularity" (pp. 161–66, 201). Rabkin similarly suggests that Marvin "Rosenberg's historical criticism, based on the history of performance, demands that we build into our understanding of the greatest tragedies the full range of interpretation that they have provoked" (pp. 26–27). An awareness of production history does increase a reader's sense of the possibilities inherent in a

dramatic sequence; I submit that it also allows the reader to speculate about what "works," and what does not.

2. The Olivier *Richard III* film was directed by Laurence Olivier, and produced in Shepperton Studios, London. Its copyright date was 1955, but its U.S. release date was 1956. It is currently distributed by Films, Inc. Graham, "Cinema," p. 841; C. B. Young, "The Stage History of *Richard III*," in CAM3, pp. xlix–l; Hankey, ed., *Richard III*, pp. 27–54; Hammond, ed., *King Richard III*, p. 68; Jorgens, *Shakespeare on Film*, pp. 142–44; Trewin, "Show Pieces," p. 994.

3. Jorgens, *Shakespeare on Film*, pp. 142–44; Thorpe, "Shakespeare and the Movies," p. 364; Schein, p. 414; Brown, "Olivier's *Richard III*," p. 31; Speaight, "Shakespeare in Britain" (1977), p. 185.

4. Bryant, "Our Notebook," p. 290; Phillips, "Some Glories and Some Discontents," p. 406.

5. Young, "The Stage History of *Richard III*," in CAM3, pp. li, lv.

6. Pettigrew, "Stratford, 1967," p. 516; Pryce-Jones, "Little Richard," p. 262; Speaight, "Shakespeare in Britain" (1963), p. 430; Berry, "Stratford Festival Canada," p. 224; Marder, "No Royal Kings," p. 33; Elsom, "Theatre Love," p. 597; Hankey, ed., *Richard III*, p. 69.

7. Edinborough, "Stratford, Ontario—1967," p. 401; Byrne, "The Shakespeare Season . . . 1957," p. 479.

8. Hankey, ed., *Richard III*, p. 45.

9. *Richard the Third* (1889), p. 8; Hankey, ed., *Richard III*, p. 62; see also W. Winter, cited in Furness, ed., *New Variorum*, pp. 602–3, and C. Alex Pinkston, Jr., "Richard Mansfield's Production of *Richard the Third*," *Theatre History Studies* 3 (1983): 3–28.

10. The British Broadcasting Company's videotape of *The Tragedy of Richard III*, directed by Jane Howell in 1982, is distributed by Time-Life Videos. Jorgens, *Shakespeare on Film*, p. 142, and Griffin, "Shakespeare Through the Camera's Eye," pp. 236–37, argue Olivier's suggestions of a richer psychological texture.

11. The seduction of Anne has often worked on stage. Kean was apparently so convincing that he seduced the audience as well as Anne. Shock greeted his subsequent soliloquy (Nicholas Brooke, "Reflecting Gems and Dead Bones," p. 128). In another success at Ontario, both were "expert duellists with words," but Anne was finally "overwhelmed by the sheer power of Richard's will" (Pettigrew, "Stratford, 1967," p. 514). In New York in the late 1950s, "Richard's very strength and cunning attracted the young woman" (Griffin, "The Shakespeare Season in New York," p. 532). Finally, Martha Henry's Anne "was visibly stirred by this sexually ravenous creature" in Ontario in the late 1970s (Berry, "Stratford Festival Canada," pp. 222–26).

12. Several reviewers of the Olivier film have noticed its largely gratuitous "contribution to the impression that the church is hardly fulfilling its function as a moral force" in Richard's world. A good example is the Archbishop's saying the Mayor's cynical line about Mistress Shore and Hastings's guilt "just as he acquiesces in Hastings's execution" (Brown, "Olivier's *Richard III*," p. 30). Of the music, Jorgens, *Shakespeare on Film*, similarly says, "Throughout, the religious music serves as an

incongruous backdrop for treachery, treason, and murder" (p. 146). He adds that even the "helpless painted angels, recall, look on as Richard ensnares Hastings" (p. 146). To Jorgens, then, the supernatural forces of providence are emasculated along with the human representatives of the church in Olivier's film. I saw the angels rather as an ironic emblem of the Last Judgment, an emblem which would finally touch Richard as much as his victim. Is not the last impression of this fresco a death's head?

13. Dent, "Richard III: A Disclaimer," p. 30, quotes Olivier on cutting: "I've cut the wooing-of-Lady-Anne scene in two, in an attempt to make it more credible and possible."

14. Roy Walker likes Claire Bloom's portrayal as "a young woman hypnotized by the serpent that destroys her," but thinks her "surrender to Richard much less credible" because she is mourning her husband rather than her father-in-law ("Bottled Spider," pp. 63, 68). Phillips dislikes Olivier's scene. He finds a gradual breakdown in Shakespeare's Anne from hatred to vanity to fear of killing to puzzlement to conviction that Richard is repentant. To Olivier it is "sheer sexual appeal." "Only when sexual desire can be made acceptable to [Anne] in terms of a moral or religious rationalization [viz. repentance] does it become convincing" ("Some Glories and Some Discontents," p. 405).

15. Reviewers of Olivier's film are almost unanimous on this point. Griffin finds it an "artistic success," but faults it for sacrificing "the larger significance of the work." Margaret is the focus of her complaint: "He cuts out the character of the virago Queen Margaret, who runs like a thread through Shakespeare's text, reminding Richard, his fellow sinners, and the audience, that retribution will come. And in so doing, Olivier narrows his scope from the execution of divine justice on doers of evil to a chronicle of Richard and his pawns, and his theme from the fall of princes to the punishment of one man" ("Shakespeare Through the Camera's Eye," p. 235). Jorgens, *Shakespeare on Film*, p. 138, agrees that "cutting foreknowledge and Margaret's curses ... shifted the emphasis away from history and the working out of Divine Justice." (Nicholas Brooke, "Reflecting Gems and Dead Bones," p. 124) finds Margaret's curses, at least during the 1964 season at Stratford-upon-Avon, to be "in echo of liturgical forms, such as the ancient 'ubi sunt' theme to which Margaret proceeds." See also Phillips, "Some Glories and Some Discontents," pp. 401-2; Young, "The Stage History of *Richard III*," CAM3, p. xlix; and Roy Walker, "Bottled Spider," pp. 63-64. Brown, in contrast, has the curiously modern comment that eliminating Margaret eliminates "superstition" from the play, which a "modern [audience] can do without" ("Olivier's *Richard III*," p. 24). Olivier apparently agreed, if he considered it so deeply. According to Dent, "*Richard III*: A Disclaimer," he was merely eliminating "that old cursing Queen Margaret" (p. 30).

16. Byrne, "The Shakespeare Season," calls it "flying in the face of providence" to cut Margaret's lines completely or even significantly. She urges: "It is time we had a chance to gauge the effect in the theatre of this 'musically massed' stone wall of opposition to Richard" (p. 478). Recently successful Margarets illustrate how

much Olivier sacrificed by eliminating Margaret from this film. In Tony Church's *Richard* III at The Other Place, in Stratford-upon-Avon, 1975, Brenda Bruce's Margaret "was rightly interpreted as a chorus of moral indignation in a play which has much in common with a morality" (Speaight, "Shakespeare in Britain" [1977], p. 184). The Franklin and Marshall college "production stressed the curse of Margaret as the principal organizing device" (Griffin, "Current Theatre Notes," p. 80). Dame Peggy Ashcroft was "a great tragic creation" in Stratford-upon-Avon in 1963 (Speaight, "Shakespeare in Britain" [1963], p. 429).

17. Hankey, ed., *Richard* III, briefly discusses the theatrical tradition of the comic Mayor (pp. 179-80).

18. Nichols, "The Oregon Shakespeare Festival, 1967," p. 422; Crouch, "The Colorado Shakespeare Festival," p. 466; Thompson, "A Necessary Theatre," p. 120; Marder, "No Royal Kings," p. 33; Horobetz, "Shakespeare at the Old Globe—1970," p. 406.

19. See note 12, this chapter.

20. "Lift out scenes" was Olivier's recipe for cutting Shakespeare for production (Thorpe, "Shakespeare and the Movies," p. 362).

21. Nicholas Brooke, "Reflecting Gems and Dead Bones," p. 133; Hammond, ed., *King Richard* III, pp. 71 ff., and others notice this ritual pattern in the play and lament its absence in the Olivier film. Sprague, "Shakespeare on the New York Stage," p. 312, finds "regrettable" a similar cutting in the theater. Tyrone Guthrie's 1953 *Richard* III, on the other hand, apparently "intensified the ritualistic aspect" of the play in the first season of the Ontario festival. The "inexorable dramatic logic" of the conclusion, for example, was supported by a "stealthy circling of the Lady Anne and Richard around the bier," the "stylized cursings and frenzies of the four queens," and a "clustering of ghosts around Richard on the battle-eve" (Edinborough, "A New Stratford Festival," [1953], p. 49). Similarly potent was the "sense of structure and ritual" in the play Edinborough witnessed at the same festival fourteen years later ("Stratford, Ontario—1967," p. 401). Dorothy E. Nichols describes a similar effect in the *Richard* III in Oregon in the same year. There was the "formality of Gothic symbolism in the kneeling queens ... and the supernatural rising of the ghosts at Bosworth Field" ("The Oregon Shakespeare Festival, 1967," p. 423). A production in the Rockies four years earlier also gave us the queens "in all their contrapuntal strength, and a pattern, customarily obscured, emerged with great power" (Perkin, "Shakespeare in the Rockies, VI," p. 464). Finally, again in Stratford, Ontario, in 1978, "The Nemesis that awaited Richard was figured powerfully in the chorus of women, as formidable a set as I have seen. Margaret Tyzack's crazed Margaret was a fearsome creation" (Berry, "Stratford Festival Canada," p. 224). Hankey adds this comment: "Tyrrel's and Clarence's set-pieces, and even more the the lamentations of the women, ... would have fallen easily upon ears accustomed to the litany" (ed., *Richard* III, p. 17). "Myself alone," of course, is Richard's phrase from III *Henry* VI, 5.6.83.

22. *Richard* III, in *Five Restoration Adaptations of Shakespeare*, p. 329; *Shakespeare's King Richard the Third*, arr. Henry Irving, p. 78.

23. Horobetz, "Shakespeare at the Old Globe—1971," p. 406; Berry, "Stratford Festival Canada," p. 224; Sykes, "Richard III in Brisbane," pp. 364-65; Dukore, "Richard III," p. 323. See also Nichols, "The Oregon Shakespeare Festival, 1967," pp. 421-23.

24. Roy Walker, "Bottled Spider," justly complains that Olivier's Buckingham was too much "the slightly ruffled and bewildered clown" before his execution (p. 67).

25. Many reviewers complained about the truncated ghosts. By not appearing to Richmond, they cannot function as a "sign that divine providence is guiding him" (Griffin, "Shakespeare Through the Camera's Eye," p. 238); Roy Walker, "Bottled Spider," p. 64, also complains that the "film short-lists these apparitions." Nicholas Brooke, "Reflecting Gems and Dead Bones," notes the supernatural condemnation that Richard challenges: in the last act it is not only the living who oppose him, but the ghosts of his victims as well" (p. 130). Two West Coast productions within a decade of the Olivier film also deemphasized the ghosts by cutting their lines and numbers, deleting their words to Richmond, or making them into nightmares rather than apparitions (Hapgood, "West Coast Shakespeare, 1961," p. 348; Whitaker, "Shakespeare in San Diego," p. 406). The loss of significance, not to mention the reduction of Richmond's role, was noticed by both reviewers.

26. See page 35 for a brief summary of these critics and their positions.

27. Coursen, "Shakespeare in Maine: 1979," p. 177, describes Paul Haggard as a "monumental" Richard who, nevertheless, conveys the "hollow rationalization" of Richard's battle orations.

28. Recent stage productions have differed radically in their presentations of Richmond. The one opposing Al Pacino's Richard was apparently as noble as the BBC's, "a strong Richmond, solidly assuring change and reconstruction" (Hodgdon, "Richard III," p. 374). Similarly, Richard Gale made Richmond a "nice sincere young Welshman, with a touch of real fervor." "When the youthful Richmond, glorious in golden armor and his red dragon helm, has won the day, there is no doubt at all about the sunburst that heralds the Tudor dawn" (Byrne, "The Shakespeare Season," pp. 477-78). In contrast, Hapgood describes a downplayed Richmond: "Denied the blessings of the ghosts, his hoarse, clumsily-delivered oration ... completely topped by Richard's, ... Richmond was scarcely an agent of right, God, and St. George; he was not even a worthy opponent" ("West Coast Shakespeare, 1961," p. 348). Likewise, Pettigrew describes a play in which both orations are "mere rant," and Richmond merely "another villain" ("Stratford, 1967," p. 515); and Aaron, "Richard III," reviews the Robin Phillips production in which "the pedestrian Richmond gives an intentionally bland victory speech" (p. 113). Though I admire many aspects of the Phillips production, I find these last Richmonds even more perverse than Olivier's.

29. *Macbeth*, directed by Roman Polanski, was produced at Shepperton Studios, London, in 1971. Its U.S. release date was 1972. The film is currently distributed

by Swank Motion Pictures. Warren, "Shakespeare in England," p. 340, agrees with my criticism of the BBC videotape.

30. Virginia McNamee's typed transcription of the Olivier film in the Folger Shakespeare Library indicates another twenty lines which may have been edited out of my print of the film. Sixteen, however, are Stanley's lines to Richmond (lines 3525 ff.); Richmond is still mute and largely invisible after his prayer.

31. Brown, "Olivier's *Richard* III," p. 30; Hunter, *Shakespeare and the Mystery of God's Judgments*, p. 73.

32. Roy Walker, "Bottled Spider," p. 60, refers to the "butchery of Richmond's part." Brown, "Olivier's *Richard* III," p. 30, sees it as part of Olivier's (and Cibber's) systematic elimination of attractive alternatives to Richard: family, church, state are all diminished in the film, if not depraved, and Richmond is "not overwhelmingly appealing." Whitaker, "Shakespeare in San Diego," mentions a similar loss of significance in the San Diego *Richard* III in 1961. Because the ghosts appear only to Richard, the ladies have little dignity, and Richmond is not sufficiently impressive, "God's purposes were lost sight of" (p. 404).

33. Hammond, ed., *King Richard* III, mentions how Olivier's extensive cuts "cannot fail to damage the play's internal structure, its patterns of imagery, rhetoric and tone, and its moral and historical fabric" (p. 72). Diether, "*Richard* III: The Preservation of a Film," pp. 288–89, disagrees. He argues that the film's musical score successfully replaces these excisions: "What 'booms majestically' is the main march subject, in E flat minor, which . . . is the motif of . . . Richmond, who symbolizes in the play the hope of England. . . . It expresses in musical terms what Henry does not say in words." Diether's pp. 291 ff., incidentally, are excellent on other musical motifs in the film.

34. Roy Walker, "Bottled Spider," p. 64, calls this soliloquy omitted. Brown, "Olivier's *Richard* III," p. 32, similarly mentions that no one hears "Have mercy, Jesu," which is, however, distinct in my print of the film.

35. In striking contrast, in the Champlain (Vermont) *Richard* III of 1973, when Richard awakes, "we beheld the terrible spectacle of a man looking inside himself and finding nothing, absolutely nothing, to admire, pity, or even cling to" (Jorgens, "Champlain Shakespeare Festival 1973," p. 429). Similarly, John Hirsch directed a Richard in Ontario who "having put aside all superstition, suddenly lapses back into it at the most crucial moment in his history" (Edinborough, "Stratford, Ontario—1967," p. 400). I would quarrel with the "suddenly," and Edinborough's choice of "lapse," but not the general thrust of the action.

36. Roy Walker, "Bottled Spider," p. 66, observes that Olivier's film "is so blind to the celestial orchestration of the theme . . . [that it] follows Richard's ominous line 'The sun will not be seen today'—that is the eclipse of the sun of York—by fighting the battle immediately afterwards in bright Spanish sunshine."

37. Hammond, ed., *King Richard* III, p. 72, urges that "balletic rather than naturalistic action suits better the sacrificial nature of the elimination of Richard

from the world." Jorgens complains in *Shakespeare on Film*, p. 141, that in Olivier's film "the soldiers brutally tear at Richard like mad dogs." This is "far from the neat, orderly rites of Christianity" which should be suggested here.

38. Brown, "Olivier's *Richard III*," p. 26, similarly sees a "cross framed by the hilt of the sword."

39. In Irving's version, as in Olivier's, "A Horse, . . ." is the last line of the play. The rest is visual interpretation of the Folio stage directions: "*Enter Richard and Richmond, they fight, Richard is slaine. Retreat and flourish. Enter Richmond, Derby bearing the Crowne, with divers other Lords*" (11.3841–44). Kean's acting version retains a number of lines after Richard's death, including some of Richmond's final speech (according to Cibber) (Downer, ed., *King Richard III*, pp. 97–100); so does Cooke's (*Richard III*, ed. W. Oxberry).

40. Hankey, ed., *Richard III*, pp. 12–13, 30–31.

Chapter 2

1. Tillyard, *Shakespeare's History Plays*, pp. 201–2; Jones, *The Origins of Shakespeare*, pp. 231, 204. Hunter, *Shakespeare and the Mystery of God's Judgments*, p. 73; Palmer, *Political Characters of Shakespeare*, p. 116; Reese, *The Cease of Majesty*, p. 212; Rossiter, "Angel with Horns," pp. 71–75, 80. See also Clemen, *A Commentary on Shakespeare's Richard III*, pp. 199–200.

2. Frey, *The First Tetralogy*, pp. 130–32; Nicholas Brooke, *Shakespeare's Early Tragedies*, p. 78; Sanders, *The Dramatist and the Received Idea*, p. 109.

3. See chapter 1, note 28.

4. Bullough, ed., *Narrative and Dramatic Sources of Shakespeare*, 3:225–26, 228. As Bullough says (3:224–25), though Holinshed, *The . . . Chronicles of England, Scotlande, and Irelande . . .* , is better known as the source for Shakespeare's historical material, and though both Hall and Holinshed derived their material from Sir Thomas More's *History of King Richard III* "almost word for word," Shakespeare is most likely to have used Hall. Hall is therefore the primary source Bullough and I use.

5. Hall, *The union of the two noble and illustre famelies of Lancastre & Yorke*, fol. liiii. Subsequently Hall will be cited in the text.

6. The first Folio; see introduction, note 1.

7. *I Henry IV*, 2.4.489–90; 3.3.2–3.

8. Bullough, ed., *Narrative and Dramatic Sources of Shakespeare*, 3:247.

9. Machiavelli, *The arte of warre*, sig. R1.

10. Tuchman, *A Distant Mirror*, p. 73.

11. Sutcliffe, *The practice, proceedings, and lawes of armes*, pp. 37–38; Platonico, *Of the generall captaine, and of his office*, sig. B3; Machiavelli, sig. R1verso; Garrard, *The arte of warre*, p. 145, also prescribes exploiting "the love toward God."

12. This Quarto notation indicates added lines from the first Quarto of 1597, and will subsequently occur in the text.

13. Machiavelli, *The arte of warre*, sig. R1verso; Sutcliffe, *The practice, proceedings, and lawes of armes*, p. 157; Hurault, *Politicke, moral, and martial discourses*, p. 424.

14. Hurault, *Politicke, moral, and martial discourses*, p. 398.

15. Sutcliffe, *The practice, proceedings, and lawes of armes*, p. 157; Garrard, *The arte of warre*, p. 145.

16. Sutcliffe, *The practice, proceedings, and lawes of armes*, p. 157; Garrard, *The arte of warre*, p. 145; Machiavelli, *The arte of warre*, sig. R1.

17. Sutcliffe, *The practice, proceedings, and lawes of armes*, p. 157; Machiavelli, *The arte of warre*, sig. R1verso; Garrard, *The arte of warre*, p. 145.

18. Garrard, *The arte of warre*, p. 145.

19. Proctor, *Of the Knowledge and Conducte of Warres*, sig. K1verso.

20. *I Henry IV*, 5.1.134.

21. Rich, *A path-way to military practise*, sig. H2.

22. Bevington, *Action Is Eloquence*, similarly notices the "dissonance and incongruity" that results at the coronation when Richard tries to "project a real connection between himself and the [usurped] signs of his office" (p. 149).

Chapter 3

1. Quoted in Furness, ed., *New Variorum*, note 210, p. 337. Clemen, *A Commentary on Shakespeare's Richard the Third*, agrees, p. 190.

2. Chambers, *Shakespeare: A Survey*, p. 18; Tillyard, *Shakespeare's History Plays*, p. 214.

3. See note 210, p. 337 in Furness, ed., *New Variorum*, for early disagreement. Cf. Hudson's comment, in HUD1, note 450, p. 355 (most critics to 1872 think "Elizabeth is really beguiled"; he does not). See also Tanner, "Richard III Versus Elizabeth: An Interpretation," pp. 468–72; Dollarhide, "Two Unassimilated Movements of *Richard III*: An Interpretation," pp. 40–46. The former finds Richard deceived, the latter Elizabeth. See also Ornstein, *A Kingdom for a Stage*, pp. 75, 78, and Clemen, *A Commentary on Shakespeare's Richard the Third*, who thinks Elizabeth may pretend to yield.

4. The first Folio; see introduction, note 1.

5. See discussion in chapter 1, and note 23.

6. Hunter, *Shakespeare and the Mystery of God's Judgments*, p. 74.

7. In Boswell's *Life of Johnson*, 1:463.

8. Pope, *Paradise Regained: The Tradition and the Poem*, p. 88. See also Stein, *Heroic Knowledge*, pp. 118–19; Tillyard, *Milton*, p. 263; Lewalski, *Milton's Brief Epic*, p. 305.

9. Andrewes, *Ninety Six Sermons*, 5:483.

10. Hall, *The union of the two noble and illustre famelies of Lancastre & Yorke*.

11. Legge, *Richardus Tertius*, pp. 441–42. See also Bullough, 3:310–12. The last two phrases are quoted from Bullough's more dramatic translation. Lordi has "foolishly" and "put off these things."

12. *The true tragedie of Richard the Third*, sigs. G1, H4.

Chapter 4

1. See chapter 1, notes 17 and 18.

2. Heilman, "Satiety and Conscience," pp. 60–62; Rossiter, "Angel with Horns," p. 7; Frey, *The First Tetralogy*, pp. 106–9.

3. Quoted in Furness, ed., *New Variorum*, note 8, p. 242.

4. Tillyard, *Shakespeare's History Plays*, pp. 244–45; W. J. Birch, quoted in Furness, ed., *New Variorum*, note 48, p. 260.

5. Stopford Brooke, *On Ten Plays of Shakespeare*, p. 113.

6. Legge, *Richardus Tertius*, p. 340; subsequently Legge will be cited in the text, in Lordi's translation.

7. Alexander Pope, *An Essay on Criticism*, line 297, in *English Poetry of the Eighteenth Century*, ed. Cecil A. Moore (New York: Henry Holt and Co., 1935).

8. All cited in Furness, ed., *New Variorum*, notes 2 and 4, pp. 252–53. Clemen, *A Commentary on Shakespeare's Richard the Third*, agrees about the wisdom of the Scrivener and the Citizens, but calls the Mayor "a particularly feeble and gullible person" (pp. 147–49).

9. For example, Cibber's adaptation, like Olivier's film, cuts the Scrivener entirely (Spencer, ed., *Five Restoration Adaptations of Shakespeare*).

10. The instinct to protect the myth of Richard's perfect villainy is clear in the discomfort of several critics with the failed slander against the princes. Horace Walpole rationalizes that "Clarence is the first who is said to have propagated this slander, and it was much more consonant to his levity and indigested politics, than to the good sense of Richard." C. Wessel argues similarly, "It has been said that Dr. Shaw, at the bidding of Richard, accused the Duchess of York of faithlessness. It is only possible to explain this fact by Dr. Shaw's acting without Richard's authorization, but it is more likely still that the whole tale is a myth invented by Richard's enemies." The possibility of a strategic blunder on the part of this artist in evil is apparently inconceivable to these apologists. Cited in Furness, ed., *New Variorum*, note 92, p. 250.

11. In Holinshed, Pynkie is corrected to Penker. That Shakespeare gets the name right suggests to Bullough, *Narrative and Dramatic Sources in Shakespeare*, that Shakespeare is using Holinshed as well as Hall at this moment (p. 227). The sources are all nearly identical on *Richard III*. Hall, fols. xx–xxii, makes it clear that both Friars Shaa and Penker were totally unconvincing during this deception, and totally discredited thereafter. The Citizens "stoode as they had been turned into stoones for wonder of [Shaa's] shamefull sermonde"; both were of "more learnyng then vertue . . . [or] trueth"; both "had no scrupulous conscience" (fols. xx, xvii). These are stated as matters of common knowledge.

12. Goldberg, *James I and the Politics of Literature*, and Greenblatt, *Renaissance Self-Fashioning*, offer other historical insights into the Citizens' cautious and ironic detachment from Richard's charade. Goldberg discusses (pp. 113–209, 262–63) "the familiar metaphor of the king as actor," and "the theatricality of power and the power of the theater" (p. xiii). Greenblatt argues that self-fashioning is commonly accepted as a part of effective ruling in the Renaissance. Bevington, *Action Is Eloquence*, p. 103, has interesting comments on this "scene" that Richard plays and its relationship to political iconography in the Renaissance.

Chapter 5

1. See chapter 1, notes 12, 15, 16, 21, 25, 31, and 32.

2. Tillyard, *Shakespeare's History Plays*, p. 199; Reese, *The Cease of Majesty*, p. 208; Jones, *The Origins of Shakespeare*, pp. 204–5; Prior, *The Drama of Power*, p. 56; Patrides, *The Phoenix and the Ladder*, p. 119; Hammond, ed., *King Richard III*, p. 72; Rossiter, "Angel With Horns," p. 67; Hunter, *Shakespeare and the Mystery of God's Judgments*, p. 67.

3. See introduction, note 8, for a brief discussion of this turmoil in the interpretive community. See note 17 in this chapter for a discussion of another aspect of this turmoil, what has been called the "new historicism," and its relationship to this discussion of providence as a theological issue in the Renaissance.

4. Frey, *The First Tetralogy*, pp. 87, 153; Wilders, *The Lost Garden*, pp. 57–58; Sanders, *The Dramatist and the Received Idea*, pp. 88, 108. Nicholas Brooke, *Shakespeare's Early Tragedies*, pp. 78–79.

5. Rossiter, "Angel with Horns," p. 84; Prior, *The Drama of Power*, p. 58; Hunter, *Shakespeare and the Mystery of God's Judgments*, p. 80.

6. Rossiter, "Angel with Horns," p. 84; Sanders, *The Dramatist and the Received Idea*, p. 76.

7. Prior, *The Drama of Power*, pp. 44–58.

8. This + notation indicates lines from the first Quarto of 1597, and will subsequently occur in the text. Otherwise, all quotations of *Richard III* will continue to refer to the first Folio. See introduction, note 1.

9. Hunter, *Shakespeare and the Mystery of God's Judgments*, pp. 70–79.

10. Frey, *The First Tetralogy*, p. 120.

11. Clemen, *A Commentary on Shakespeare's Richard III*, p. 215, and Garber, *Dream in Shakespeare*, pp. 8–9, 21, 67, both illustrate the complexity of the issue of the ghost's subjective and/or objective reality. Frye, *The Renaissance Hamlet*, pp. 15–24, discusses conflicting Renaissance understandings of ghosts; several sightings apparently tended to confirm a ghost's objective reality.

12. I allude, of course, to West, *Shakespeare and the Outer Mystery*.

13. Reed, *Crime and God's Judgment in Shakespeare*, and Frye, *The Renaissance Hamlet*, p. 181, both discuss conscience as a manifestation of God's providence in Renaissance theology.

14. Hawkins, *The Devil's Party*, p. 43, concludes that Richard "is not shown to suffer as much as his victims." This perspective must ignore his tortured soliloquy after seeing the ghosts, his confusion and embarrassment after the coronation, his loss of alacrity and wit before the battle, his despair, his fear, his death, and God knows what else. Surely Richard is finally shown to suffer much more intensely and variously than his victims. Garber, *Dream in Shakespeare*, pp. 19–20, decisively counters Hawkins here, as does Norman Rabkin, *Shakespeare and the Common Understanding* (New York: The Free Press, 1967), p. 251, when he says that Richard comes in his final soliloquy "to recognize the emptiness of his ambition and the self-destruction he has made inevitable, that is, the futility of the very principle of his energy."

15. Sanders, *The Dramatist and the Received Idea*, p. 109; Frey, *The First Tetralogy*, pp. 130-31; Nicholas Brooke, *Shakespeare's Early Tragedies*, p. 78. Reese, *The Cease of Majesty*, p. 212; Hunter, *Shakespeare and the Mystery of God's Judgments*, p. 73.

16. Nicholas Brooke, *Shakespeare's Early Tragedies*, p. 78.

17. Greenblatt, *Renaissance Self-Fashioning*, p. 5, is particularly concerned about reconstructing the complex "struggles and harmonies of culture that influence its literature." Though he is as aware as Levin (*New Readings of Old Plays*) and Frye (*The Renaissance Hamlet*) of the impossibility of fully entering and reconstructing that culture, like Frye he is still committed to hazard the "impurities" of the historical method because of its attendant uses. Frye, pp. 3-10, 254 ff., and 281-92, also defends the historical method when it is applied with tact to interpretation. Like Greenblatt, Jonathan Dollimore (*Radical Tragedy*) concedes "providentialism as a dominant discourse," but concentrates on the radical and revolutionary aspects of its cultural context (pp. 3-12, 82). The difference between Frye's discussion of traditional Renaissance attitudes towards providence and those of Greenblatt and Dollimore, both "new historicists," is an instructive illustration of the different conclusions responsible scholars can draw from similar materials. Greenblatt and Dollimore are most interested in "discontinuity," the intellectual impact of radical and abrupt historical change. Frye, a more traditional historicist like myself, concedes some dissent but emphasizes a continuity of belief in fairly conservative doctrines. Richard Rorty's *Philosophy and the Mirror of Nature* discusses the hermeneutics of these new historicists. The contrast between his discussion of this "traditional" image of the "mirror up to nature" and Frye's is also revealing.

18. Frey, *The First Tetralogy*, pp. 75, 87, 96-97; Sanders, *The Dramatist and the Received Idea*, pp. 98, 103, 108-9. See, however, note 39 of this chapter on the agnosticism that might be attributable to the absoluteness of Calvin's theological position.

19. Calvin, *The institution of Christian religion*, trans. Thomas Norton, 1.17. fol. 61; subsequently referred to as *Inst.*; Ralph Walker, *A learned and profitable treatise*, pp. 51-55.

20. Jewel, *The Works*, 1:501; Calvin, *Inst.*, 1.16.fols. 57, 58.

21. Veron, *A fruteful treatise of predestination*, sig. L8.verso.

22. Calvin, *Inst.*, 1.17.fol. 61, verso; 1.16.fol. 60 verso.

23. Hunter, *Shakespeare and the Mystery of God's Judgments*, p. 68.

24. Frey, *The First Tetralogy*, pp. 96-97.

25. Wilders, *The Lost Garden*, p. 58; French, "The Mills of God and Shakespeare's Early History Plays," pp. 313-24. French is also concerned about the "scandalously natural" operation of providence (p. 320); Frey, *The First Tetralogy*, pp. 96-97.

26. Wilders, *The Lost Garden*, p. 58.

27. See, e.g., Ralph Walker, *A learned and profitable treatise*, pp. 307-9; Andrewes, *Ninety Six Sermons*, 3:326, 328; and Calvin, *Inst.*, 3.20. There are many other such references to this commonplace.

28. Marbeck, *A book of notes and common places*, p. 846; Andrewes, *Institutiones piae*, p. 8.

29. Marbeck, *A book of notes and common places*, p. 845; Calvin, *Tracts and Treatises on the Doctrine and Worship of the Church*, 2:146; Nowell, *A catechisme*, p. 182.

30. Becon, *The Early Works*, p. 138; Nowell, *A catechisme*, p. 200; Andrewes, *Institutiones piae*, pp. 11-13.

31. Becon, *The Early Works*, pp. 151, 137; Marbeck, *A book of notes and common places*, p. 845.

32. Shakespeare may have Richmond allude to Revelation as he prays as God's minister of wrath, "Looke on my Forces with a gracious eye, / Put in their hands thy bruising Irons of wrath." Of God's Messiah, his champion "faithful and true" in Rev. 19.15, it is said that "he shal rule them with a rodde of yron: for he it is that treadeth the wine presse of the fiercenes and wrath of almightie God" (Rev. 6.2— *The Geneva Bible*). This allusion can increase our sense of both the apocalyptic and the providential dimensions of Richmond's potency in *Richard III*.

33. Frey, *The First Tetralogy*, p. 120; Sanders, *The Dramatist and the Received Idea*, p. 101.

34. Calvin, *Inst.*, 3.24.fol. 259 verso; 1.17.fol. 67; see also 3.24, passim; and 1.18.fol. 68-69; and Walker, *A Learned and profitable treatise*, p. 244. Calvin, *Inst.*, 1.17.fol. 67; Calvin, *Sermons from Job*, p. 259.

35. Ralph Walker, *A learned and profitable treatise*, pp. 246-47; Calvin, *Inst.*, 1.18.fol. 70 verso. The occasional alternative translation in parentheses is that of John Allen's 1936 edition of Calvin's *Institutes*.

36. Ralph Walker, *A learned and profitable treatise*, pp. 254-55.

37. Calvin, *Inst.*, 1.17.fol.63; 1.18.fols. 67, 69-70. The last quotation Calvin translates from Augustine. See also Martin Luther, *Sermons*, 1:169, 295; and Calvin, *The Mystery of Godliness and Other Selected Sermons*, p. 188.

38. Veron, *A fruteful treatise of predestination*, sig. L8.verso; Calvin, *Inst.*, 1.17.fol. 62.

39. Elton, *King Lear and the Gods*, p. 31. Dollimore, *Radical Tragedy*, pp. 84-86, points out with Elton that atheists as well as the devout could invoke the idea of an inscrutable, baffling providence. In fact, he suggests that the uncompromising theological positions of a Calvin on this issue tended to provoke agnosticism.

40. Frey, *The First Tetralogy*, pp. 96-97; French, "The Mills of God and Shakespeare's Early History Plays," pp. 321-24.

41. See also Ralph Walker, *A learned and profitable treatise*, p. 308.

42. Luther, *Sermons*, 1:169.

43. These questions are discussed in greater detail in chapter 6.

44. Sanders, *The Dramatist and the Received Idea*, p. 109.

Chapter 6

1. See chapter 1, note 32.

2. "Substantive variants" are defined in the *Shakespeare Variorum* editors' handbook as "all verbal changes that affect meaning." "Semi-substantive variants" are "changes of accidental details [i.e. punctuation]... that affect meaning" (p. 35). Kristian Smidt's well-received *Iniurious impostors and Richard III* has challenged the

long-accepted arguments in favor of Folio authority, presented most exhaustively by Patrick, *The Textual History of Richard* III. The consensus still favors the Folio, but the margin has diminished. A good recent discussion can be found in Hammond's introduction to the New Arden edition of *Richard* III. This discussion, and most of the reviews of Smidt's study, reveal how effectively Smidt has dispelled the notion of Q1 as a "bad" quarto, even though he did not establish its authority over the Folio.

3. See the introduction to chapter 2 for a survey of these critics. In this chapter on textual cruxes, I have resisted the "urge to closure" (Rabkin, *Shakespeare and the Problem of Meaning*, p. 25) to play with what Hawkins has called "a multiplicity of dramatic and poetic effects and responses" (*The Devil's Party*, p. 3). The complex interplay of the textual, theatrical, and interpretive traditions seemed to mandate such an approach. Because I usually share with most readers a tendency to "crush, conclude, and quell," to paraphrase bully Bottom, it has proven exhilarating to participate in such a brief exercise of "indeterminacy."

4. For convenience, refer to Smidt's parallel text edition of *Richard* III. I continue to cite the first Folio, unless Q (Quarto 1) or another quarto is indicated; see introduction, note 1. CAM1, GLO, WH2, CAM2, RID, DYCE2, HUD2, and WORD1 follow the Q1 "shrinke." To save much space, I will use in the notes only the most abbreviated forms of the major editions. Their abbreviations, order, and dates are provided in the Textual Bibliography. The format will finally be that of the *Shakespeare Variorum* textual notes, but I will start with a discursive format in the text and notes.

5. KTLY, HUD2, and CAM3 follow CAP's "spoils" in 3413 (5.2.8).

6. Unlike the "flye] shrinke" variant, these originate not in the first Quarto but in early eighteenth-century and nineteenth-century editions. Their interest to the interpreter is therefore greater than their textual authority, though some have proven remarkably resilient in the textual tradition.

7. When such references occur in the text, they will always refer to the *Oxford English Dictionary* (OED). The same editions that follow Q1 in note 4 follow Q1 "partie." With the Q1 "foe," the followers are limited to CAM1, GLO, WH2, CAM2, and RID. I will subsequently refer to these five editions as the "CAM group." STAU has "our foe."

8. POPE–JOHN, V1773, and the "CAM group" follow the Q1 "signall." The influential CAM1 and GLO (Globe) editions of 1864 both reverse the earlier textual tradition by choosing Q1 as their copy-text. As a result, hundreds of additional Q1 variants have been introduced into the textual history of *Richard* III.

9. First Folio readings that originate in Quartos 2-6 are of doubtful textual authenticity because they probably slipped into those quartos, and therefore into the first Folio, by accident. For example, there are several cases when the compositor of the first Folio uses Quarto 6 as his copy-text. When he does, the accidental changes that have accumulated since Quarto 1 slip unauthorized into the otherwise more authoritative first Folio text. As Evans says (PEL2, p. 597), in such cases we "approach more nearly to Shakespeare's original by reverting to Quarto 1." Evans

adds this interesting comment: "This is the theory, but in practice some editorial judgment in the choice of readings has to be admitted."

10. SIS, EVNS(3), and BEV are unusual in giving the lines to Norfolk, following Q1 and F1. Here and later "EVNS(3)" will refer to Evans's three editions of *Richard III*, PEL1, PEL2, and the *Riverside*. IRV and RLTR mark the aside.

11. DYCE1 and 2, V1821, STAU, "CAM group," HUD2, WORD1, ARD1, and most of the important editions from 1935 through 1985 follow Q1 in this. Like the "soyle] foile" variant above, this one may originate in a Quarto misprint (Q2 this time). Unlike it, the possible misprint, "you to," has often been preferred by editors.

12. Namely BLAIR, JOHN-RANN(-MAL), SING2, COL2, KTLY, DYCE2, HUD2, WORD1, and CAM3 all use "distraine." Only MAL in the group JOHN-RANN does not.

13. PEL2, p. 596n.

14. For three radically different views of their exchange, see the introduction to chapter 3.

15. Ridley is the only editor I have found who follows Q1 here in either variant.

16. CAP, STAU, GLO, CAM1, 2, and 3, WORD1, WH2, and RID all go with the Q1 "love." The editors from POPE1-JOHN2, and HUD 2, emend to "now."

17. POPE, HAN, CAP, and MAL stick with the Folio "Too." Only THEO, WARB, JOHN, and the "CAM group" go along with the Q1 "grave."

18. See Hassel, *Faith and Folly in Shakespeare's Romantic Comedies*, pp. 28–51.

19. ALEX, CAM3, and ARD2. Bevington, *Action Is Eloquence*, does many interesting things with such added and implied stage directions in Shakespeare's texts.

20. Q1, NLSN, and OXF1 read "shallow changing"; THEO1-KTLY, WH2, CAM2, RID, and all collated editions after him except CAM3 read "shallow, changing."

21. See the introduction to chapter 5 for the issues and the participants.

22. 649 all] *Om.* Q3, F2–F4; now ROWE1-JOHN2 (1.3.179). In this *Shakespeare Variorum* format, we have the TLN, the Folio lemma, the variant(s), and their editions listed or grouped chronologically. "*Om.*" indicates that "all" is omitted. (I continue to add act, scene, line numbers from EVNS for the general reader's convenience.) The Textual Bibliography must be consulted for the chronological order. I will use this form in most of the subsequent notes, explaining possibly confusing conventions as they occur.

23. 651 Given to Margaret ROWE1-THEO2, THEO4; given to Elizabeth MAL, V1793+(-KIT1) (1.3.181). Here all editions in my list except KIT1 and those indicated before the semicolon give the line to Elizabeth. The + means "and all editions following."

24. 666 Though] If Q1, POPE1-V1773(-CAP), STAU, "CAM group." 673 live,] live$_\wedge$ Q1, ROWE1-V1773(-CAP), DYCE1, WH1, STAU+(-HAL, KTLY). 676 dayes,] dayes$_\wedge$ Q1, POPE1+ (1.3.196, 203, 206). This last, with the caret, indicates that all editions collated since POPE have omitted the comma.

25. 750 live] lives SING2, KTLY. 761–66 *Marked as an aside* WH2, NLSN, CAM3 (1.3.277, 288–93).

26. 758 breath] breathe ROWE1+(–CAP). 771 sooth] soothe KNT, COL2+(–COL3, HAL). 777 *given to Hastings* CAP, MAL, V1793–CAM3(–NLSN, ALEX) (1.3.285, 297, 303).

27. 1083 Have you] Hast thou Q1, CAP–SING1, STAU–CAM2 (–HAL, KTLY), RID. 1083 your soules] thy soule Q1, CAP, MAL, V1793–SING1, STAU–CAM2(–HAL, KTLY), RID. 1085 are you . . . your] art thou . . . thy Q1, CAP–SING1, CAM1–CAM2 (–KTLY), RID; art thou . . . your STAU. 1086 you will] thou wilt Q1, CAP–SING1, STAU–CAM2 (–HAL, KTLY), RID (1.4.250–53).

28. 1028 shalt] shall F2 (1.4.197). 1028 Will you] And wilt thou Q1, "CAM group"; Wilt thou CAP–SING1, STAU.

29. 1021 for any goodnesse] to have redemption Q1, POPE1–JOHN2, V1773–RANN, V1821, SING1, COL1, HUD1+. 1021+1 *Line added by* Q1, MAL, V1793+(–KNT, HUD2, NLSN) (1.4.189, 190).

30. 990 Soft, he wakes] Harke he stirs, shall I strike Q1, STAU, "CAM group"; Shall I strike POPE1–JOHN2, V1773. 991 *Om.* Q1, POPE1–JOHN2, V1773, STAU, "CAM group." The same cluster gives 992 to *Two*; so does NLSN. 994 *Given to* I Q1, CAP V1778–HAL, KTLY–OXF1(–WH2), NLSN, ARD1, KIT1, SIS (1.4.158–62).

31. 1004 given to *Ambo* Q1, THEO, WARB, JOHN, V1773, MAL, V1793–SING1, COL1, HUD1–CAM2, ARD1, RID, KIT1, PEL1; given to II BEV. 1082; given to I Q1, "CAM group." 1080–81 given to II Q1, "CAM group." 1102 *Om.* Q1, CAP, HUD2, WORD1; degr. POPE, HAN, DYCE2, STAU (1.4.172, 247–49, 269).

32. 983 fram'd] in fraud Q1, RID. 974 (by chance)] *Om.* Q1, STAU, "CAM group," OXF1. 954 passionate] holy POPE1–JOHN2, MAL, V1793–V1813, SING1, COL4, SIS; compassionate CAP–RANN(–MAL), COL2 (1.4.150, 140, 118).

33. 5 lowr'd] lour'd CAP, SING1, STAU, GLO, DYCE2–RID, ALEX–CAM3, ARD2; lowered COL1, HUD1–WH1, HAL, KTLY, PEL1, EVNS(3), BEV (1.1.3).

34. 1181 unwillingly] unwittingly Q1, POPE1+. 1183 To] By Q1, POPE1+(–COL1, ALEX) (2.1.57).

35. All but three major editions since CAM1 have included the Q1 "Zounds" and Richard's response. They are KTLY, OXF1, and NLSN. 2463 given to *Mayor* Q1; given to *Mayor and Citizens* BEV (3.7.241).

36. 3592 lance] hurtless lance CAP; pointless lance COL3, DYCE2, HUD2, WORD1, OXF1. 3620 edgelesse Sword] powerless arm COL2 and COL3 (5.3.142, 164).

37. 3645 I am I] I and I Q1, RID, ARD2 (5.3.183).

38. 3671 Who's there] Zoundes, who is there Q1, CAP, CAM1, GLO, OXF1–ARD1, RID+ (5.3.208).

39. 3828 Daring an] Daring, an HAN; a daring BLAIR; Daring and Q8, CAP, RANN, CAM3 (5.4.3).

40. 3841–42 Richard is slaine] Exeunt, *fighting* CAP, MAL, V1793–SING1, COL1, HUD1, DYCE1–HAL(–COL3), DYCE2–OXF1.

41. 1320 nere-changing night] perpetuall rest Q1, POPE1–SING1, STAU–CAM2 (–HAL, KTLY), RID. 1320 night] light COL2 (2.2.46).

42. 2839 franticke] tragicke Q1, POPE1–SING1, SING2, STAU–CAM2 (–HAL), RID. 2876 whirl'd] whe'eld Q1, POPE1–JOHN2, V1773–SING1, DYCE1, WH1, STAU–CAM2 (–HAL, KTLY, OXF1), RID (4.4.68, 105).

43. HAN omits only 3390. 3396 in] on Q1, POPE1–KNT2 (–COL1), SING2, DYCE1, STAU–CAM2 (–KTLY), RID (5.1.18, 24). *Macbeth*, 1.7.8–10.
44. 3881 Abate] Rebate HUD1, SING2, COL3, KTLY (5.5.35).
45. See notes 5–7, chapter 5.

Epilogue
1. Michael Billington, *Guardian*, 21 June 1984; J. C. Trewin, *Birmingham Evening Mail*, 20 June 1984.
2. Tinker, *Daily Mail*, 21 June 1984.
3. Ratcliffe, *Observer*, 24 June 1984.
4. Billington, *Guardian*.
5. Masters, *Times*, 21 June 1984.
6. Ratcliffe, *Observer*.
7. Peter McGarry, *Coventry Evening Telegraph*, 20 June 1984.
8. Billington, *Guardian*.
9. Kahn, *New Statesman*, 6 July 1984.
10. Coveney, *Financial Times*, 21 June 1984.
11. Ratcliffe, *Observer*; Tinker, *Daily Mail*.
12. Ratcliffe, *Observer*.
13. Masters, *Times*; Tinker, *Daily Mail*.
14. Coveney, *Financial Times*; Wells, *Times Literary Supplement*, 21 June 1984.
15. King, *Sunday Telegraph*, 24 June 1984.
16. Tinker, *Daily Mail*.
17. Trewin, *Birmingham Evening Mail*.
18. Ratcliffe, *Observer*; McGarry, *Coventry Evening Telegraph*.
19. Billington, *Guardian*.
20. Gordon, *Spectator*, 7 July 1984.
21. Billington, *Guardian*.
22. Coveney, *Financial Times*, describes him here as a "loathsome bat" with his "midnight snack."
23. Hankey (ed., *Richard III*) briefly discusses the theatrical tradition of the comic Mayor (pp. 179–80). The promptbooks of two other Royal Shakespeare Company productions of *Richard III* illustrate alternative readings of the scene. In Terry Hand's play in 1970, Norman Rodway as Richard "swirls around with an axe, missing the Mayor's head who has ducked." Later in 3.5, the Mayor's attempted exit is blocked by Catesby, with Buckingham's sword. Then "Richard throws head to Mayor who faints." And 3.7 is equally full of physical intimidation of a surprisingly stubborn Mayor. First he is pushed about by Buckingham, Ratcliffe, and Lovell. Then Ratcliffe twists his hands, picks him up, steps on his fingers, and finally "flattens" him. The Aldermen are cynical cowards throughout, in contrast to their Mayor. The conspirators must come off badly, even though the charade is literally successful. In 1975 at The Other Place, Stratford-upon-Avon, the whole scene is done as a meaningless charade, with the Mayor a willing accomplice. "Props [are] handed out" ("the Mayor and Buck. [receive] a book"); Buckingham

gives several stage directions to the Mayor, who dutifully follows them as the scene proceeds. On this note of widespread cynicism comes the interval. Cruelty in the one case, cynicism in the other, both undercut the charade in telling and historically accurate ways. Such touches, or the even grimmer version of gross intimidation at San Diego in 1972 would also have been more consonant with the vision of Alexander's *Richard* III, though less hilarious theatrically.

24. Masters, *Times*; King, *Sunday Telegraph*.

25. Interview with Bill Alexander, November 1984, Stratford-upon-Avon. Patricia Routledge played an unusually animated and energetic Margaret; Yvonne Coulette was effectively stern and strong as Richard's mother. See chapter 1, note 23, about other Elizabeths.

26. Coveney, *Financial Times*; Kahn, *New Statesman*.

27. Coveney, *Financial Times*; Kahn, *New Statesman*.

28. Coveney, *Financial Times*.

29. Masters, *Times*.

30. Coveney, *Financial Times*; interview with Bill Alexander, November 1984, Stratford-upon-Avon; Ratcliffe, *Observer*; Gordon, *Spectator*.

31. Wells, *Times Literary Supplement*. This theatrical reassertion of an identity between aesthetics and morality, and between the particularity of events on the stage and their meaning is an eloquent response to the theoretical questions raised about meaning, irony, and historical context by Levin (*New Readings of Old Plays*) and Hawkins (*Poetic Freedom and Poetic Truth* and *The Devil's Party*).

32. Wells, *Times Literary Supplement*.

33. See also Coveney, *Financial Times*, and Gordon, *Spectator*, on these details.

34. The two standard definitions of "charisma" illustrate its curious relevancy to problems of interpretation and performance in *Richard* III. On the one hand, it is "a spiritual gift or talent regarded as divinely granted to a person as a token of grace and favor." On the other, it is an "attribute of awesome and almost magical power and capacity ascribed by followers to the person and personality of extraordinarily magnetic leaders. Such leaders may be political and secular as well as religious" (*Webster's Third International Dictionary*). Richard's traditional impact upon the audience of *Richard* III, in the stage and the study, can be described by the second definition, and most of that captivated audience maintains that he has a similar power over his gulls and victims in the play itself. Paradoxically, Richard's chief opponent, Richmond, has the spiritual gifts the first definition describes, but far less theatrical magnetism. Margaret has something of both gifts, and she is Richard's formidable rival in 1.3. Alexander was scrupulous about distinguishing between Richard's false charisma and Richmond's true in this production.

35. See, however, Gordon, *Spectator*: "At Bosworth, Richmond (. . . jolly good chap) stabs him in the back." Wells, *Times Literary Supplement*, observes of this back stabbing: "We need to have believed Richmond's claim to be one of God's 'ministers of chastisement' not to find a destructive irony in this."

36. Anthony Masters, *Times*, reveals how difficult it is to respond to Ravenscroft's Richmond when he calls him a "febrile, uneasy Richmond."

37. See chapter 1, note 28 for other portrayals of Richmond.
38. B. H., *Leamington Spa Courier*, 22 June 1984.
39. McGarry, *Coventry Evening Telegraph*.
40. Tinker, *Daily Mail*.
41. Billington, *Guardian*; Trewin, *Birmingham Evening Mail*.
42. Ratcliffe, *Observer*.
43. Coveney, *Financial Times*.
44. Gordon, *Spectator*.
45. John Keats, "The Eve of St. Agnes," in *English Romantic Poets*, ed. James Stephens, Edwin L. Beck, and Royall H. Snow (New York: American Book Co., 1952), lines 16, 215.
46. Ratcliffe, King, Billington, Coveney, and Gordon all mentioned the symbolic power of this religious imagery, and found it impressive.
47. Interview with Antony Sher, November 1984, Stratford-upon-Avon.

Textual Bibliography

Editions Fully Collated, with Abbreviations

Q1   *The Tragedy of King Richard the Third*. London: Valentine Sims, 1597.
F1   *Mr. William Shakespeares Comedies, Histories, & Tragedies*. London: Isaac Jaggard and Ed. Blount, 1623.
F2   *[Plays]* (Second Folio.) London: Thomas Cotes, 1632.
F3   *[Plays]* (Third Folio.) London: 1663–64.
F4   *Comedies, Histories, & Tragedies*. (Fourth Folio.) London, 1685.
ROWE1   *Works*. Revised and corrected by Nicholas Rowe. 6 vols. London: J. Tonson, 1709.
ROWE2   *Works*. Revised and corrected by Nicholas Rowe. 2d ed. 6 vols. London: J. Tonson, 1709.
ROWE3   *Works*. Revised and corrected by Nicholas Rowe. 3d ed. 8 vols. London: J. Tonson, 1714.
POPE1   *Works*. Edited by Alexander Pope. 6 vols. London: J. Tonson, 1723–25.
POPE2   *Works*. Edited by Alexander Pope. 10 vols. London: J. Tonson, 1728.
THEO1   *Works*. Edited by Lewis Theobald. 7 vols. London: A. Bettesworth, 1733.
THEO2   *Works*. Edited by Lewis Theobald. 2d ed. 8 vols. London: H. Lintott, 1740.
HAN1   *Works*. Edited by Thomas Hanmer. 6 vols. Oxford, 1743–44.
WARB   *Works*. Edited by William Warburton. 8 vols. London: J. and J. Knapton, 1747.
THEO4   *Works*. Edited by Lewis Theobald. 4th ed. 8 vols. London: C. Hitch, 1757.
JOHN1   *Plays*. Edited by Samuel Johnson. 8 vols. London: J. and R. Tonson, 1765.
JOHN2   *Plays*. Edited by Samuel Johnson. 2d ed. 8 vols. London: J. and R. Tonson, 1765.
CAP   *Comedies, Histories, and Tragedies*. Edited by Edward Capell. 10 vols. London: Dryden Leach, 1767–68.

182   Textual Bibliography

V1773   Plays. Edited by Samuel Johnson and George Steevens. 10 vols. London: C. Bathurst, 1773.
V1778   Plays. Edited by Samuel Johnson and George Steevens. 10 vols. London: C. Bathurst, 1778.
V1785   Plays. Edited by Samuel Johnson, George Steevens, and Isaac Reed. 10 vols. London: C. Bathurst, 1785.
MAL   Plays and Poems. Edited by Edmond Malone. 10 vols. London: H. Baldwin, 1790.
RANN   Dramatic Works. Edited by Joseph Rann. 6 vols. Oxford: Rivington, 1786–[94].
V1793   Plays. Edited by George Steevens and Isaac Reed. 15 vols. London: T. Longman, 1793.
V1803   Plays. Edited by Isaac Reed. 21 vols. London: J. Johnson, 1803.
V1813   Plays. Edited by Isaac Reed. 21 vols. London: J Nichols and Son, 1813.
V1821   Plays and Poems. Edited by James Boswell. 21 vols. London: F. C. and J. Rivington, 1821.
SING1   Dramatic Works. Edited by Samuel W. Singer. 10 vols. Chiswick: Charles Whittingham, 1826.
KNT1   Works. Edited by Charles Knight. (Pictorial Edition.) 8 vols. London: Charles Knight & Co., 1838–[43].
COL1   Works. Edited by John Payne Collier. 8 vols. London: Whitaker & Co., 1842–44.
KNT2   Comedies, Histories, Tragedies, and Poems. Edited by Charles Knight. 2d ed. 12 vols. London: Charles Knight & Co., 1842–44.
HUD1   Works. Edited by Henry Hudson. 11 vols. Boston: James Munroe & Co., 1851–[56].
SING2   Dramatic Works. Edited by Samuel W. Singer. 10 vols. London: Bell and Daldy, 1856.
DYCE1   Works. Edited by Alexander Dyce. 6 vols. London: Edward Moxon, 1857.
COL3   Comedies, Histories, Tragedies, and Poems. Edited by John Payne Collier. 6 vols. London: Whittaker and Co., 1858.
WH1   Works. Edited by Richard Grant White. 12 vols. Boston: Little, Brown, and Co., 1857–66.
STAU   Plays. Edited by Howard Staunton. 3 vols. London: George Routledge & Co., 1858–60.
HAL   Works. Edited by James O. Halliwell. 16 vols. London: C. and J. Adlard, 1853–65.
CAM1   Works. Edited by William George Clark and William Aldis Wright. (Cambridge Shakespeare.) Cambridge: Macmillan and Co., 1863–66.
GLO   Works. Edited by William George Clark and William Aldis Wright. (Globe Edition.) Cambridge: Macmillan and Co., 1864.
KTLY   Plays. Edited by Thomas Keightley. 6 vols. London: Bell and Daldy, 1864.
DYCE2   Works. Edited by Alexander Dyce. 9 vols. London: Chapman and Hall, 1864–67.

HUD2	*Complete Works*. Edited by Henry N. Hudson. (Harvard Edition.) 20 vols. Boston: Ginn & Heath, 1880–81.
WH2	*Comedies, Histories, Tragedies, and Poems*. Edited by Richard Grant White. (Riverside Shakespeare.) 3 vols. Boston: Ginn, Heath, & Co., 1883.
WORD1	*History Plays*. Edited by Charles Wordsworth. 3 vols. Edinburgh: William Blackwood and Sons, 1883.
OXF1	*Complete Works*. Edited by W. J. Craig. (Oxford Shakespeare.) London: Henry Frowde, [1891] 1904.
CAM2	*Works*. Edited by William Aldis Wright. (Cambridge Shakespeare.) 9 vols. London: Macmillan and Co., 1891–93.
NLSN	*Complete Dramatic and Poetic Works*. Edited by William A. Neilson. Boston: Houghton, Mifflin and Co., 1906.
ARD1	*Works. The Tragedy of Richard the Third*. Edited by A. H. Thompson. (Arden Shakespeare.) Indianapolis: Bobbs Merrill, 1907.
RID	*Richard III*. Edited by Maurice R. Ridley. (New Temple Shakespeare.) 40 vols. London: J. M. Dent and Sons, 1935.
KIT1	*Complete Works*. Edited by George Lyman Kittredge. Boston: Ginn, 1936.
ALEX	*Works*. Edited by Peter Alexander. London: Collins, 1951.
SIS	*Complete Works*. Edited by Charles J. Sisson. London: Odhams, 1954.
CAM3	*Richard III*. Edited by John Dover Wilson. (New Cambridge Shakespeare.) Cambridge: University Press, 1954.
PEL1	*The Tragedy of Richard the Third*. Edited by G. Blakemore Evans. Penguin: Baltimore, 1959.
PEL2	*Richard III*. In *William Shakespeare: The Complete Works*. Edited by Blakemore Evans. General Editor Alfred Harbage. (The Pelican Shakespeare.) Baltimore: Penguin, 1969.
EVNS	*The Riverside Shakespeare*. Edited by G. Blakemore Evans and Harry Levin. Boston: Houghton Mifflin, 1974.
BEV	*The Complete Works of Shakespeare*. Edited by David Bevington. 3d Edition. Glenview, Ill.: Scott Foresman, 1980.
ARD2	*King Richard III*. Edited by Antony Hammond. (New Arden Shakespeare.) New York: Methuen, 1981.

Editions Occasionally Consulted, with Abbreviations

Q2	*The Tragedy of King Richard the Third*. (Second Quarto.) London: Thomas Creede, 1598.
Q3	———. (Third Quarto). London: Thomas Creede, 1602.
Q4	———. (Fourth Quarto). London: Thomas Creede, 1605.
Q5	———. (Fifth Quarto). London: Thomas Creede, 1612.
Q6	———. (Sixth Quarto). London: T. Purfoot, 1622.
Q7	———. (Seventh Quarto). London: I. Norton, 1629.
Q8	———. (Eighth Quarto). London, 1634.
HAN2	*Works*. Edited by Thomas Hanmer. 2d ed. 6 vols. London: J. and P. Knapton, 1745.

BLAIR	*Works.* Edited by Hugh Blair. 8 vols. Edinburgh: Sands, 1753.
HAN3	*Works.* Edited by Thomas Hanmer. 6 vols. Oxford, 1770–71.
COL2	*Plays.* Edited by John Payne Collier. London: Whitaker and Co., 1853.
KNT3	*Works.* Edited by Charles Knight. 8 vols. London: George Routledge and Sons, 1867.
HTR	*Richard* III. Edited by John Hunter. (Longman's Series.) London: Longman, Green and Co., 1869.
IRV	*Works.* Edited by Henry Irving and Frank Marshall. 8 vols. London: Blackie & Sons, 1888–90.
RLTR	*Richard* III. Edited by E. K. Chambers. (Red Letter Shakespeare.) London: Blackie & Sons, [1904–8].

General Bibliography

Aaron, Jules. "Richard III." *Educational Theater Journal* 30(1978): 113.
Adelman, Janet. *The Common Liar*. New Haven: Yale University Press, 1973.
Andrewes, Lancelot. *Institutiones piae, or Directions to pray*. London: Henry Seile, 1630.
———. *Ninety Six Sermons*. Reprint of 1843 ed. 5 vols. New York: AMS Press, 1967.
Babula, William. *Shakespeare in Production: 1935-1978*. New York: Garland Press, 1981.
Beckerman, Bernard. "The 1964 Season at Stratford, Connecticut." *Shakespeare Quarterly* 15 (1964): 397-407.
Becon, Thomas. *The Early Works*. Edited by John Ayre. Cambridge: Cambridge University Press, 1853.
Berry, Ralph. "Stratford Festival Canada." *Shakespeare Quarterly* 29 (1978): 222-26.
Bevington, David. *Action Is Eloquence*. Cambridge: Harvard University Press, 1984.
Boswell, James. *The Life of Johnson*. Edited by G. B. Hill. Revised by L. F. Powell. Oxford: Clarendon Press, 1934.
Brooke, Nicholas. "Reflecting Gems and Dead Bones." *Critical Quarterly* 7(1965): 123-34.
———. *Shakespeare's Early Tragedies*. London: Methuen, 1968.
Brooke, Stopford. *On Ten Plays of Shakespeare*. Reprint of 1905 ed. New York: AMS Press, 1971.
Brown, Constance A. "Olivier's Richard III: A Re-evaluation." *Film Quarterly* 20 (1967): 23-32.
Bryant, Arthur. "Our Notebook." *Illustrated London News* 228 (14 April 1956): 290.
Bullough, Geoffrey, ed. *Narrative and Dramatic Sources of Shakespeare*. 8 vols. London: Routledge & Kegan Paul, 1957-75.
Byrne, Muriel St. Clare. "The Shakespeare Season . . . 1957." *Shakespeare Quarterly* 8 (1957): 461-92.
Calvin, John. *Institutes of the Christian Religion*. Translated by John Allen. Edited by B. B. Warfield and T. C. Pears, Jr. 2 vols. Philadelphia: Board of Christian Education, 1936.

———. *The institution of Christian religion*. Translated by Thomas Norton. London: Reinolde [W]olfe & Richarde Harison, 1561.

———. *The Mystery of Godliness and Other Selected Sermons*. Reprint of 1830 ed. Grand Rapids, Mich.: William B. Eerdmans, 1950.

———. *Sermons from Job*. Translated by Leroy Nixon. Grand Rapids, Mich.: William B. Eerdmans, 1952.

———. *Tracts and Treatises on the Doctrine and Worship of the Church*. Translated by Henry Beveridge. Edited by Thomas F. Torrance. 3 vols. Grand Rapids, Mich.: William B. Eerdmans, 1958.

Chambers, E. K. *Shakespeare: A Survey*. London: Sidgwick & Jackson, 1951.

Clemen, Wolfgang. *A Commentary on Shakespeare's Richard III*. Translated by Jean Bonheim. London: Methuen, 1968.

Coursen, H. R. "Shakespeare in Maine: 1979." *Shakespeare Quarterly* 31(1980): 176–79.

Crouch, J. H. "The Colorado Shakespeare Festival—1970." *Shakespeare Quarterly* 21(1970): 465–66.

Dent, Alan. "Richard III: A Disclaimer." *Illustrated London News* 228(7 Jan. 1956): 228–30.

Diether, Jack. "Richard III: The Preservation of a Film." *Film Quarterly* 11(1956–57): 280–93.

Dollarhide, Louis. "Two Unassimilated Movements of *Richard III*: An Interpretation." *Mississippi Quarterly* 14(1960): 40–46.

Dollimore, Jonathan. *Radical Tragedy*. Chicago: University of Chicago Press, 1984.

Donne, John. *The Sermons*. 10 vols. Edited by George R. Potter and Evelyn M. Simpson. Berkeley and Los Angeles: University of California Press, 1962.

Downame, John. *The Christian warfare against the Devill, world, and flesh*. 4th ed. London: William Stansby, 1634.

Downer, Alan S., ed. *King Richard III*. London: Society for Theatre Research, 1959.

Dukore, Bernard F. "Richard III." *Educational Theater Journal* 22(1970): 323–24.

Edinborough, Arnold. "A New Stratford Festival." *Shakespeare Quarterly* 5(1954): 47–50.

———. "Stratford, Ontario—1967." *Shakespeare Quarterly* 18(1967): 399–404.

Elsom, John. "Theatre Love." *The Listener* 89(1973): 596–97.

Elton, William R. *King Lear and the Gods*. San Marino, Calif.: Huntington Library, 1966.

French, A. L. "The Mills of God and Shakespeare's Early History Plays." *English Studies* 55(1974): 313–24.

Frey, David L. *The First Tetralogy*. The Hague: Mouton, 1976.

Frye, Roland Mushat. *The Renaissance Hamlet*. Princeton: Princeton University Press, 1984.

Garber, Marjorie B. *Dream in Shakespeare*. New Haven: Yale University Press, 1974.

Garrard, William. *The arte of warre*. Corrected by Captain Hitchcock. London: Roger Warde, 1591.

The Geneva Bible. Introduction by Lloyd E. Berry. Madison: University of Wisconsin Press, 1969.

Goldberg, Jonathan. *James I and the Politics of Literature*. Baltimore: Johns Hopkins University Press, 1983.

Graham, Virginia. "Cinema." *Spectator* 195 (16 Dec. 1955): 841.
Greenblatt, Stephen. *Renaissance Self-Fashioning*. Chicago: University of Chicago Press, 1980.
Griffin, Alice. "Current Theatre Notes, 1959-60." *Shakespeare Quarterly* 12(1961): 73-85.
———. "The Shakespeare Season in New York." *Shakespeare Quarterly* 9(1958): 531-34.
———. "Shakespeare Through the Camera's Eye." *Shakespeare Quarterly* 7(1956): 235-40.
Haefner, Paul. *A Critical Commentary on Shakespeare's Richard the Third*. London: Macmillan, 1966.
Hall, Edward. *The union of the two noble and illustre famelies of Lancastre & Yorke. . . .* [London], 1548.
Hapgood, Robert. "West Coast Shakespeare, 1961." *Drama Survey* 2(1962): 344-50.
Hassel, Chris. *Faith and Folly in Shakespeare's Romantic Comedies*. Athens: University of Georgia Press, 1980.
Hawkins, Harriet. *The Devil's Party*. Oxford: Oxford University Press, 1985.
———. *Poetic Freedom and Poetic Truth*. Oxford: Oxford University Press, 1976.
Heilman, Robert. "Satiety and Conscience: Aspects of *Richard III*." *Antioch Review* 24(1964): 57-73.
Hodgdon, Barbara. "*Richard III*." *Educational Theater Journal* 25(1973): 374-75.
Holinshed, Raphaell. *The . . . Chronicles of England, Scotlande, and Irelande*. London: [H. Bynneman], 1577.
Horobetz, Lynn. "Shakespeare at the Old Globe—1970." *Shakespeare Quarterly* 23(1972): 405-7.
Hunter, Robert G. *Shakespeare and the Mystery of God's Judgments*. Athens: University of Georgia Press, 1976.
Hurault, Jaques. *Politicke, moral, and martial discourses*. Translated by William Golding. London: Adam Islip, 1595.
Jewel, John. *The Works*. Edited by John Ayre. 4 vols. Cambridge: Cambridge University Press, 1845-50.
Jones, Emrys. *The Origins of Shakespeare*. Oxford: Clarendon Press, 1977.
Jorgens, Jack J. "Champlain Shakespeare Festival 1973." *Shakespeare Quarterly* 24(1973): 428-34.
———. *Shakespeare on Film*. Bloomington: Indiana University Press, 1977.
Kilfoil, Thomas F. "Current Theatre Notes, 1960-61." *Shakespeare Quarterly* 13(1962): 99-128.
Legge, Thomas. *Richardus Tertius*. Translated by Robert J. Lordi. New York: Garland Press, 1979.
Levin, Richard. *New Readings of Old Plays*. Chicago: University of Chicago Press, 1979.
Lewalski, Barbara. *Milton's Brief Epic*. Providence: Brown University Press, 1966.
Luther, Martin. *Devotional Writings*. Philadelphia: Fortress Press, 1969.
———. *Sermons*. 2 vols. Philadelphia: Muhlenberg Press, 1959.
———. *Works*. Edited by Hilton C. Oswald. St. Louis: Concordia Press, 1973.
Machiavelli, Niccolo. *The arte of warre*. Translated by Peter Whitehorne. London, 1560.

Marbeck, John. A *book of notes and common places*. London: Thomas East, 1581.
Marder, Louis. "No Royal Kings." *Shakespeare Newsletter* 20(1970): 33.
Nichols, Dorothy E. "The Oregon Shakespeare Festival, 1967." *Shakespeare Quarterly* 18(1967): 421-23.
Nowell, Alexander. A *catechisme*. Translated by Thomas Norton. Cambridge: Cambridge University Press, 1843.
Ornstein, Robert. A *Kingdom for a Stage: The Achievement of Shakespeare's History Plays*. Cambridge: Harvard University Press, 1972.
Palmer, John. *Political Characters of Shakespeare*. London: Macmillan, 1945.
Patrick, D. L. *The Textual History of Richard III*. London: Oxford University Press, 1936.
Patrides, C. A. *The Phoenix and the Ladder*. Berkeley and Los Angeles: University of California Press, 1964.
Perkin, Robert L. "Shakespeare in the Rockies, VI." *Shakespeare Quarterly* 14(1963): 461-66.
Pettigrew, John. "Stratford, 1967." *Queen's Quarterly* 74(1967): 509-21.
Phillips, James E. "Some Glories and Some Discontents." *Film Quarterly* 10(1955-56): 399-407.
Platonico, Onosandro. *Of the generall captaine, and of his office*. Translated by Peter Whytehorne. London: W. Seres, 1563.
Pope, Elizabeth. *Paradise Regained: The Tradition and the Poem*. Baltimore: Johns Hopkins University Press, 1947.
Prior, Moody. *The Drama of Power*. Evanston: Northwestern University Press, 1973.
Proctor, Thomas. *Of the Knowledge and Conducte of Warres*. London: Richard Totelli, 1578.
Pryce-Jones, David. "Little Richard." *Spectator* 211 (30 Aug. 1963): 262.
Rabkin, Norman. *Shakespeare and the Problem of Meaning*. Chicago: University of Chicago Press, 1981.
Reed, Robert Rentoul. *Crime and God's Judgment in Shakespeare*. Lexington: University Press of Kentucky, 1984.
Reese, M. M. *The Cease of Majesty*. London: Edward Arnold, 1961.
Rich, Barnabe. A *path-way to military practise*. London: John Charlewood, 1587.
Rorty, Richard. *Philosophy and the Mirror of Nature*. Princeton: Princeton University Press, 1979.
Rossiter, A. P. "Angel with Horns." In *Shakespeare: The Histories*. Edited by Eugene Waith. Englewood Cliffs, N.J.: Prentice-Hall, 1965.
Sanders, Wilbur. *The Dramatist and the Received Idea*. Cambridge: Cambridge University Press, 1968.
Schein, Harry. "A Magnificent Fiasco?" *Film Quarterly* 10(1955-56): 407-15.
Shakespeare Variorum Handbook. Compiled by Richard Hosley, Richard Knowles, and Ruth McGugan. New York: Modern Language Association, 1971.
Shakespeare, William. *King Richard III*. Arranged by Henry Irving. London: E. S. Boot, 1877.
―――. *Richard the Third*. (Kean's version.) London: John Cumberland, n.d.

———. *Richard the Third*. (Mansfield's acting version.) New York: Metropolitan Job Print, 1889.
———. *Richard III*. Edited by Julie Hankey. London: Junction Books, 1981.
———. *Richard III*. Edited by W. Oxberry. London: E. Simpkin, 1819.
———. *The tragedy of Richard the Third*. Edited by Horace Howard Furness. 2d ed. Philadelphia: J. B. Lippincott, 1909. (*New Variorum*).
Shaw, George Bernard. *Our Theatres in the Nineties*. 3 vols. London, 1932.
Smidt, Kristian. *Iniurious impostors and Richard III*. New York: Humanities Press, 1964.
———. *The Tragedy of King Richard the Third*. New York: Humanities Press, 1969.
Speaight, Robert. "The Old Vic and Stratford-upon-Avon, 1960–61." *Shakespeare Quarterly* 12(1961): 425–41.
———. "Shakespeare in Britain." *Shakespeare Quarterly* 14(1963): 419–32.
———. "Shakespeare in Britain." *Shakespeare Quarterly* 28(1977): 184–90.
Spencer, Christopher, ed. *Five Restoration Adaptations of Shakespeare*. Urbana: University of Illinois Press, 1965.
Sprague, Arthur Colby. "Shakespeare on the New York Stage 1953–54." *Shakespeare Quarterly* 5(1954): 311–15.
Stein, Arnold. *Heroic Knowledge*. Hamden, Conn.: Archon Books, 1965.
Sutcliffe, Matthew. *The practice, proceedings, and lawes of armes*. London: Christopher Barker, 1593.
Sykes, Alrene. "Richard III in Brisbane." *Shakespeare Quarterly* 32(1981): 364–65.
Tanner, Stephen L. "Richard III Versus Elizabeth: An Interpretation." *Shakespeare Quarterly* 24(1973): 468–72.
Thomson, Peter. "A Necessary Theatre." *Shakespeare Survey* 24(1971): 117–26.
Thorpe, Margaret Farrand. "Shakespeare and the Movies." *Shakespeare Quarterly* 9(1958): 357–66.
Tillyard, E. M. W. *Milton*. London: Longmans Green, 1959.
———. *Shakespeare's History Plays*. New York: Macmillan, 1947.
Trewin, J. C. "Show Pieces." *Illustrated London News* 238 (1 June 1961): 994.
The True Tragedie of Richard the Third. London: Thomas Creede, 1594.
Tuchman, Barbara. *A Distant Mirror*. New York: Alfred A. Knopf, 1978.
Veron, John. *A fruteful treatise of predestination*. J. Tisdale, 1561.
Walker, Ralph. *A learned and profitable treatise of Gods providence*. London: Felix Kyngston, 1608.
Walker, Roy. "Bottled Spider." *Twentieth Century* 159(1956): 58–68.
Warren, Roger. "Shakespeare in England: 1982–83." *Shakespeare Quarterly* 34(1983): 334–40.
Wells, Stanley. "Television Shakespeare." *Shakespeare Quarterly* 33(1982): 261–77.
West, Robert. *Shakespeare and the Outer Mystery*. Lexington: University of Kentucky Press, 1968.
Whitaker, Virgil K. "Shakespeare in San Diego—the Twelfth Season." *Shakespeare Quarterly* 12(1961): 403–8.
Wilders, John. *The Lost Garden*. Towota, N.Y.: Rowman and Littlefield, 1978.

Index of Authors

Aaron, Jules, 166 n. 28
Adelman, Janet, 162 n. 8
Andrewes, Lancelot, 112

Becon, Thomas, 112
Berry, Ralph, 2, 163 n. 11, 165 n. 21
Bevington, David, 169 n. 22, 170 n. 12, 175 n. 19
Billington, Michael, 145, 148–49, 157, 179 n. 46
Brooke, Nicholas, 2, 35, 89, 90, 106, 115, 163 n. 11, 164 n. 15, 165 n. 21, 166 n. 25, 167 nn. 32, 33
Brooke, Stopford, 75
Brown, Constance, 29, 89, 163 n. 12, 164 n. 15, 167 nn. 32, 33
Bryant, Arthur, 7
Bullough, Geoffrey, 36, 79, 168 n. 4
Byrne, Muriel St. Clare, 164 n. 16, 166 n. 28

Calvin, John, 109, 110, 112, 115, 116
Chambers, E. K., 57
Clemen, Wolfgang, 169 n. 3, 170 n. 8
Coursen, Herb, 166 n. 27
Coveney, Michael, 146, 148, 153, 157, 177 n. 22, 179 n. 46

Cowden-Clark, Charles, 74, 81

Dent, Alan, 164 nn. 13, 15
Diether, Jack, 167 n. 33
Dollarhide, Louis, 169 n. 3
Dollimore, Jonathan, 162 n. 8, 172 n. 17, 173 n. 39

Edinborough, Arnold, 165 n. 21, 167 n. 35
Elton, William, 116, 173 n. 39
Evans, G. Blakemore, 127, 174–75 n. 9

French, A. L., 111, 117, 172 n. 25
Frey, David L., 35, 74, 90, 98, 100, 106, 108–9, 110, 111, 114–15, 117, 118
Frye, R. M., 104, 162 n. 8, 171 nn. 11, 13, 172 n. 17
Furness, H. H., 75

Garber, Marjorie B., 171 nn. 11, 14
Garrard, William, 51, 52, 168 n. 11
Goldberg, Jonathan, 162 n. 8, 170 n. 12
Gordon, Giles, 149, 154, 157, 178 n. 35, 179 n. 46
Greenblatt, Stephen, 162 n. 8, 170 n. 12, 172 n. 17

Index of Authors

Griffin, Alice, 89, 163 n. 10, 164 n. 15, 165 n. 16, 166 n. 25

Hall, Edward, 36–45, 48, 50, 51, 55, 57, 69, 70–71, 72, 78–81, 85–86, 88, 123, 150
Hammond, Antony, 1, 2, 89, 90, 155, 157, 160, 167 nn. 33, 37, 174 n. 2
Hankey, Julie, 9, 16, 32, 162 n. 1, 165 nn. 17, 21, 177 n. 23
Hapgood, Robert, 166 nn. 25, 28
Hassel, Chris, 175 n. 18
Hawkins, Harriet, 162 n. 8, 171 n. 14, 174 n. 3, 178 n. 31
Heilman, Robert, 74
Hodgdon, Barbara, 166 n. 28
Holinshed, Raphael, 36, 57, 150
Hunter, Robert G., 29, 35, 90, 91, 99, 110
Hurault, Jacques, 49–50

Jewell, John, 109
Johnson, Samuel, 57, 66
Jones, Emrys, 35, 90
Jorgens, Jack, 1, 7, 89, 163–64 nn. 10, 12, 15, 167 n. 35, 168 n. 37

Kahn, Naseem, 146, 153
King, Francis, 148, 179 n. 46

Lamb, Charles, 7, 9
Legge, Thomas, 70, 72, 78–81, 86
Levin, Richard, 162 nn. 8, 1, 172 n. 17, 178 n. 31
Luther, Martin, 116, 117

McGarry, Peter, 148
Machiavelli, Niccolo, 46, 48, 49, 51, 52
Marbeck, John, 112
Marder, Louis, 16
Marshall, F. A., 74–75
Masters, Anthony, 146, 151, 178 n. 36
More, Sir Thomas, 168 n. 4

Nichols, Dorothy E., 165 n. 21
Nowell, Alexander, 112

Ordish, F. A., 81

Palmer, John, 35
Patrick, D. L., 173–74 n. 2
Patrides, C. A., 90
Perkin, Robert L., 165 n. 21
Pettigrew, John, 163 n. 11, 166 n. 28
Phillips, James E., 1, 7–8, 164 nn. 14, 15
Prior, Moody, 90, 91, 95, 144
Proctor, Thomas, 53
Pryce-Jones, David, 9

Rabkin, Norman, 162 n. 1, 171 n. 14, 174 n. 3
Ratcliffe, Michael, 145, 146, 148, 153
Reed, Robert Rentoul, 171 n. 13
Reese, M. M., 35, 90, 108
Ribner, Irving, 108
Rich, Barnabe, 46, 54
Rorty, Richard, 172 n. 17
Rosenberg, Marvin, 162 n. 1
Rossiter, A. P., 35, 74, 90–91, 108, 144

Sanders, Wilbur, 35, 90, 91, 106, 108–9, 114–15, 121
Schein, Harry, 1
Shakespeare, William: *Antony and Cleopatra*, 133; *As You Like It*, 86; *Hamlet*, 76, 115; I *Henry IV*, 39, 51; III *Henry VI*, 76–77, 131; *Julius Caesar*, 52; *King Lear*, 58, 60, 62, 63; *Love's Labor's Lost*, 129; *Macbeth*, 27, 28, 84, 118, 141, 166 n. 29; *Merchant of Venice, The*, 58; *Midsummer Night's Dream, A*, 63, 86
Sher, Antony, 3, 34, 145–60, 179 n. 47
Smidt, Kristian, 161 n. 1, 173 n. 2
Speaight, Robert, 2, 164–65 n. 16
Sprague, Arthur Colby, 165 n. 21
Sutcliffe, Matthew, 46–47, 48, 50, 52

Index of Authors

Tanner, Stephen L., 169 n. 3
Thorpe, Margaret Farrand, 165 n. 20
Tillyard, E. M. W., 35, 57, 58, 63, 75, 90, 108, 160
Tinker, Jack, 145, 146, 148, 157
Trewin, J. C., 7, 148, 157
True Tragedie of Richard the Third, The, 70, 72
Tuchman, Barbara, 46

Veron, John, 109

Walker, Ralph, 109, 115
Walker, Roy, 1, 2, 89, 164 nn. 14, 15, 166 nn. 24, 25, 167 nn. 32, 33, 36, 168 n. 38
Walpole, Horace, 170 n. 10
Wells, Stanley, 2, 148, 154, 178 n. 35
Wessel, C., 170 n. 10
Whitaker, Virgil K., 166 n. 25, 167 n. 32
Wilders, John, 90, 111
Wright, W. A., 74

Index of Actors, Characters, and Directors

Alexander, Bill, 3, 34, 145, 149, 151, 153–54, 154–55, 157, 158, 159, 160, 178 nn. 25, 34
Allam, Roger, 155
Anne, Lady, 10, 11, 12–13, 26, 30, 33, 48, 64, 87, 93, 98, 107, 108, 117, 118, 119, 146, 158, 163 n. 11, 164 nn. 13, 14, 165 n. 21
Archbishop, 163 n. 12
Ashcroft, Dame Peggy, 165 n. 16

Bates, Alan, 9
Bedford, Brian, 9
Blessed, Brian, 159
Bloom, Clare, 1, 12–14, 15, 30, 164 n. 14
Blunt, 44–45, 52, 123
Brackenbury, 93
Browne, Anthony, 25
Buckingham, 4, 16–21, 24, 26, 30, 33, 48, 58, 74–88, 94, 95, 96, 97, 102–3, 104, 107, 108, 117, 119, 132–33, 134, 138–39, 141, 142–43, 144, 146, 149–50, 155, 158, 159, 166 n. 24
Byrne, Michael, 24

Catesby, 18, 20, 52, 66, 71, 80, 84, 88, 138–39, 141

Christopher (Urswick), Sir, 71
Church, Tony, 165 n. 16
Cibber, Colley, 2, 3, 7, 9, 10, 21, 23, 29, 31, 33, 34, 35, 74, 75, 89, 122, 141, 145, 170 n. 9
Citizens, 2–3, 4, 16–21, 33, 74–88, 95, 138–39, 149–51, 155, 158, 160, 170 nn. 8, 11, 12, 176 n. 35, 177–78 n. 23
Clarence, 10, 21, 25, 30, 59, 64, 87, 92–93, 94–95, 96, 97, 98, 100, 103, 104, 107, 108, 113–17, 119, 120, 134–37, 143, 146, 155, 157–58, 159, 165 n. 21, 170 n. 10
Clunes, Alec, 1
Cook, Ron, 6, 10–12, 13, 15–19, 22–23, 25–28
Cooke, George Frederick, 9, 168 n. 39
Cooper, Rowena, 22–23
Coulette, Yvonne, 178 n. 25
Cox, Arthur, 16–19
Crosbie, Annette, 21

Deacon, Brian, 25–28, 56
Dorset, 60, 61, 70–71, 94, 98, 119
Downie, Penny, 153
Duchess of York, 21, 60, 62, 99–100,

101, 104, 107, 151, 153, 158, 170 n. 10, 178 n. 25
Dudley, William, 157
Edward IV, 59, 60, 61, 82, 92, 94, 97–98, 100, 119, 132, 146
Elizabeth, Princess, 72, 119
Elizabeth, Queen, 2, 3, 4, 5, 11, 19, 21–24, 33, 37, 44, 57–73, 88, 91, 93, 94, 98, 99–100, 101, 104, 107, 110, 111–13, 117–18, 119, 120, 122, 126, 127–31, 132, 133–34, 141, 142, 143, 144, 151–53, 155, 169 n. 3, 175 n. 23

Foster, Julia, 15

Gale, Richard, 35, 56, 166 n. 28
Garrick, David, 1, 6, 7, 8, 11
Ghosts, the, 3, 25–26, 30, 33, 47–48, 53, 89, 90, 91, 93, 103–4, 107, 108, 114, 119–21, 122, 139, 146, 158, 159, 171 n. 11
Gielgud, Sir John, 1
Grey, 20, 21, 26, 48, 60, 96, 98, 100, 108, 117, 119, 155, 158
Guthrie, Tyrone, 165 n. 21

Haggard, Paul, 166 n. 27
Hands, Terry, 9, 177 n. 23
Hastings, 17, 20, 26, 30, 33, 48, 58, 75–80, 84, 85, 94–95, 95–97, 98, 100, 102–3, 104, 107, 108, 117, 119, 133, 134, 142–43, 144, 149–50, 155, 158, 163 n. 12, 176 n. 26
Helpman, Robert, 9
Henry VI, 59, 108, 146
Henry, Martha, 163 n. 11
Herbert, 44–45, 52
Hirsch, Robert, 9
Holms, Ian, 9
Howell, Jane, 6

Irving, Henry, 6, 7, 23, 168 n. 39

Kean, Edmund, 1, 6, 7, 8, 11, 16, 161 n. 1, 163 n. 11, 168 n. 39

Lovell, 20, 72, 84, 88

Mansfield, Richard, 9
Margaret, Queen, 2, 3, 4, 14, 15–16, 17–18, 19–20, 21, 30, 33, 58, 59, 60–62, 89, 93–94, 95, 96, 98, 99, 100–101, 102, 104, 107, 108, 110, 111–16, 117–20, 121, 122, 131–34, 141, 142, 143, 146, 148, 151, 157, 159, 164 n. 15, 164–65 nn. 16, 21, 178 n. 25
Mayor, 2–3, 4, 16–21, 33, 74–88, 138–39, 149–51, 155, 158, 160, 163 n. 12, 165 n. 17, 170 n. 8, 177–78 n. 23
Murderers, Two, 21, 88, 93, 94–95, 97, 100, 107, 120, 134–37, 144, 155, 159

Naismith, Laurence, 1
Norfolk, 31, 52, 125

Olivier, Laurence, 1–5, 6–34, 35, 58, 74, 89, 90, 96, 122, 141, 145, 160, 163–68 nn. 2–39 passim, 170 n. 9
Oxford, 44–45, 52

Penker, Friar, 84, 170 n. 11
Phillips, Robin, 166 n. 28
Polanski, Roman, 28, 166–67 n. 29
Porteous, Lynne, 24, 57–58, 66–67
Princes, Two, Edward and Richard, 30, 64, 108, 111, 119, 128, 146, 170 n. 10

Ratcliffe, 20, 25, 27, 52, 66, 71, 104, 158
Ravenscroft, Christopher, 154–55
Richard: and the 1955 film, 1–5, 6–34, 35, 58, 74, 89, 90, 96, 122, 141, 145, 160, 162–68 nn., 170 n. 9; and historical sources, 35–45, 69–73, 78–88; and the Mayor and Citizens,

Richard (continued)
74–88; and military manuals, 46–56; and the 1982 BBC videotape, 3, 4, 6, 10–12, 15–16, 16–19, 21–23, 24–26, 27–28, 30, 74, 84–85, 159, 163 n. 10; and the 1984 Sher-Alexander RSC production, 3, 4, 127, 145–60; his perceptions and use of providence, 25–27, 31, 48, 53–54, 85, 88, 91–94, 97–99, 103–7, 110, 119–21, 131–32, 137–44, 153–57, 158; providence opposed to Richard, 25–34, 53–54, 63–65, 89–91, 100, 101–2, 107–8, 108–11, 113–14, 114–16, 117–21, 131–34, 157–60; and Queen Elizabeth's characterization, 57–67; and Queen Elizabeth's temptation, 67–69; and textual cruxes, 122–23, 123–27, 127–31, 131–34, 137–41, 143–44
Richardson, Ralph, 1, 20–21, 24
Richard III, productions. *See* Richard *for Olivier's film, the 1982 BBC videotape, and the 1984 RSC Sher-Alexander production; see Bibliography for a list of the other productions that are mentioned*
Richmond, 3–4, 5, 24–34, 35–56, 70, 88, 89, 91, 103, 106, 108, 113–14, 120–22, 123–27, 141, 143, 144, 145, 154–55, 156–57, 158, 159, 160, 166 nn. 25, 28, 167 nn. 30, 32, 33, 168 n. 39, 173 n. 32, 178 n. 36

Risso, Richard, 16
Rivers, 20, 21, 26, 48, 60, 64, 94, 96, 98, 100, 108, 111, 112, 117, 119, 158
Rodway, Norman, 9, 177 n. 23
Routledge, Patricia, 178 n. 25

Scrivener, 2–3, 17–18, 19, 77, 79–82, 83, 84, 85, 88, 122, 149, 155, 170 n. 8
Shaa, Friar, 84, 170 n. 11
Shore, Mistress, 58, 77, 163 n. 12
Smith, Maggie, 24, 57–58, 66–67
Stanley, 23, 28, 31, 32, 52, 59, 71, 95, 96, 119, 167 n. 30
Storry, Malcolm, 159
Surrey, 52, 119

Tomelty, Frances, 151, 152
Tyrrel, 25, 155, 165 n. 21
Tyzack, Margaret, 165 n. 21

Vaughan, 20, 21, 26, 48, 60, 96, 98, 100, 108, 117, 119, 155

Walker, William, 1
Wanamaker, Zoe, 12
Wheeler, David, 36
Woolfenden, Guy, 158